LINCOLN UNBOUND

Also by Rich Lowry

FICTION

Banquo's Ghosts (with Keith Korman)

NONFICTION

Legacy: Paying the Price for the Clinton Years

BROADSIDE BOOKS
An Imprint of HarperCollins*Publishers*
www.broadsidebooks.net

LINCOLN UNBOUND

How an Ambitious Young
Railsplitter Saved the
American Dream—and How
We Can Do It Again

RICH LOWRY

LINCOLN UNBOUND. Copyright © 2013 by Rich Lowry. All rights reserved. Printed in the United States of America. No part of this book may be used or reproduced in any manner whatsoever without written permission except in the case of brief quotations embodied in critical articles and reviews. For information, address HarperCollins Publishers, 10 East 53rd Street, New York, NY 10022.

HarperCollins books may be purchased for educational, business, or sales promotional use. For information, please e-mail the Special Markets Department at SPsales@harpercollins.com.

Title page image © Library of Congress

FIRST EDITION

Designed by William Ruoto

Library of Congress Cataloging-in-Publication Data has been applied for.

ISBN: 978-0-06-212378-7

13 14 15 16 OV/RRD 10 9 8 7 6 5 4 3 2 1

To Edward D. Lowry,

MY DEAR FATHER.

Acknowledgments

Writing a book is a solitary pursuit that is only possible through the kindness and generosity of others. My wife Vanessa, my friend and my rock, was patient, encouraging, and willing to lend a hand whenever and wherever necessary. I started this project when we were engaged, and it was our constant companion for the first two years of our marriage. She hates clutter, but tolerated the ever-growing stack of Lincoln books in our apartment. She likes relaxing weekends, but understood when the book took my Saturdays and then my Sundays, too. She showed more understanding than I could have expected when I was tired and distracted. Every day she shows me what love means, and for that I am grateful beyond words.

My assistant, Madison Peace, who is unshakably cheerful and incredibly diligent, aided in research and a dozen other tasks related to the project. I couldn't have finished without her.

My brilliant agent, hilarious friend, and sometime co-author Keith Korman was willing to do anything to advance the project. He always lent a sympathetic ear, even when he was telling to me to "Shut up and write."

Adam Bellow was encouraging when he needed to be and (constructively) critical when he needed to be, and made the book better for it. He is an exceptionally talented editor.

Lewis Lehrman is a Lincolnian to the core who has done so much to aid the study and understanding of our sixteenth president. As far as I'm concerned, the flaw in David Herbert Donald's

Acknowledgments

book, *We Are Lincoln Men: Abraham Lincoln and His Friends* is that he left out Lew. He was unfailingly generous, always willing to do a favor, always willing to provide guidance.

I have the privilege of working with some of the smartest and most interesting people on the planet at *National Review.* They provided characteristically good-humored support. I'm especially indebted to our publisher, Jack Fowler, who has the heart of Mother Teresa and the accent of a cop from Bronx Police District 12.

Noah Glyn and Scott Reitmeier provided early research and editorial help, as did Christeleny Frangos. I am grateful to those who read portions of the draft: Michael Burlingame, Bradford Short, Charles Kesler, Danilo Petranovich, Yuval Levin, Scott Winship, Mario Loyola, Charles C. W. Cooke, Adam White, Adam Keiper, Frederick Hess, and Abby Thernstrom. Of course, any and all errors are my own.

Joe and Lorraine Palo were generous as always. I appreciate the support of Nicholas and Noel Vassallo.

My friend Ric Andersen was there when it counted most and I will never forget it.

I will never be able to repay my mom's boundless love. My brother Robert is my friend and my joy.

I dedicate this book to my dad, who passed away when it was nearing completion. An English professor and history buff, he was a great reader and lover of books. It is because of him and his library in the basement that I will always have the best associations with the smell of old, musty books. By his example, he taught me lifelong lessons in patience and much else. He is missed, but not gone.

Contents

Contents

"Why if the old Greeks had this man, what trilogies of plays—what epics would have been made out of him!"

—Walt Whitman, "Death of Abraham Lincoln," 1879

LINCOLN
UNBOUND

Introduction

"An Inestimable Jewel":
Lincoln's America

"He knew the American people better than they knew themselves."
—Frederick Douglass, "Oration in Memory of Abraham Lincoln," 1876

In the summer of 1864, President Abraham Lincoln welcomed the 166th Ohio Regiment to the White House. His words that day didn't make it onto the Lincoln Memorial. No schoolchildren ever recited them. But they capture the essence of Lincoln and of his idea of America.

"I suppose you are going home to see your families and friends," he said by way of greeting the regiment. These men were representatives of the Union army, whose camps and hospitals he visited, who were fighting and suffering for the Union and who would vote for him in overwhelming numbers in the November election, a contest that, at that moment, Lincoln believed he would lose. The day after seeing the regiment on August 22, Lincoln wrote his "blind memorandum" stipulating that it is "exceedingly probable that this Administration will not be re-elected."

The Ohio troops had been mustered for a hundred days in the spring and had done garrison duty around Washington, D.C. Lincoln offered the soldiers "sincere thanks for myself and the country," and then got to the point. "I almost always feel inclined, when I happen to say anything to soldiers," he told them, "to impress upon them in a few brief remarks the importance of success in this contest."*

"It is not merely for to-day," he said of the significance of the war, "but for all time to come that we should perpetuate for our children's children this great and free government, which we have enjoyed all our lives." This was a more pedestrian expression of the rousing sentiment from the finale of the Gettysburg Address the prior November—"that government of the people, by the people, for the people, shall not perish from the Earth."

"I beg you to remember this," he continued, "not merely for my sake, but for yours. I happen temporarily to occupy this big White House. I am a living witness that any one of your children may look to come here as my father's child has." Lincoln characteristically refrained from saying "as I have," with its whiff of immodesty. Free government is so valuable, he insisted, because it affords us an open, fluid society where anyone can ascend to the highest office in the land. Or at least ascend higher than where he started.

"It is in order," Lincoln said, "that each of you may have through this free government which we have enjoyed, an open field and a fair chance for your industry, enterprise and intel-

---

*Almost all direct quotes from Lincoln are drawn from the *Collected Works of Abraham Lincoln*, a project of the Abraham Lincoln Association and edited by Roy P. Basler. It is searchable online and a stupendous resource. I have preserved misspellings, strange punctuation, and other idiosyncrasies, including all of the italics.

ligence; that you may all have equal privileges in the race of life, with all its desirable human aspirations. It is for this the struggle should be maintained, that we may not lose our birthright—not only for one, but for two or three years. The nation is worth fighting for, to secure such an inestimable jewel."

The priceless treasure is opportunity. It is the cause so dear that it was worth a conflagration that made the country, in the title of historian Drew Gilpin Faust's moving book on wartime death, "this republic of suffering." In Lincoln's telling, America exists to give all people the chance to rise. We are, by birthright and through our free institutions, a nation of aspiration.

This theme wasn't patriotic pap for the boys. Lincoln believed it in the marrow of those strong bones with which he had labored all during his youth. It had suffused his determination, as a boy and into his early adulthood, to read and to learn, so he could do something besides chop and plow all his life. It had been the touchstone of his politics as a Whig and then as a Republican, in the Illinois House of Representatives, in Congress, and in his antislavery leadership in the 1850s that marked the beginning of the heroic phase of his career.

Decades earlier, if the youthful Lincoln had been asked, upon his election as captain by his fellow Illinois militiamen in the Black Hawk War, to speak about the meaning of America, his remarks might not have been much different than they were to those Ohio troops. (Not that his fellow militiamen would have particularly cared. Lincoln's first order to his roughneck troops, described by one observer as "the hardest set of men he ever saw," was supposedly met with a hearty "Go to the devil, sir!") A commitment to the fulfillment of individual potential—his own and that of others—was Lincoln's true north, the bright thread running from his first statement as a novice political candidate in his early twenties to his utterances as one of the world's greatest statesmen.

If there is one thing to know about Lincoln, it is this. It isn't his war leadership or his martyrdom, although they both have launched a thousand books, documentaries, and journal articles. Lincoln's vision for the country goes deeper than either of those— needless to say, highly compelling and consequential—things. So much else about Lincoln is the *how* or *what*. This is the *why*.

We might romanticize his background, the log cabins and all the rest of it. Lincoln didn't. He didn't want to be poor; he wanted to be respectable. He summarized his early life for a biographer with the dismissive phrase "the short and simple annals of the poor," in a line he borrowed from a well-known poem of the time. "That's my life," Lincoln said, "and that's all you or any one else can make of it."

From his first stirrings as a politician, Lincoln committed himself to policies to enhance opportunity. He wanted to build canals and railroads to knit together the nation's markets. He wanted to encourage industry. He wanted to modernize banking. He hated isolation, backwardness, and any obstacles to the development of a cash economy of maximal openness and change. He thrilled to steam power and iron, to invention and technology, to the beneficent upward spiral of a commercial economy. With Emerson, he celebrated "men of the mine, telegraph, mill, map, and survey."

From his youth, he exemplified a middle-class morality at the core of the Whig and the Republican ethic. Self-control and self-improvement, rationality and abstemiousness were the necessary personal ingredients to economic advancement. Lincoln hewed to these qualities and evangelized for them. His characteristic advice to aspiring lawyers, to discouraged friends, and to penurious relatives came down to exhortations to work, and then to work some more.

His opposition to slavery was caught up in his exalted view of work. He constantly invoked a verse from Genesis 3:19: "In the sweat of thy face shalt thou eat bread, till thou return unto the ground." In God's sentence for Adam's sin, Lincoln saw the most elementary justice. It was simply wrong for anyone to take the fruits of someone else's labor, someone else's *property*. Every fiber in his being revolted against what he called in the Second Inaugural "unrequited toil."

He made it his project in life to dissolve the isolation of the backwoods of his upbringing, and to unravel slavery in the South. In its separation from the market and the enlivening churn of commerce, the backwoods could only limit possibilities for individual advancement. In its aristocratic pretension and heinous system of human bondage, the slave South substituted for the true American creed a society built, in Lincoln's words, on "classification" and "caste."

He prevailed in both contests. More and more of the country was enveloped in the net of the new, relentlessly modernizing economy. As for slavery, Lincoln had hoped to limit its spread as a means of effecting its ultimate extinction. Instead, in his words, as the Southern states broke from the Union, "the tug" came. The Civil War preserved a united America oriented around Lincoln's democratic capitalism and defined by the truths of the Declaration of Independence, although the race-based economic and social system of the South wouldn't be fully dismantled for another century.

For all of Lincoln's rustic associations, contemporary America is much closer to his vision of the country than the world of his youth. It is the dense, creative commercial network that he imagined, but on steroids—a heavily urbanized population of more than 300 million, robustly democratic yet highly educated and technologically proficient, featuring some of the most innovative companies in the world. It is open to talent and relatively free of irrational discrimination based on race or birth.

Yet all is not well and everyone—right, left, and in-between—feels it, even if they disagree about the exact problem and the nature of the solution. The American Dream is generally considered under threat, and rightly so. We suffer from a lack of mobility up from the bottom, from stagnating working-class wages, and from a growing dependence on government. Above all, we are experiencing an erosion of the bourgeois virtues that undergird aspiration. America will exist as a great nation for a long time to come. It has a vast store of economic and military capital that it will take time to spend down even in the worst of circumstances and even under the worst policies. But it risks losing the fluidity and dynamism that have made it so admirable and the best place in human history for the pursuit of happiness.

This is not simply a matter of income inequality, although that is part of the picture. The share of the national income going to the top 1 percent has increased since the 1970s, a trend that holds across the Western world. The rise in inequality in the United States comes in the context of slowing economic growth and diminished prospects for the non-college-educated. Men with only a high-school diploma saw their earnings decline from the early 1970s to the mid-to-late first decade of the 2000s.

We are not quite the highly mobile society we imagine ourselves. Forty percent of those starting in the bottom fifth of the economic distribution stay there, when, if it were a matter of perfect chance, only 20 percent would. Nordic countries, Canada, Australia, and some Western European countries are more mobile than we are. If he were writing today, Horatio Alger might set his stories in Finland.

Social capital in the form of family stability and bourgeois habits is increasingly the preserve of the best-educated third of the country (a college degree or more). It is woefully scarce in the least-educated third (no high-school diploma) and is eroding in the middle third (a high-school degree or some college). All of this points to a slow-motion social and economic evisceration of a swath of Middle America and a divide between the classes that risks becoming more and more unbridgeable.

It is in this context that it is important to recapture the essential Lincoln. His keen political sense, his deft statesmanship, his stalwart war leadership, his martyrdom—all of these are important but incidental to his animating purpose of enhancing opportunity. Lincoln argued that the Declaration of Independence existed to exert a gravitational force pulling the country always back toward its ideals. Such is the totemic power of our sixteenth president that his life and example serve the same function.

We all know the Lincoln of the Second Inaugural and the Gettysburg Address. We need to know the Lincoln of the Address before the Wisconsin State Agricultural Society and of the Lecture on Discoveries and Inventions, both talks in which he vents his favorite enthusiasms. We need to understand his thirst for economic and industrial development. We need to realize that he was a lawyer for corporations, a vigorous advocate of property rights, and a defender of an "elitist" economics against the unreflective populist bromides of his age. We need to focus on his love for the

Founders as guides to the American future. We need to grapple with his ferocious ambition, personal and political.

The vast archipelago of this (relatively) unknown Lincoln is the foundation for his greatness. Another man might have saved the Union; only Lincoln could have grasped and defined so precisely and profoundly what made it worthy of the saving. He felt it. He understood it. He had *lived* it.

It is famously said that Lincoln is the second-most written-about figure in history after Jesus Christ. Yet it is easy to lose the true Lincoln in the haze of celebration. He wasn't an Everyman. He wasn't "out of the very earth," in the words of James Russell Lowell, or an "aboriginal man," in the words of Emerson. He was exceptional from his youth, possessed of a rigorous mind and an uncanny memory. For all his generosity of spirit, he was a slashing partisan for much of his political career and even after he mellowed, a merciless polemicist. He wasn't an accidental president, or an accidental anything else in politics. He burned with a white-hot desire for political distinction, and was a legislative mechanic, quasi-campaign operative, and dispenser of patronage before anyone thought to build a monument to him. About to be dispatched to London as ambassador during the war, Charles Francis Adams was shocked when in a meeting with Lincoln and Secretary of State William Seward, the president exulted to Seward about finally resolving a knotty patronage appointment: "Well, Governor, I've this morning decided that Chicago post-office appointment!"

Decades ago, the distinguished Lincoln biographer David Herbert Donald coined the phrase "getting right with Lincoln" to describe the impulse nearly everyone feels to appropriate Lincoln for his political agenda. This is better than the alternative. What kind of country would it be if people felt compelled to get right with Jefferson Davis or John C. Calhoun? But this tendency often means doing violence to Lincoln's memory.

In Barack Obama's stump speeches, Lincoln is often boiled down to his support for infrastructure projects. His fellow Illinoisan, he insists, would have been an enthusiast for subsidies for green energy and high-speed rail and the like. Lincoln did indeed back infrastructure "improvements" throughout his career. His beloved railroads, though, genuinely represented the economic future rather than a fashionable lark. Even so, the results of the subsidies he supported for transit were decidedly mixed.

One of the more egregious examples of getting Lincoln wrong while "getting right" with him is a little book called *Why Lincoln Matters*, by the liberal lion Mario Cuomo. His Lincoln is all in favor of sharing, inclusion, diversity, and whatever else Cuomo deems valuable and important. He ends the book with an imaginary 2004 State of the Union address by Lincoln that intersperses Lincoln quotes with Cuomo's predictable policy positions. Lincoln comes out against the Bush tax cuts and in favor of more spending on education, job training, health care, and foreign aid. Lincoln opposes the Iraq War because he would have given United Nations weapons inspectors more time to work. He argues that attacking terrorists creates more terrorism. And he counsels against letting wartime exigencies impinge at all on civil liberties despite his very own wartime example. In short, Cuomo's Lincoln is John Kerry with a beard. As an interpreter of Lincoln, Cuomo is a great former governor of New York.

N ot everyone feels a need to get right with Lincoln. A school of conservatives excoriates him for the same reason Cuomo embraces him: He was allegedly a proto–New Dealer. An intellectual giant of mid-twentieth-century conservatism, Willmoore Kendall, averred that modern liberalism "is Lincoln's legitimate offspring." Another major thinker of the right in that period, Frank Meyer, seconded this verdict: "Were it not for the wounds that Lincoln inflicted upon the Constitution, it would have been infinitely more difficult for Franklin Roosevelt to carry through his revolution, for the coercive welfare state to come into being and bring about the conditions against which we are fighting today."

Kendall and Meyer think Lincoln should have let the South merrily go its own way in 1861. Contemporary libertarians take a similar tack. Rejecting praise for Lincoln as "one of our greatest presidents," Ron Paul wonders why Lincoln didn't forestall the war by simply buying up all the slaves and freeing them—a market solution to the sectional conflict. With his usual sense of realism, Paul ignores the fact that Lincoln repeatedly advanced schemes for just such a compensated emancipation. Lincoln argued for these proposals as "the cheapest and most humane way to end the war." Except in the District of Columbia, they went precisely . . . nowhere. The border states weren't selling, let alone the South. Even little Delaware, which was selected as a test case because it had only 587 slaveholders out of a white population of 90,500 in 1860, couldn't be persuaded to cash out of slavery. One plan proposed by Lincoln would have paid four hundred dollars or so per slave and achieved full abolition by 1893. A version of the scheme failed in the state's legislature.

The Lincoln-hating libertarian Thomas DiLorenzo expands this line of criticism in a rancid book-length prosecution of Lincoln as the Whore of Springfield. In his telling, Lincoln was a racist dictator who didn't care about ending slavery so much as aggrandizing the central government and crushing federalism and states' rights. Lincoln, DiLorenzo concludes with his typical judiciousness, "was an even worse tyrant than George III was."

Where to begin? These critiques from the right amount to the contention that the Constitution was so precious and inviolate that half the country should have been permitted to exit from it, and write a new explicitly proslavery one. In contrast to the U.S. version, the foundational governing document of the Confederacy didn't tiptoe around the issue. It was full of explicit references to slavery, or as Article IV, section 2 put it, "slaves and other property." It accorded the so-called peculiar institution high, protected status: "No bill of attainder, ex post facto law, or law denying or impairing the right of property in negro slaves shall be passed." It guaranteed slavery in new territories.

The South seceded to protect human bondage, not to vindicate liberty. Prior to the Civil War, it didn't even honor that most elemental political freedom, free speech, which it trampled to suppress the expression of abolitionist opinions. Its commitment to federalism was highly situational. It insisted on a federal Fugitive Slave Act to tighten the screws on anyone in the Northern states who was insufficiently zealous about returning runaways. Southern Democrats walked out of the 1860 Democratic convention, in a foreshadowing of secession, when the party couldn't forge a consensus on a platform demanding *federal* protection for slavery in the territories.

The ensuing war necessarily entailed the growth of the state, but this hardly makes Lincoln a forerunner to FDR or LBJ. The income tax to fund the war, instituted in 1861 and soon made into a progressive tax with higher rates for the wealthy, was eliminated in 1872. (The Confederacy had its own income tax, with highly progressive rates.) In 1860, the federal budget was well under $100 million. By the end of the war, it was more than $1 billion. Wars are expensive. The budget dropped back down to about $300 million, excluding payments on the debt, within five years of the end of the war.

To see the makings of the modern welfare state in any of this requires a leap of imagination. In the midst of the war, the State Department had all of thirty-three employees. The famous instances of government activism not directly related to the war—the subsidies to railroads, the Homestead Act—were a far cry from the transfer programs instituted in the twentieth century. The railroads got land and loan guarantees. The Homestead Act, as Lincoln historian Allen Guelzo argues, can be viewed as a gigantic privatization of public lands, which were sold off at a cut rate to people willing to improve their plots.*

The surges in government that presaged explosions in its growth later in the twentieth century first arrived during the Progressive Era, in the Teddy Roosevelt and the Woodrow Wilson administrations. The New Deal represented a true rupture within the American tradition, and the Great Society—born of the post-1964 liberal ascendancy and of the particular hubris of post–World War II America—doubled down on it. Lincoln never would have imagined a cradle-to-grave welfare state, or expansive government programs to support the able-bodied who aren't war widows or orphans.

---

* Guelzo is an extraordinary and prolific historian. The first sections of his biography *Abraham Lincoln: Redeemer President* place Lincoln in a political-economic context that deeply enriched my understanding of him, and is reflected in the major arguments of this book.

The likes of Mario Cuomo hang much of their case for ownership of Lincoln on a statement he wrote for himself circa 1854, in what may have been a draft note for a lecture: "The legitimate object of government, is to do for a community of people, whatever they need to have done, but can not do, *at all*, or can not, *so well do*, for themselves—in their separate, and individual capacities." In this he was referring, on the one hand, to policing and the prosecution of crimes, and on the other, to "public roads and highways, public schools, charities, pauperism, orphanage, estates of the deceased, and the machinery of government itself." In other words, functions of government that are thoroughly uncontroversial. And when Lincoln talked of government, he didn't necessarily mean the federal government.

In the same document he writes, "In all that the people can individually do as well for themselves, government ought not to interfere." He elaborated in a 1858 speech, "I believe each individual is naturally entitled to do as he pleases with himself and the fruit of his labor, so far as it in no wise interferes with any other man's rights—that each community, as a State, has a right to do exactly as it pleases with all the concerns within that State that interfere with the rights of no other State, and that the general government, upon principle, has no right to interfere with anything other than that general class of things that does concern the whole."

Obviously, Lincoln is not an exact fit with either of our two competing political ideologies. He was more favorable to government activism than conservatives are today. But progressives do him the gravest disservice by attempting to conscript him for their cause, a project that dates back to Teddy Roosevelt. Lincoln had more faith in the market and an up-by-the-bootstraps individualism; a greater tolerance for economic inequality; a deeper commitment to bourgeois moral norms; a more realistic view of human nature; and a keener sense of constitutional limits and of natural rights than liberals do today.

Lincoln's policies sought to create more robust markets, with more people better equipped to pursue their own advancement, without government interference or guarantees. Lincoln warned a delegation of workingmen during the Civil War of the peril of a "war on property, or the owners of property": "Let not him who is houseless pull down the house of another; but let him labor diligently and build one for himself, thus by example assuring that his own shall be safe from violence when built." In March 1860, he said, "I take it that it is best for all to leave each man free to acquire property as fast as he can. Some will get wealthy. I don't believe in a law to prevent a man from getting rich; it would do more harm than good. So while we do not propose any war upon capital, we do wish to allow the humblest man an equal chance to get rich with everybody else."

It is a trope to say that Lincoln never could have foreseen the post–Civil War age of large corporations and industry and would have rued its onset. In his influential essay "Abraham Lincoln and the Self-Made Myth," the historian Richard Hofstadter wrote that, had Lincoln lived, "he would have seen the generation brought up on self-help come into its own, build oppressive business corporations, and begin to close off those treasured opportunities for the little man." Booth's bullet was almost a mercy, as "it confined his life to the happier age that Lincoln understood." This is condescending to Lincoln and willfully disregards his lifelong aims.

Of course, Lincoln couldn't have predicted the exact parameters of the American economy in the decades after the Civil War. No one is clairvoyant. Nor, we can safely assume, would he have welcomed Gilded Age corruption. But the entire point of his politics was to hasten the end of the world as he had known it. He was a man utterly unburdened by nostalgia. The America that emerged in the wake of the war was different in degree, certainly, but not necessarily in kind from the one he had envisioned throughout his adult life. Nothing in what he ever said or did suggests that he would have been outraged by the rise of railroads, corporations, and financial capitalism. By the onrush of epoch-making technological changes. By big industry and big cities.

The unified country that Lincoln restored became a clamorous, unstoppable dynamo of economic development that eclipsed every other nation on earth. In 1800, its share of world manufacturing output had been .8 percent. By 1900, it was the highest in the world, at 23.6 percent. It produced by far the most iron and steel of any country. Andrew Carnegie alone produced more steel than Britain. It consumed the most energy of any nation. As a percentage of its population, it was the second-most urban country in the world, and in absolute numbers it had a greater urban population than Britain. Lincoln's optimism about the country's prospects—provided it embraced industry and banking, and fostered individual initiative—was vindicated several times over.

This growing economic might naturally led to more assertiveness abroad. Over time, our influence on the international order began to justify the grander statements Lincoln had made about the spread of liberty to all men: "The theory of our government is Universal Freedom." He forged the country that went on to win World War II. And in that war's wake, America blossomed into a broad-based middle-class society that was the envy of the world and—looking back on it from the vantage point of our current economic and social discontents—is the envy of us, too. The conditions of that mid-century moment in time, with most of the industrialized world on its back and national cohesion at a high here after we passed through the forge of World War II, can't be replicated.

The question now is what we can do to check our drift away from our status as a Lincolnian republic, with the middle struggling, the lower end left behind, and dependence on government growing. What can we do to maintain the ethic of equality of opportunity, with its attendant respect for work, self-reliance, and success? What can we do to remove obstacles to mobility, and reassert the virtues conducive to it? In short, what can we do to live up to the ideal that Lincoln rightly identified as the true center of America? And what does his Republican Party have to contribute to this project?

This book tells the story of Lincoln's rise so as to underscore those qualities most relevant to his politics, which will remain of significance to America so long as it is recognizable as America. It examines his economic policies, not because their details are exactly relevant in our different circumstances, but for their thrust. It recounts his devotion to the Founding, and especially the Declaration, as a pillar of his worldview. It traces the consequences of his achievements, and considers his lessons for addressing today's crisis of the American Dream.

The miracle of Lincoln isn't that he was a railsplitter who became president. It is that he opened the way for the upward march of those behind him and left a legacy to be honored by ensuring that, in America, the way always stays open. What was true when Lincoln spoke to those troops from the 166th Regiment is just as true now: The struggle for a free society defined by individual aspiration is not merely for today, but for all time to come.

Chapter 1

——

"An Ambition that Knew No Rest": Young Man on the Make

Good boys who to their books apply / Will make great men by & by.
— COUPLET WRITTEN BY ABRAHAM LINCOLN, 1829

For the young Abraham Lincoln, a dollar opened up a new vista on the world.

When he was about eighteen years old, Lincoln had built a little boat that idled at a landing on the Ohio River. Two men approached in carriages with trunks. They wanted to meet a steamboat coming down the river. Seeing Lincoln's conveyance, they asked if he'd take them out to meet the steamer in the middle of the river (the practice when there were no wharves). Lincoln obliged and, when they were about to steam off, yelled out that they had forgotten to pay him. To his astonishment, they each tossed a silver half-dollar onto the bottom of his flatboat. Lincoln had, as he put it, "earned my first dollar."

"In these days it seems to me a trifle," he recalled, according to a White House visitor who heard him tell the tale, "but it was a most important incident in my life. I could scarcely credit that I, a poor boy, had earned a dollar in less than a day—that by honest work I had earned a dollar. The world seemed wider and fairer before me. I was a more hopeful and confident being from that time."

The story of this fleeting incident captures many of Lincoln's lifelong concerns. Here is Lincoln on a commercial throughway, the Ohio River. Here is Lincoln rejoicing in earnings from his labor. Here is Lincoln fired with ambition by the sight of those half-dollars—all his own, a token of services rendered and rewarded in a free and fair exchange.

If we want a symbol that is true to the youthful Lincoln and what he was to become, it shouldn't be the axe (or maul) of Lincoln "the railsplitter"; it should be those half-dollars. His political boosters settled on the axe for obvious reasons. As a populist statement, redolent of earthiness and hard work, it's hard to beat a trusty old axe. But it missed the point of the man entirely. The axe represented what Lincoln wanted to leave behind; the half-dollars what he wanted to create. The axe represented the frontier; the half-dollars the commercial economy. The axe the past; the half-dollars the future.

"Lincoln the railsplitter" ranks as one of the greatest mythogenic acts of political image making of all time. His supporters at the Decatur, Illinois, Republican convention in 1860 came up with it while making him the state's favorite son for president. Two rails he had supposedly split decades earlier were hauled out in an inspired bit of stagecraft, together with a placard reading, "Abraham Lincoln, The Rail Candidate for President in 1860. Two rails from a lot of 3,000 made in 1830 by Thos. Hanks and Abe Lincoln." (They got the first name of Hanks wrong, but that's a quibble for another day). The *New York Tribune* reported that Lincoln told the ecstatic gathering that, whether or not he had split these rails, "he had mauled many and many better ones since he had grown to manhood." According to a witness, Lincoln joked: "I used to shirk splitting all the hard cuts. But if those two are honey locust rails, I have no doubt I cut and split *them*."*

Without a doubt, Lincoln split more than his share of rails. In an autobiographical statement provided to the journalist John L. Scripps in 1860, Lincoln said that when his father moved the family from Kentucky to Indiana in 1816, he settled them "in an unbroken forest." There was hardly any other kind in Indiana at that time. "Tall trees covered the whole country," one description of the state relates, "with their wide-spreading branches, depending to the ground, and the shrubbery below arose and united with the branches of the trees." Traveling to the new spot, Lincoln's father had to "[c]ut his way to his farm with the Axe felling the forest as he went," according to a neighbor.

The eight-year-old Lincoln "had an axe put into his hands at once," he told Scripps, referring to himself in the third person, "and from that till within his twenty-third year, he was almost constantly handling that most useful instrument." First, the family built a cabin out of logs, and then Abraham and his father cleared the land—the boy working on the underbrush, the father on the trees. By some accounts, what Ted Williams was to the baseball

---

* For details of Lincoln's life, I rely heavily throughout on Michael Burlingame's magisterial two-volume *Abraham Lincoln: A Life*, as definitive a biographical work as will ever be written on Lincoln. It is not only exhaustive, it is original. Burlingame has scoured the archives to come up with every last scrap related to the sixteenth president. Everyone with an interest in Lincoln is in his debt, and that includes me more than most.

bat, Abraham was to the axe. "My how he could chop," marveled a witness to his later work in the woods. "His axe would flash and bite into a sugar tree or sycamore, down it would come. If you heard him felling trees in a clearing, you would say there were three men at work, the way the trees fell."

He remained adept with it right to the end of his life. Shortly before his assassination, he visited a military field hospital and after shaking hands all day, held out an axe at arm's length—grasping it from the butt—to prove his arm wasn't tired. After he left, soldiers attempted it, but none of them could equal the feat of the president.

All of this speaks to an intense relationship with a tool that had proven most useful to man since the Paleolithic period. But Lincoln would never have been on that platform in Decatur if he hadn't been inalterably determined to escape railsplitting. To escape rural backwardness. To escape his father. Escape unrequited toil. Escape, for that matter, physical toil of any sort. "I have seen a good deal of the back side of this world," Lincoln once told a neighbor, in a remark shorn of any sentimentality for the places where he had done his chopping.

The America of Lincoln's boyhood remained, more or less, the world of the Founders (both Adams and Jefferson still lived). Although the population had been growing at a rapid clip, people still lived overwhelmingly in Atlantic coast states. As of 1815, only about 15 percent of Americans made their homes farther inland. Poor transportation acted as a great wall blocking intercourse between the middle of the country and the East Coast. Commerce largely depended on rivers and the oceans; those areas out of reach of them were isolated and economically stunted. Merchant capitalists clustered in the cities along an eastern seaboard that, historian George Rogers Taylor writes, "provided the chief highway for travel and transportation by methods surprisingly little changed from the days of the Phoenicians."

The country was almost uniformly agricultural. Cities were the exception that proved the rule. Only 5 percent of people lived in the metropolises of the time—cities with populations exceeding eight thousand. There were a grand total of thirteen of them. Many of the nation's farms were all but islands unto themselves. Historian Bruce Levine writes that "market-oriented activities remained circumscribed and subordinate aspects of life." Rural families "produced most of what they consumed or wore; purchases were few. About two-thirds of all clothes worn in the United States were homemade," and "[a]s late as 1820, only 20 percent of the farm crop ever reached urban markets."

It was a country of prodigious promise, almost entirely untapped. In the coming decades, its potential would begin to be unlocked in a series of epochal changes. A tide of migration headed out beyond the Alleghenies, dragging the country's center of gravity away from the East Coast. (Indiana became a state right around the time the Lincolns arrived there in 1816, and Illinois just two years later.) A transportation and communications revolution drew the country closer together and transformed its economy, as canals, steamboats, railroads, and the telegraph worked daily miracles and brought to bear more and more of the country's resources. Manufacturing began to take hold, the beginning of the country's transition into a great industrial powerhouse. In a matter of decades what had been a youthful, predominantly rural country became a budding world power.

Lincoln was born into the old world, but he could feel the new one arising. It was toward this new, more sophisticated world of runaway economic advancement that he bent all his effort, both personal and—eventually—political. He wanted to expand its ambit so more people could enter it together with him. But first, obviously, he had to get there himself. He managed to do it through self-discipline and perseverance, through cultural uplift and education, through a relentless ethic of self-improvement central to his worldview all his life. Lincoln's political character wasn't formed by where he came from so much as by where he went and how he got there.

His law partner and biographer William Herndon famously wrote of Lincoln's political career, "his ambition was a little engine that knew no rest." Lincoln's life invites us to put away any hesitance we may have about celebrating ambition. When we say of someone, he's *very* ambitious, there's usually a hint of disapproval or suspicion about it. But the most celebrated figure in American history felt an ambition to the very marrow of his bones—to make the most of himself and to achieve political fame. "Every man is said to have his peculiar ambition," Lincoln wrote in his first message to voters in a political campaign. "Whether it be true or not, I can say for one that I have no other so great as that of being truly esteemed of my fellow men, by rendering myself worthy of their esteem."

Herndon's engine metaphor could reach all the way back into those Indiana woods, where something helped ignite Lincoln's striving. A friend of the Lincoln family in Kentucky captured it nicely in a letter to Herndon: "To all human appearance the early life of Abraham Lincoln was as unpromising for becoming a great man as you could imagine, indeed I would say it was forbidding, and proves to me that nature bestowed upon him an irrepressible will and innate greatness of mind, to enable to break through all those barriers & iron gates and reach the portion he did in life."*

Lincoln must have had a sense of his own giftedness early on. "His mind & the Ambition of the man soared above us," a childhood friend told Herndon. "He naturally assumed the leadership of the boys." When the family arrived in Indiana, it relied on Abraham to pen the letters to friends back in Kentucky, because his mother and father couldn't write. When word got out in the area, according to one account, "little Abraham was considered a marvel of learning and wisdom by the simple-minded settlers." He performed the same service for neighbors, writing their "friendly confidential letters," recalled a friend.

His stepmother recognized him as "a Boy of uncommon natural Talents," according to a Lincoln relative. One of the hallmarks of his mind—the penetration of his insight and his ability to think things through all the way to the bottom—became evident when he was still young. Understanding constituted a kind of compulsion with him. It went beyond mere childish curiosity to an inchoate intellectual rigor.

His stepmother told Herndon, "Abe, when old folks were at

---

*Herndon (together with his collaborator Jesse Weik) conducted interviews and engaged in correspondence with hundreds of people who knew Lincoln after his death for his biography of his former law partner. All references here to someone telling Herndon something or writing to him come from *Herndon's Informants*, the indispensable collection of Herndon's raw materials edited by Douglas L. Wilson and Rodney O. Davis and published by the University of Illinois Press. Many of the accounts of old friends and neighbors also come from this work. It is a wonderful book, with an incredibly convenient searchable online version. The quotes are all as they originally appear in Herndon's letters and notes, except for the addition of some periods and some cleaned-up spacing. They often are ungrammatical or have other imperfections, idiosyncrasies, or anachronisms that reflect Herndon's method of note-taking or the shaky literacy of his correspondents or the writing style of the day. At times this makes the quotes harder to follow than if they had been fixed, but rendering them in the original preserves their distinctive flavor.

our house, was a silent & attentive observer—never speaking or asking questions till they were gone and then he must understand Every thing—even to the smallest thing—Minutely & Exactly[;] he would then repeat it over to himself again & again—sometimes in one form and then in another & when it was fixed in his mind to suit him he became Easy and he never lost that fact or his understanding of it. Sometimes he seemed pestered to give Expression to his ideas and got mad almost at one who couldn't Explain plainly what he wanted to convey."

Lincoln apparently reserved his childhood rage almost entirely for incomprehension. His inability to follow something so agitated him, it literally kept him up at night. On a triumphant tour of the Northeast after his Cooper Union address in 1860, Lincoln told a pastor he met on a train in Connecticut—and who had heard Lincoln speak the night before—about his youthful drive to understand. "I remember how, when a mere child," the pastor recalled him saying, "I used to get irritated when anybody talked to me in a way I could not understand. I don't think I ever got angry at anything else in my life. But that always disturbed my temper, and has ever since."

Lincoln remembered hearing adults discuss things he couldn't understand with his father during evenings, and staying up trying to puzzle out the meaning of what he heard: "I could not sleep, though I often tried to, when I got on such a hunt after an idea, until I had caught it; and when I thought I had got it, I was not satisfied until I had repeated it over and over, until I had put it in language plain enough, as I thought, for any boy to comprehend. This was a kind of passion with me, and it has stuck by me, for I am never easy now, when I am handling a thought, till I have bounded it north and bounded it south and bounded it east and bounded it west."

A boy who possessed such a restless and seeking mind was un-likely to be satisfied with his lot. He would strain against his limits and those of his surroundings. By the time he was a young man, Lincoln spoke openly of his ambition. Lincoln assured neighbor Elizabeth Crawford, "I don't always intend to delve, grub, shuck corn, split rails, and the like." She told Herndon later, "Abe was ambitious—sought to outstrip and override others. This I confess." A cousin remembers him vowing to "cut himself adrift from his old world." His friend Joseph Gentry agreed: "Abe wa[s]n't fond of work and often told me he never intended to make his living that way—he often said he would get some profession, in fact his whole mind seemed bent on learning and education."

Lincoln, of course, achieved what he intended. But it meant turning his back on his family—especially his father—and its way of life. A good, but limited man, Thomas Lincoln was rough-hewn like one of those famous rails. With straight black hair, a low forehead, and a large Roman nose, he was built like a line-backer at five feet ten and nearly two hundred pounds. A relative told Herndon that he was "so compact that it was difficult to find or feel a rib in his body." Before there was "Honest Abe," there was "Honest Thomas." He was "a plain unpretending plodding man," "peaceable good and good natured," according to someone who had known him in Kentucky. He loved to hunt and fish. A talented storyteller, he was considered "brilliant as a storebox whittler and leader of grocery-store dialogue" (saloons, at the time, were called groceries). He obviously passed along a gene for folksy humor to his son.

A carpenter and farmer, Thomas Lincoln didn't particularly distinguish himself at either role. A neighbor called him a "pid-dler," someone who was "always doing but doing nothing great."

He chose his land poorly and cultivated just enough of it to get by. He once let "a pair of sharpers" rip off a load of pork he planned to take on a flatboat down the Mississippi to sell in New Orleans. Another neighbor said, pungently, that he was "lazy & worthless," "an excellent spec[imen] of poor white trash."

His son evaluated him harshly, too. He wrote in the autobiographical sketch for Scripps that his father, born around 1778 in Virginia's Shenandoah Valley, "never did more in the way of writing than bunglingly sign his own name." His mother, Nancy Hanks, signed her name with an X and his stepmother couldn't sign her name, either. The adverb *bunglingly* is pregnant with contempt. The description sounded so harsh that Scripps left it out of his biography. Lincoln's statement to Scripps wasn't a one-time lapse. "In all of his published writings," historian David Herbert Donald points out, "and, indeed, even in reports of hundreds of stories and conversations, he had not one favorable word to say about his father."

Thomas Lincoln didn't have much of a start in life, nor much of a middle. His lament that "everything I ever teched either died, got killed or was lost" captured it all too accurately. It applied to his father, infant son, wife, and daughter.

When Thomas was a boy growing up in Kentucky, Indians attacked his family while they were planting a cornfield. The attack killed his own father, Abraham, grandfather of the future president. An Indian was about to snatch Thomas when his older brother Mordecai, who returned to the cabin for a rifle, aimed for a pendant on the Indian's chest and shot him dead. Primogeniture meant that all the property went to Mordecai, and so Thomas was left, as his son put it to Scripps, "a wandering laboring boy."

With what he scratched together from three-shilling-a-day

labor and some carpentry, Thomas bought his first farm and started a family. He and Nancy lost a son—Abraham's younger brother—in infancy. Two years after their move to Indiana another tragedy struck. Along with her aunt and uncle who had moved to the vicinity, Nancy fell ill with the horrific, mysterious "milk sickness." They were poisoned with the milk of cows that ate a toxic weed while wandering in the forest. The illness galloped in about a week from dizziness and nausea, to irregular respiration and pulse, then coma and death. She died without a physician and was buried on a hill near the cabin in a wooden coffin fashioned by Thomas and his son. There wasn't a funeral sermon until months later.

The family fell into a "sad, if not pitiful condition," in Lincoln's words. His twelve-year-old sister Sarah kept house, sometimes so despairing she sat and wept. A first cousin of Lincoln's mother who lived with the family at this time, Dennis Hanks, remembered that to try to lift her spirits, "Me 'n' Abe got 'er a baby coon an' a turtle, an' tried to get a fawn but we couldn't ketch any." Shortly thereafter, Lincoln's father left the children to head back to Kentucky to find a new wife.

At this time and place, women tended to work ceaselessly and men might outlive two or more of their wives, for whom childbirth was a mortal threat. An English traveler called it "a hard country for women and cattle." When Lincoln's sister later married, she died shortly afterward in childbirth. The Lincolns blamed her in-laws, but they claimed that the nearest doctor had been too drunk to care for her.

That heartbreak was in the future, when Lincoln's father returned from his mission with Sarah Bush Johnston Lincoln, who found his children hungry tatterdemalions. Sarah described the children when she first met them as "wild—ragged and dirty." A widow, she brought three children of her own and provided a welcome dose of order and cleanliness to a suddenly overcrowded household desperately in need of female attention. Lincoln adored his stepmother and called her "mama."

It was a symptom, though, of his larger discontent with his family (not to say his embarrassment over it) that he later told William Herndon that his biological mother, Nancy, was the illegitimate child of a Virginia nobleman. The mystery squire was presumably the source of her talent—she was widely regarded as intelligent—and his own. Lincoln underestimated his family stock.

Lincoln's great-grandfather had enough means to give his son 210 prime acres in Virginia. Lincoln's grandfather sold them and made the fateful move to Kentucky, where he accumulated more than five thousand acres. As mentioned earlier, his oldest son, Mordecai, inherited the property after his death at the hands of the Indians. He lived comfortably in Kentucky, a respected man and a slave owner with an interest in horse breeding. Lincoln liked to say, "Uncle Mord had run off with all the talents of the family"—another gibe at his father.

Lincoln was too hard on him. Despite much adversity, his father managed to provide for his family and was a solid, respected member of the communities where he lived. In the Kentucky county where he resided with his family in 1814, he ranked on the higher end of property owners. He served on juries and in the militia, and was active in church. In 1821, in Indiana, he was charged with supervising the construction of the local Little Pigeon Baptist Church, where he served as a trustee. He said grace before meals: "Fit and prepare us for humble service for Christ's sake, Amen." (After one grace for a meal of little besides potatoes, Lincoln blurted out, these are "mighty poor blessings.")

Thomas Lincoln was by no means a reprobate. But his virtues were refracted through an environment of rural isolation. Spencer County, where he took the family in Indiana, was a vast expanse roughly the size of Rhode Island. Yet only a couple of hundred people lived there. Lincoln later wrote a poem that described the wilderness: "When first my father settled here, / 'Twas then the frontier line: / The panther's scream, filled night with fear / And bears preyed on the swine." The Lincolns may have gotten their light at night partly through a wick lit in a cup of bear's grease. Another family in the vicinity recalled seeing the glowing eyes of wolves reflecting its fire through spaces in its cabin walls at night. A few years before the Lincolns arrived, a brother and sister picking grapes were attacked by a panther. The girl was killed before her brother could kill the beast with a tomahawk to the skull.

Places like this were all but untouched by the swim of commerce or the quickening effects of the cash economy. The Lincoln household, like so many others at this time, was largely self-sufficient. A. H. Chapman, who was familiar with the family, reported to Herndon: "They taned there own Leather & Young Hanks made them Shoes out of their rude Leather. There clothing was all made at home & the Material from which it was made was also made at home." The Lincolns could trade for other goods they needed, but it was mostly a barter economy, or as Dennis Hanks told Herndon, "Hogs and Venison hams was a Legal tender and Coon Skins all so." According to Hanks, Thomas Lincoln sold his place in Kentucky for three hundred dollars "and took it—the $300—in whiskey."

Thomas Lincoln was a pre-market man. He was blissfully untouched by what much later would be called "consumerism." A neighbor told Herndon that he "was happy—lived Easy—& contented. Had but few wants and Supplied these." Dennis Hanks put it in similar terms to Herndon: "He was a man who took the world Easy—did not possess much Envy. He never thought that gold was God." Yet another observer makes the connection between these qualities in Thomas Lincoln and economic isolation: "Well, you see, he was like the other people in that country. None of them worked to get ahead. There wasn't no market for nothing unless you took it across two or three states. The people raised just what they needed."

It was this very contentment that must have so vexed his son. Thomas Lincoln wasn't indolent or irresponsible; he was *content* and therefore lacked all ambition. For his son, it was a contentment of stagnation and wasted potential, of mindless labor and equally mindless leisure. In this difference of perspective yawned a vast, unbridgeable gap in worldview.

Historian Jean Baker writes of the contrast between the "rusticity," with its "pre-modern sense of things," of Lincoln's family and what would become his own "bourgeois" mentality. Lincoln had no interest in learning his father's carpentry, and, as his stepmother said, "he didn't like physical labor." Even if his stepmother is right that her husband never interfered with Lincoln's reading—at least "if he could avoid it"—the gap between the unlettered father and his increasingly lettered son had to be another source of tension. One study of the autobiographies of self-made men in the eighteenth and nineteenth centuries found the dynamic that characterized the relationship between Lincoln and his father was so familiar it was a cliché: "The son's ambitions juxtaposed against the father's failure," while "the opportunity to quit the family farm is presented as a deliverance."

Lincoln found the beginning of his deliverance in words. Books lifted Lincoln's sights beyond the constraints of his immediate environs and gave him the skills to transcend his upbringing. It fell to him to discover and master them mostly on his own. As Lincoln said later of his frontier surroundings, "If a straggler supposed to understand latin, happened to so-journ in the neighborhood, he was looked upon as a wizzard. There was absolutely nothing to excite ambition for education." Famously, Lincoln had little in the way of formal schooling, less than a year total by his estimate. In a brief biographical sketch that he wrote as a congressman, he captured the matter in two words: "Education defective." In another autobiographical account, he noted, "What he has in the way of education, he has picked up. . . . He regrets his lack of education, and does what he can to supply the want."

As a child, he went to a tiny schoolhouse briefly in Kentucky, about two or three miles from his cabin, and not for the last time made an impression with his inappropriate attire. He came home crying the first day after the other kids made fun of him for wearing a sunbonnet. Subsequently, a man named Caleb Hazel became his instructor. A friend of the Lincoln family at the time wrote Herndon a letter noting how "Abraham Commenced trugging his way to school to Caleb Hezle—with whom I was well-acquainted & could perhaps teach spelling reading & indifferent writing & perhaps could Cipher to the rule of three—but had no other qualifications of a teacher except large size & bodily Strength to thrash any boy or youth that came to his School, and as Caleb lived in hazel nut switch country, no doubt but that young Abraham received due allowances."

Once in Indiana, Lincoln attended "ABC schools" on and off. Reading, writing, and very basic math—the so-called ciphering to the rule of three—made up the curriculum in these schools. Teachers might beat the hell out of offending students. The equivalent of a gold star to reward a student might be a plug of tobacco or draft of whiskey. Teachers emphasized reading aloud (hence the term "blab" schools) and rote memorization.

Lincoln captured the pedagogical atmosphere with a story he told in the White House. A little boy named Bud was behind in his reading and had the misfortune to be selected to read aloud the story of Nebuchadnezzar and the Golden Image from the book of Daniel. The poor child mangled the names Shadrach, Meshach, and Abednego. The instructor cuffed the lad in the head and he dissolved into tears. After the rest of the class had read, his turn again approached and he began to blubber. The teacher asked him what was wrong. He pointed at the impending verse and cried: "Look there marster, there comes them same damn three fellers again."

Spelling was an obsession and even a public entertainment, with Fridays devoted to contests. Lincoln bested his classmates in spelling, but he hardly mastered it. He never stopped writing the possessive of "it" as "it's." Well into his adulthood he spelled very "verry." He lacked all self-consciousness about his deficiency, even in the White House. He once asked a group of visitors how to spell "missile" and told Supreme Court justice David Davis at a reception in 1865 that he had only just learned the correct spelling of *maintenance*.

Altogether, Lincoln proved a diligent and impressive student. In his raccoon cap and too-short buckskin pants—one fellow student recalled how "there was bare & naked 6 or more inches of Abe Lincoln shin bone"—he outpaced his teachers by some accounts. According to John Hanks, another first cousin of Lincoln's mother who lived in the Lincoln household, he "*worked* his way by toil: to learn was hard for him, but he walked Slowly, but Surely." Lincoln explained to other students things he had read, in the kind of simple, illustrative terms that became his signature as a public communicator.

His education, though, had fundamentally to be self-directed, "picked up." He worked out sums on a wooden shovel, scraping and wiping it off and repeating. He practiced writing letters on whatever surface happened to be at hand. Above all, he read. Into spare moments as a boy and young adult he poured his appetite for books. He read aloud walking to and from school. He read during lunch breaks while working. He read during meals. He read during his free time on Sundays. He read, by one account, at the end of each plow furrow while allowing his horse to "breathe."

John Hanks called Lincoln "a Constant and voracious reader." When he got home from work, according to Hanks, "he would go to the Cupboard—Snatch a piece of Corn bread—take down a book—Sit down on a chair—Cock his legs up as high as his head and read." The popular image of him reading by firelight is irresistible, although false according to his stepmother. She said he "studied in the day time," and "got up Early and then read."

His stepmother describes his self-devised and -enforced program: "Abe read all the books he could lay his hands on—and when he came across a passage that Struck him he would write it down on boards if he had no paper & keep it there till he did get paper—then he would re-write it—look at it repeat it—He had a copy book—a kind of scrap book in which he put down all things and this preserved them. He ciphered on boards when he had no paper or no slate and when the board would get too black he would shave it off with a drawing knife and go on again: When he had paper he put his sums down on it."

He read the Bible (the family copy had been published in 1799 and its original price was twenty-seven shillings), from which his mother had told him stories even before he could read. He recalled hearing the sound of her voice when he later came across certain verses. He read, among other books, Aesop's Fables, the *Arabian Nights*, *Pilgrim's Progress*, and biographies of George Washington and Henry Clay. He borrowed a biography of Washington from a farmer named Josiah Crawford. When it was damaged by rain, Crawford made Lincoln work it off. He had to "pull fodder"—stripping the leaves off corn for cattle fodder—in Crawford's field as recompense.

Lincoln's fare also included schoolbooks and anthologies that could be extraordinarily rich. They contained literary excerpts and exhortations to upright behavior. Lincoln insisted that Lindley Murray's *English Reader*—featuring readings from Cicero, St. Paul, Lord Mansfield, and much more—was "the greatest and most useful book that could be put in the hands of a child at school." His stepmother is reported to have brought to Indiana with her *Lessons in Elocution*; its excerpts from Shakespeare may have given Lincoln his first introduction to the Bard. Dennis Hanks claimed that "Abe was so attached to reading we had to buy him . . . the Columbian Orator or American Preceptor" (the subtitle of the *Orator* was, in part, "Rules Calculated to Improve Youth and Others in the Ornamental and Useful Art of Eloquence").

Lincoln began consuming newspapers by the late 1820s. His stepmother recalled, "I think newspapers were had in Indiana as Early as 1824 & up to 1830 when we moved to Ills—Abe was a

Constant reader of them." They provided a ready window into national affairs, and presumably an early education in politics. Lincoln neighbor William Wood told Herndon: "I took news papers—some from Ohio—Cincinnatie—the names of which I have now forgotten—One of these papers was a temperance paper. Abe used to borrow it—take it home and read it & talk it over with me."

Another neighbor, John Romine, remembered a similar experience: "Abe borrowed a newspaper from me which contained a long editorial about Thomas Jefferson, and read the entire paper by firelight. The next morning he returned the paper, and it seemed to me that he could repeat every word in that editorial, and not only that. [H]e could recount all the news items, as well as tell all about the advertisements." Romine said that "while but a boy [he] had the best memory of any person I ever knew."

If Lincoln's studiousness entered lore as evidence of his determined striving, it didn't strike all of those around him as particularly admirable—certainly not compared to what was considered honest labor. A neighbor in Illinois remembered they "uset to think he would n't amount to much. You see, it war n't book-readin' then, it war work, that counted." An acquaintance from Illinois commented later, "Lincoln was a mighty lazy man. Why, I've seen him under a tree with a book in his hand and too mortal lazy to move around when the sun came around." A former employer recalled in a similar vein that "Abe was awful lazy: he worked for me—was always reading & thinking—used to get mad at him." Another neighbor noted, "He was no hand to pitch in at work like killing Snakes."

Despite the assurance of Lincoln's stepmother, his father may well have shared this estimate of his son's bookishness. Dennis Hanks told Herndon that Lincoln "was a Constant and I m[a]y

Say *Stubborn* reader, his father having Sometimes to slash him for neglecting his work by reading." According to Hanks, Lincoln's father said that when it came to his son's reading he initially had "to pull the old sow up to the trough," but "then and now he had to pull her away." After Abraham left home, Thomas Lincoln remarked, if one account is to be believed, "I suppose that Abe is still fooling hisself with eddication. I tried to stop it, but he has got that fool idea in his head, and it can't be got out."

As Abraham got older and Thomas became more frail, his father relied on him more for physical tasks. Thomas still had a large household to support, and when a friend defaulted on a loan he had endorsed, it added to the finacial strain. He began to hire Lincoln out, which was his legal right until his son reached age twenty-one. Abraham worked; Thomas took his wages for the family.

Abraham was enlisted in every kind of job imaginable, from cutting corn to digging wells. Long afterward he recalled that he had "fought until his twentieth year . . . with the trees and logs and grubs." Lincoln worked for as little as ten cents a day, and at least once was paid in corn. At one point, he got thirty-one cents a day butchering hogs, a brutal and nasty business even prior to the horrors of the age of Upton Sinclair's *The Jungle*. When it came to all this toil, Lincoln's flesh was strong but his spirit wasn't so willing. He said that "his father taught him to work but never learned him to love it."

Lincoln labored under a sense of injustice. He worked hard, stealing time from pursuits he found more congenial and productive, yet he couldn't keep the proceeds for himself. "I used to be a slave," he said in a speech in 1856, a rank exaggeration tinged with not a little self-pity. But the statement spoke to how deeply he felt a principle that would come to define his antislavery advocacy at its core: A person, as a basic matter of justice, deserved to keep what he earned. A friend from Illinois who heard the 1856 speech remembered him arguing that "we were all slaves one time or another." The difference was "that white men could make themselves free and the [N]egroes could not."

As an avenue of freedom, the water beckoned. If books were an intellectual escape, the rivers were a physical one. They were the interstate highways of the time. The roads themselves were atrocious. It's a symptom of their general state that an Ohio law set the maximum height for a stump in the road at one foot. And bridges hardly existed. Because shipping by land was too time-consuming and expensive, rivers provided the avenue to markets.

It was one thing to get downriver, with the current carrying rafts or flatboats and their cargo to their destinations. It was quite another to get back upriver. According to George Rogers Taylor, you could get to New Orleans from western Pennsylvania in about a month, but it would take four times as long to get back up—with keel-boats or barges that were poled, pulled, rowed, or sailed back upriver. Often men who took flatboats down to New Orleans had to walk back to where they started. A. H. Chapman said that Thomas Lincoln walked back to Kentucky after two trips to New Orleans.

The advent of the steamboat changed everything. "By 1830," Taylor writes, "it dominated American river transportation and for two decades thereafter was the most important agency of internal transportation in the country." It was not only faster and could carry more than primitive boats; it also could power its way back upriver. It took roughly three months to get from New Orleans to above Louisville by keelboat; by the 1850s, a steamboat could do it in about a week. The steamboat was especially important in the Mississippi River valley. "No section of the country," he explains, "was so completely dependent upon steam for effective transportation, and in no other part of the world were so many steamboats built and operated."

Lincoln got caught up in the riverine commercial current. One summer, he and Dennis Hanks chopped wood on the bank of the Ohio River to sell for fuel to passing steamboats. They ended up trading nine cords of firewood for nine yards of white domestic cloth. According to Hanks, "Abe had a shirt made, and it was positively the first white shirt which . . . he had ever owned or worn." Subsequently, and close to the spot where he and Hanks had tried to sell their wood, Lincoln worked for a farmer named James Taylor, who ran a packinghouse and ferry across the Anderson River. Among other tasks, Lincoln operated the ferry. One customer recalled that at low tide he could power the boat across the river "with one sweep of the oars."

Nearby was the town of Troy, where Lincoln surely spent time and which, compared to his home, might as well have been Paris. "Steamboat traffic brought a cosmopolitan touch to the river towns," Lincoln biographer Louis Warren writes. "Arrivals and departures provided never-ending excitement. On board were prospective settlers and immigrants with their families and curious travelers from the East and Europe, as well as merchants and boatmen."

In 1828, he took a flatboat down to New Orleans on behalf of the merchant James Gentry, together with Gentry's son. The owner of a store in what was still basically a barter economy, Gentry accumulated produce and then found a market for it farther south. Lincoln and Gentry floated down the Ohio and Mississippi rivers, on a trip of twelve hundred miles that would take about two months all told. They traded with the plantations on the banks as they went, before reaching New Orleans. It was one of the biggest cities in the country, a bustling outlet for the products of the lower South and Ohio River valley and the second-largest exporter in the country after New York. "Everybody makes money here," one observer wrote of the city. "Raw materials are all cheap and labor of every kind dear. The whole western world must come here and they do come and leave their money."

Shortly after he got back—in all likelihood, via steamboat—Lincoln asked a neighbor for help escaping from his family, to work on a steamboat even though he was still a minor legally obligated to his father. William Wood told Herndon that "Abe came to my house one day and stood around about timid & Shy. I Knew he wanted Something. I said to him—Abe what is your Case. Abe replied—'Uncle I want you to go to the River—(the Ohio) and give me Some recommendation to some boat.' I remarked—'Abe—your age is against you—you are not 21 yet.' 'I Know that, but I want a start' said Abe. I concluded not to go for the boys good."

Lincoln accompanied his family on another move, this time to Macon County, Illinois, near Decatur. Two yoke of oxen drew the family wagon, which had been put together with wooden pins and had rawhide tires. (According to one account, they stopped in a town where Lincoln saw his first printing press.) After a miserable winter, Lincoln's father proposed to move again, and Lincoln instead struck out on his own with a bundle of his belongings. He departed a "friendless, uneducated, penniless boy," in his oft-quoted words, sure of nothing, perhaps, except that he wasn't going to be a farmer or carpenter, or do anything that entailed working with his hands if he could help it. He had left his family, and he was well and truly gone.

"He never once," Michael Burlingame writes, "invited Thomas or his wife to Springfield during the entire twenty-four-year span Lincoln lived there." He didn't visit his father in 1851 when the latter was dying. In a letter to his stepbrother, he pleaded the press of business and Mary's illness. However, he added that his stepbrother should tell his father "that if we could meet now, it is doubtful whether it would not be more painful than pleasant."

When Lincoln left home, he got his "start" with a figure, the merchant Denton Offutt, who was the opposite of his father in every important respect, for good and mostly ill. Unlike Thomas Lincoln, Offutt was a hard-drinking, unreliable, and improvident huckster. Unlike Thomas Lincoln, he always had an eye on the main chance and lurched from one get-rich-quick scheme to another. Unlike Thomas Lincoln, he saw only limitless possibilities in the young Lincoln and bootstrapped him into his business ventures.

Offutt hired Lincoln, along with two others, to take a flatboat with produce down to New Orleans with him. John Hanks, part of the entourage, described the journey to Herndon and painted a picture of the multifaceted ardors of such a trip at the time. First, "I and Abe went down the Sangamon River from Decatur to Springfield in a canoe." (Lincoln explained in his own account that melting snows made the roads impassable.) They found a spot where they "cut & cared—& hewed timber to frame a flat boat—80 feet long & 18 feet wide." They floated the timbers down to Sangamon town in a raft and built the boat while they camped out—"done our own Cooking—mending & washing."

Then the completed boat was "loaded with bacon—pork—Corn & live hogs," and on its way.

On the return trip, according to Hanks (although Lincoln remembered him not making it all the way to New Orleans), he and Lincoln got back to St. Louis together, and from there they walked. They got "out to Edwards afoot and there the Roads parted, he taking the Charleston–Coles Co Road & I the Decatur Road—both afoot all the way."

During the trip, Offutt grew quite enamored with Lincoln, who cleverly saved the boat when it got hung up on the mill dam at New Salem, Illinois, on the Sangamon River. He enthused that "Lincoln can do any thing. I really believe he could take the flat-boat back again up the river." As Lincoln remembered it, Offutt "conceved a liking for A. and believing he could turn him to account, he contracted him to act as a clerk for him." Lincoln worked in the store Offutt opened in the promising village of New Salem.

People moved into Illinois starting in the south, and at the time of its establishment two years prior to Lincoln's arrival, New Salem didn't have many appreciable settlements to its north. Perched on a bluff above the Sangamon, it began with the typical nucleus of a pioneer village—a mill, a store, and a saloon—and catered to the commercial needs of farmers in the vicinity. It had a tiny population consisting of a couple of dozen families, including a large contingent who were, like Lincoln, originally from Kentucky. Its structures were mostly one-story high, one- or two-room log houses. After social gatherings at night, hosts and guests might all bed down to sleep on the floor together.

A major urban center compared to his former homes, New Salem constituted a perfect launching pad for Lincoln. "Like

Westerners in general," historian Benjamin Thomas writes, "the people of New Salem were young, enthusiastic, self-reliant, willing to take a chance. Equality of opportunity was in large degree a fact, and courage, endurance, and ingenuity were the requisites of success." Conscientious and courteous, Lincoln impressed people and won friends at Offutt's (short-lived) store. He had two qualities that served him well in this coarse, male-dominated world. Big, strong, and athletic, he had the physical prowess on which labor and manly prestige depended. And he could make men laugh.

He had always been an unusual physical specimen. His father had said, as only a carpenter could, that he "looked as if he'd been chopped out with an axe an' needed a jack-plane tuk to him." At six feet four, 180 pounds as a grown man, Lincoln excelled in the competitions that were a running strongman contest on the frontier. He could outrun, outjump, and outlift his peers, or as Stephen Douglas put it in his first debate with Lincoln in 1858, "he could beat any of the boys wrestling, or running a foot race, in pitching quoits or tossing a copper."

Lincoln brought an irresistible sense of humor to gatherings of men. He had a limitless supply of stories, some so ribald—or "on the vulger order," as an old listener put it—that friends hesitated to repeat them for posterity's sake after he had achieved greatness. He could be an inspired practical joker. When he was the local postmaster, Lincoln was irked by an illiterate man named Johnson Elmore who repeatedly asked if he had any letters. Knowing that the man would take it to friends to read for him, Lincoln finally wrote a fake letter to Elmore from a black woman in Kentucky in a familiar tone that concluded, "Johns—Come & see me and old master won't Kick you out of the Kitchen any more."

Lincoln's trustworthiness made him a natural umpire in the competitions that enlivened the community. He refereed the horse races, and a witness attests it was his disinterestedness in judging these contests that first earned him the sobriquet "Honest Abe." According to one story, Lincoln was the judge of a cockfight involving a rooster of one Babb McNabb. When it came time for the match, McNabb's rooster ran off and perched itself on a fence, where it displayed itself proudly. McNabb upbraided the bird: "Yes, you little cuss, you're great on dress parade, but not worth a damn in a fight." During the war, Lincoln compared the impressive-looking but battle-shy General McClellan to Babb McNabb's rooster.

"Lincoln *had nothing only plenty of friends*," someone who knew him in New Salem recalled. Historian William Miller notes that once Lincoln set out on his own, "it is striking how rapidly his life opens out and heads upward. How easily the doors open for him. How few barriers there appear to be. How readily he finds sponsors, and supporters—including persons in the upper ranks." Lincoln himself wrote of New Salem, "Here he rapidly made acquaintances and friends."

Some of them convinced him to run for the state legislature in 1832. During this, his first race, he was just twenty-three and had been away from home for a year. To go from rootless flatboat operator and store clerk to elected official—even in the decidedly non-august Illinois legislature—represented a giant leap. Not everyone may have taken it seriously. One friend said of Lincoln's promoters, "He was so uncouth and awkward, and so illy dressed, that his candidacy afforded a pleasant diversion for them, but it was not expected that it would go any further."

But Lincoln knew the Sangamon River, the artery on which the future of the town depended. Could it become a viable throughway, putting New Salem on the commercial map and providing easier access to textiles and farm implements from the east? Whether the river could be improved was as important, in mid-nineteenth-century terms, as whether an interstate highway would be built nearby with an exit at the town. As it stood, the Sangamon was a sorry and sinuous river fit only for flatboats. It had to be improved and become navigable for light-draft steamboats if New Salem were to realize its potential. The Sangamon reputedly took 150 miles of river to cover forty-five miles as the crow flies. Lincoln joked that he once headed downriver and ended up camped at exactly the same spot three straight nights.

As an aspiring representative of the village's interests, candidate Lincoln opposed a railroad project that would bypass the burg. He instead pumped for straightening and deepening the Sangamon. Early in 1832, he joined the men wielding long-handled axes who helped chop the river clear for a steamboat to make its way up it past New Salem, to much fanfare. But then the river fell. Lincoln assisted on the boat during its desultory retreat. It struggled to make its way back downriver, its cabin raked by low-hanging trees. The ballyhooed voyage, which had held out the prospect of freight arriving from St. Louis at a much diminished cost, ended in a fizzle.

In a notice of his candidacy in the *Sangamo Journal*, Lincoln declared his support for education and "internal improvements" (or, in modern parlance, infrastructure). In other words, he wanted people better educated for a world beyond subsistence agriculture, and he wanted to aid the development of the connective tissue of transport and communication to hasten that world's emergence. These are themes that would carry through Lincoln's politics throughout the decades.

"For my part," he wrote, "I desire to see the time when education, and by its means, morality, sobriety, enterprise and industry, shall become much more general than at present." On improvements, he argued, "With respect to the county of Sangamo, some more easy means of communication than we now possess, for the purpose of facilitating the task of exporting the surplus products of its fertile soil, and importing necessary articles from abroad, are indispensably necessary." And if he weren't elected, well, "I have been too familiar with disappointments to be very much chagrined."

Even in this first campaign, we can see in rough outline what would become the trademark Lincoln formula: a high-minded program of uplift and improvement (both personal and collective), presented with a winsome political touch.

The emphasis on "more easy means of communication" was latent with revolutionary economic potential. The extension of modern transportation networks would take a sledgehammer to the subsistence economy of Lincoln's youth. It would make it obsolete, impossible even. "Members of inland communities found it hard to resist the high-quality manufactures that good roads, canals, and railroads made available at unprecedented low prices," historian Bruce Levine writes. "But the extra money needed to buy such items compelled them to sell still more goods and increasingly to focus their efforts on raising crops that would command the highest price in distant markets." In its remorseless logic, newly open markets drove specialization. They meant it no longer made sense for farmers even to grow all their own food, let alone make their own agricultural implements. The enmeshment of farmers "with commerce grew into a dependence upon the market and subordination to its rhythms."

Whatever the merits of his vision, Lincoln didn't have much time to campaign. As Offutt's store died (it was the kind of venture that might have benefited if New Salem had been better connected to St. Louis via the Sangamon), Lincoln joined the militia for the Black Hawk War. When his service ended uneventfully, he made his way back to New Salem by hook and crook after someone stole his horse the night before his departure. Out on the hustings, he cut quite the figure, as usual. "I well remember," a prospective constituent said later, "how he was dressed he wore flax & tow linnen pantaloons—I thought about 5 inches too short in the legs and frequently he had but one Suspender—no vest or Coat he Wore a Calico Shert Such as he had in the black Hawk War he wore coarse Brogans Tan Couler Blue Yarn Socks & straw Hat—old style and without a band."

He didn't win, place, or show, or even finish seventh. He polled eighth out of thirteen candidates. The top four finishers won seats in the legislature. He didn't do so well in the broader county, where he wasn't well-known and didn't get enough of a chance to introduce himself. But he nearly swept the votes of New Salem.

Lincoln opened his own store with a friend, before it, too, "winked out," in Lincoln's words. The business failure saddled him—together with some minor speculative ventures that went nowhere—with a lawsuit-spawning mess of liabilities. He called it his "national debt" and it dogged him for years. Herndon maintained that even as a congressman Lincoln still worked to pay it off, although he was probably free of it by then.

He won appointment as the local postmaster for a time, a minor post, but one that supplied a trickle of income and—gratifyingly—access to newspapers. Based in Samuel Hill's store, Lincoln ran his operation informally if conscientiously. He kept receipts in an old blue sock. There were not yet any envelopes or stamps, and his first year on the job, a post rider still brought the mail to town. Lincoln was known to tuck letters into his hat and deliver them on foot to people who didn't come to get them.

He also became a deputy to the county surveyor, a job, as he put it later, that "procured bread, and kept body and soul together." In another act of self-education, he boned up on plane geometry and trigonometry, studying such texts as Abel Flint's *A System of Geometry and Trigonometry with a Treatise on Surveying*, and Robert Gibson's *Treatise on Practical Surveying*. He bought a fifty-dollar horse on credit and, wearing an old straw hat, dove into the brush with surveyor's compass and chain. One farmer sold him two buckskins, which a friend's wife used to "fox" his pants to protect them from getting shredded in the brambles.

A talented and scrupulous surveyor, Lincoln found himself a sought-after umpire of land disputes in a growing area in need of constant surveying. This was Lincoln's granular experience with the property rights to which he would become so firmly committed. As he worked throughout the area, he was a kind of walking billboard for himself. "Not only did his wit, kindliness, and knowledge attract people," said his friend Coleman Smoot, "but his strange clothes and uncouth awkwardness advertised him, the shortness of his trousers causing particular remark and amusement. Soon the name 'Abe Lincoln' was a household word."

He ran again for the legislature, introducing himself far and wide. When one group of men harvesting grain vowed not to vote for anyone who couldn't work, Lincoln took up and adeptly wielded a cradled scythe in the field: "Boys if that is all i am shure of your votes," a witness recalled him saying. He gave out candy and nuts to kids. William Butler said he made such a good candidate because he was "genial, kind, sympathetic, open-hearted," and when he gave an answer to a question "it was always characteristic, brief, pointed, *à propos*, out of the common way and manner, and yet exactly suited to the time place and thing."

This time, he finished second among all candidates, and within fifteen votes of first. He was headed to the state capital of Vandalia, and a four-dollar-a-day salary, the most he had ever earned in his life. He was still just twenty-five years old, and before he reached thirty, would be his party's nominee to become Speaker of the Illinois House. He borrowed two hundred dollars from the well-off Coleman Smoot (paid back as promised) and plowed sixty dollars into his first suit of clothes, remembered by one witness as "a very respectable looking suit of jeans."

The legislature exposed Lincoln to a level of attainments he had never before encountered. Lincoln nonetheless returned to New Salem nearly as desperate as he had left it. William Butler, who boarded Lincoln for a time, remembered noticing his unease on the way home. "All the rest of you have something to look forward to," Lincoln explained, "and all are glad to get home, and will have something to do when you get there. But it isn't so with me. I am going home, Butler, without a thing in the world." His partner in the failed store had died, and he committed to paying off this other half of the debt as well. A judge attached Lincoln's surveying equipment, cutting off that source of income. It was put up to auction and one of Lincoln's boosters bought it for $120 and returned it to him.

Around this time, Lincoln resolved to study the law. He had arrived in New Salem with his commitment to reading intact.

It filled his spare moments. New Salemite Robert B. Rutledge recalled: "While clerking for Offatt [Offutt] as Post Master or in the pursuit of any avocation, An opportunity would offer, he would apply himself to his studies, if it was but five minutes time, would open his book, which he always kept at hand, & study, close it recite to himself, then entertain company or wait on a Customer in the Store or post office apparently without any interruption. When passing from business to boarding house for meals, he could usually be seen with his book under his arm, or open in his hand reading as he walked." Another resident remembered that the first time he saw Lincoln "he was lying on a trundle bed rocking a cradle with his foot—was almost covered with papers and books."

A friend reported that "History and poetry & the newspapers constituted the most of his reading." But Lincoln also undertook a concerted self-directed program of the study of grammar. He walked some six miles, so the story goes, to procure a copy of Samuel Kirkham's *English Grammar* from a farmer. The text wasn't exactly inviting. At the beginning, it explained, "Grammar is divided into four parts; 1. Orthography, 2. Etymology, 3. Syntax, 4. Prosody." Lincoln asked a local schoolteacher for help when something stumped him, and had friends drill him. By one account, he mastered it in a matter of weeks and told a friend, "if that is what they call a science I'll subdue another."

When one of his old friends who had quizzed him, William Greene, visited him in Washington during the war, Lincoln introduced him to Secretary of State William Seward as the man who taught him grammar. Embarrassed, the friend objected to Lincoln afterward that all he had done was hold the book to see if Lincoln could give the right answers, and "that was not teaching you grammar." Lincoln replied, "Well, that was all the teaching of grammar I ever had."

All of this was only a warm-up for his most momentous program of self-education, as a lawyer. Legal contention had been part of his upbringing. His father was drawn into lawsuits over land titles back in Kentucky. And Lincoln sought out courtroom experiences. On the frontier, court day provided the occasion, as an observer put it, for "bustle, business, energy, hilarity, novelty, irony, sarcasm, excitement, and eloquence." Dennis Hanks said of Lincoln back in Indiana, "He attended trials—went to Court—read the Rev. Statutes of Indiana dated 1824—Heard law Speeches & listened to law trials &c &c."

However much Lincoln enjoyed the verbal pyrotechnics, the law must have represented to him the definitive step into a world above and beyond farming and related labor. "The law was the only profession within his reach," Brian Dirck writes in his book on Lincoln as a lawyer, "where reading and talking were not the mark of laziness, but of merit—that, and politics." Of course, the two were intertwined. Years later, in notes for a lecture on the law, Lincoln wrote of the "extent confidence and honors are reposed in and conferred upon lawyers by the people." Herndon maintained Lincoln always thought of the law "as a stepping stone to a political life."

At first he hesitated, doubting whether he had the education to make a go of it as a lawyer. He said he thought about becoming a blacksmith instead. But mentors encouraged him. One of them was the colorfully named local justice of the peace, Bowling Green, a "reading man" whose girth earned him the nickname "Pot." He allowed Lincoln to argue minor matters in his court, partly for the amusement value. Lincoln could always be counted on to make him laugh, so "as to produce," one witness to the proceedings remembered, "a spasmatic shaking of the very fat sides of the old law functionary." Still, he had the highest regard for the abilities of the young man some twenty years his junior, for whom he was a mentor and "almost Second Farther," according to a friend.

A friend of Lincoln from the Black Hawk War and the state legislature, the polished and accomplished Springfield lawyer John Stuart, urged him to take up the law. Lincoln borrowed Stuart's law books, and then bought at auction a copy of Sir William Blackstone's *Commentaries on the Laws of England* (the legend maintains that he found the copy at the bottom of a pile of junk he bought to help out a hard-pressed traveler). At the time, there were no law schools in the state of Illinois. Studying on his own, as Lincoln put it, he "went at it in good earnest." He may have mastered forty pages of Blackstone on the first day, and read it through twice.

The book was read by almost every aspiring American lawyer of the time. An effort to make the law something "to be cultivated, methodized, and explained," it must have appealed to the orderliness of Lincoln's mind. This is a man, after all, who went on to study geometry in his free time, and by his account, "nearly mastered the six books of Euclid."

Lincoln picked up other standard volumes of law and read them whenever he could, even as he kept surveying "to pay board and clothing bills." People remembered seeing him studying barefoot under a tree. Russell Godbey, an acquaintance, told Herndon "the first time I Ever Saw him with a law book in his hands he was Sitting astraddle of Jake Bails wood pile in New Salem—Said to him—'Abe—what are you studying' 'Studying law'—replied Abe. 'Great God Almighty—' Said Godbey." One New Salemite thought, "he read so much—was so studious— took so little physical exercise—was so laborious in his studies that he became Emaciated & his best friends were afraid that he would craze himself."

By 1837, Lincoln was officially enrolled as a lawyer. That year, he borrowed a horse, packed his few belongings in his saddlebags, and left a dying New Salem. He headed to Springfield. There he became law partners with the already-established John Stuart, a boon to the neophyte barrister. The first case we know that he handled involved a disagreement over payment to James P. Hawthorn for breaking the sod on thirty-eight acres of David Wooldridge's land.

It was the kind of suit you could imagine entangling his father, who once had to sue for payment for hewing timbers. In the speech recalled by John Roll noting his own putative slavery, Lincoln supposedly called out, "There is my old friend John Roll. He used to be a slave, but he has made himself free, and I used to be a slave, and now I am so free they let me practice law." For him, the law office felt like a liberation, from out of the bondage of toil for others into the fresh free air of making the most of his talents.

Lincoln had risen above drudgery. He would be paid for his knowledge and analytical prowess. He would read, write, and argue for a living. He wasn't a man of the axe, but of the book— and of those silver half-dollars. He was a lawyer and a politician, though of a particular type. By habit, outlook, and partisan commitment, Lincoln emerged from the backwoods, not a Jacksonian Democrat like so many of his neighbors, but a devoted Whig.

Chapter 2

"The Sober, Industrious, Thriving People": A Devoted Whig

He loved the struggling masses—all uprising towards a
higher Civilization had his assent & his prayer.
—David Davis, Interview with William
Herndon, 1866

When Lincoln was offered his deputy surveyorship in 1833 he wasn't in a position to be picky. He needed to eat. Yet delighted as he was by the opportunity, he made a stipulation before taking it. A man named John Moore Fisk related the story to Herndon: A friend of Lincoln's named Pollard Simmons knew Lincoln "was very poor at that time" and so wanted to do Lincoln a favor. He asked the surveyor of Sangamon County, John Calhoun, to give Lincoln the deputy job. Calhoun agreed. So far, so good. But Calhoun was a Democrat and it was a political appointment, although a minor one.

Fisk tells the rest: "Simmons got on his horse and went on the hunt of Lincoln whom he found in the woods mauling rails. Simmons Said 'Lincoln I've got you a job' and to which Lincoln replied—'Pollard, I thank you for your trouble, but now let me ask you a question—Do I have to give up any of my principles for this job? If I have to surrender any thought or principle to get it I wouldn't touch it with a ten foot pole.' 'No, you do not Lincoln,' said Pollard Simmons, and to which Lincoln replied—'Ill accept the office and now I thank you and my superior for it.' "

At this point in his life, Lincoln wasn't established in anything—except, apparently, his Whig principles. The surveying job fell into his lap like manna from heaven. It made it possible for him to earn a living. But that didn't trump his political commitments. Years later, in 1844, Lincoln ended up engaging Calhoun in a series of debates over tariff policy. According to one witness, "they were the best debaters—most Logical & finest debates on the Tariff question in the State."

In Illinois in the 1830s, there wasn't much reason to be a Whig other than principle and personal predilection. It was a heavily Jacksonian state, far from the party's political and cultural stronghold in New England. The Whigs never elected a governor or senator in Illinois. They always lost the state in presidential elections. "From 1830 up to 1837 the tendency in Illinois was for every man of ambition to turn Democrite," Lincoln's early law partner John Todd Stuart told Herndon. "There was a fear," he explained, "that the Yankees about 1832 to 1837 imigrating to Ills would be whig—but when they got here were no more than democrats."

Lincoln especially disdained the opportunists who switched from Whig to Democrat to better make their way in the state. Joshua Speed wrote a letter to Herndon recounting an incident from Lincoln's campaign for the legislature in 1836. Lincoln gave a speech in Springfield that thrilled the Whigs in attendance and dispirited the Democrats. George Forquer, a Democrat of some prominence, decided to rebut Lincoln and teach him a lesson. Speed writes, "Forquer had been a whig—one of the Champions of the party—But had then recently joined the Democratic party and Almost simultaneous with his change—had been appointed Register of the land office—which office he then held."

Forquer had apparently made the most of it: "Just about that time Mr F had Completed a neat frame house—the best house then in the village of Springfield and upon it had erected a lightning rod—the only one in the place and the first one Mr Lincoln had evr observed."

When Forquer rose at the event to counter Lincoln he "commenced by saying that this young man would have to be taken down and was sorry that the task devolved upon him." According to Speed, during his answer "his whole manner asserted & claimed superiority." When Forquer finished, Lincoln replied in turn. He homed in on Forquer's party switch: "The gentleman has alluded to my being a young man—I am older in years than I am in the tricks and trades of politicians—I desire to live—and I disire place and distinction as a politician—but I would rather die now than like the gentleman live to see the day that I would have to erect a lightning rod to protect a guilty Conscience from an offended God."

A few years later, Lincoln lampooned another party-switcher named Josiah Lamborn with a story of the misadventure of a slave in Kentucky. The slave was supposed to deliver two puppies to a neighbor, but when he stopped for a drink on his way, pranksters substituted piglets for the puppies, unbeknownst to him. Surprised by the advent of the piglets when he arrived to make his delivery, he turned around to go back home with them. When he stopped for another drink, the jokesters switched the puppies back. The slave exclaimed to his master when he arrived home, "I isn't drunk, but dem dar puppies can be pigs or puppies just when dey please!" Lamborn, too, Lincoln charged, could change parties "just when he pleased."

Lincoln's Whiggery wasn't subject to change. It derived from a place deep within his character. Lincoln felt drawn to the kind of people who tended to be Whigs, the "better sort," people who were firmly embedded within the commercial economy and welcomed its ethos. As the great historian of the Whigs Daniel Walker Howe points out, Lincoln's partisan commitment to the Whigs was the political expression of his individual drive, and the means by which he hoped to help his countrymen elevate themselves. He was a Whig out of aspiration—both for himself and the nation.*

This same spirit would eventually be transferred to his Republicanism, but his Whig politics matter on their own terms. He was a Whig during the entire existence of the party, for about twenty years in total. He was a proto-Whig before he ran for office and a Whig during the party's breakup in the sectional tensions of the 1850s. He was a Whig for all of his legislative career, in the Illinois House and during his one term in Congress (his central Illinois was more favorable territory for the party). He worked to build the Whig Party in Illinois, to defend and refine its doctrines, and to elect its presidential candidates. If above all else Lincoln was a politician, he was first and foremost a Whig.

And that meant, a Henry Clay man. J. Rowan Herndon, a

---

* Howe's work on the Whigs is brilliant and endlessly interesting. It informs my discussion of Whig politics and culture throughout.

cousin of William Herndon who lived in New Salem, called Lincoln, "one of the most Devoted Clay whigs in all the State. Henry Clay was his favorite of all the great men of the Nation[—] he allbut worshiped his name." Lincoln would cite Clay in his famous debates with Douglas dozens of times. In the first debate, he called Clay "my beau ideal of a statesman, the man for whom I fought all my humble life." In a letter from the White House in 1861, he referred to Clay as "him whom, during my whole political life, I have loved and revered as a teacher and leader."

A gentleman farmer from Kentucky, the charismatic Clay inspired intense devotion. He occupied the commanding heights of American politics for decades, as Speaker of the House, as a senator, and as a frequent contender for the presidency. Clay is often said to have originated the phrase "self-made man," which eventually became synonymous with Lincoln. Confronted with the argument that one of his policies—the tariff—would only support the well-heeled, Clay replied: "In Kentucky, almost every manufactory known to me, is in the hands of enterprising and self-made men, who have acquired whatever wealth they possess by patient and diligent labor." Clay depicted his own ascent as a rise up by the bootstraps. If he didn't come from poverty, he was self-educated. In his youth, he had taken the grain to the mill in an area referred to as the "slashes." Hence, he was the "Millboy of the Slashes," who had ascended to the status of great statesman.

Elected to Congress in 1810, Clay started his career as a Jeffersonian hater of banks and Great Britain. A "War Hawk," he agitated for hostilities with Britain—and got them good and hard in the War of 1812. The United States suffered serial humiliations stemming from its military and financial weakness. The White House burned and the government nearly went bankrupt, while New England threatened to secede. A dismayed Clay turned around after the war and championed his famous "American System"—banks, tariffs, and infrastructure—to strengthen the economy and the union. It became the signature program of the Whigs.

The Whigs can't be pinned down cleanly in terms of contemporary political taxonomy. Daniel Walker Howe points to a possible very rough shorthand. One might say that the Whigs supported the "positive liberal state" (affirmatively working to increase opportunity and promote the public welfare), while the Democrats believed in the "negative liberal state" (leaving people to their own devices). Howe objects to this schema, though, because it makes Whigs sound too much like contemporary liberals, when the Whigs were much more concerned with upholding moral standards and imposing discipline.

While the Whigs opposed executive power, they supported government action in furtherance of economic development. They believed in commerce and industrialization, saw a harmony of interests in all classes of society, and thought a rising tide lifts all boats. Denounced as the party of the rich, the Whigs countered via one of their newspapers: "Who are the rich men of our country? They are the enterprising mechanic, who raises himself by his ingenious labors from the dust and turmoil of his workshop, to an abode of ease and elegance; the industrious tradesman, whose patient frugality enables him at last to accumulate enough to forego the duties of the counter and indulge a well-earned leisure."

Henry Clay's program, Howe writes, embodied the Whig values of "order, harmony, purposefulness, and improvement." The Whigs championed an evangelical-inflected bourgeois morality.

Their vision of economic progress meshed with a commitment to moral progress. A mass gathering of Whigs at Bunker Hill in 1840 professed, "We believe especially, in the benign influence of religious feeling and moral instruction on the social, as well as on the individual, happiness of man." The Whigs encouraged both individual efforts at improvement, through self-discipline and work, and collective efforts, exemplified by reform movements like temperance. They considered themselves the champions of the "sober, industrious, thriving people."

As the historian of the Whigs Michael Holt relates, a fissure within the dominant Jeffersonian Republicans of the early nineteenth century ultimately created the Whigs. On the one hand, there were the moderate nationalists like Clay who supported a Hamiltonian economic program and stronger central government. On the other, there were the Old Republicans or Radicals who opposed any government centralization as a betrayal of the American Revolution.

The fiery spokesman for the latter tendency loved the simplicity of the yeoman farmer and hated the alleged greed and superficiality fostered by the economic development of the nationalists. They distrusted banks, financiers, and paper money, and therefore opposed the Clay agenda. They were egalitarians—at least when it came to the privileges of corporations or the wealth of businessmen (the riches of Southern planters were something else entirely).

The nationalists, Holt notes, had the advantage until the panic of 1819 stoked a populist reaction against the banks and the political establishment. In 1824, five different candidates ran for president. Andrew Jackson, the hero of the War of 1812, won a convincing plurality. But the election was thrown into the House, where John Quincy Adams, who had finished second in the presidential race, prevailed. An also-ran in the campaign, Henry Clay lent crucial backing to Adams in the House. President Adams subsequently made him secretary of state.

The Jackson forces screamed, "Corrupt bargain!" The charge had powerful overtones from Anglo-American history, since the king in England and colonial governors in America had sought to influence—or "corrupt"—the Parliament and colonial legislatures through alluring appointments. The slogan dogged Adams throughout his presidency and Clay for the rest of his career.

The rival Adams-Clay and Jackson alignments—destined to become the National Republicans and the Democratic Republicans (in other words, Democrats) respectively—now faced off. Jackson was the anti-establishment, anti-eastern champion, the scourge of corruption and vindicator of republican virtue. He characterized the fight as a "struggle between the virtue of the people and executive privilege." Jackson considered himself an opponent of "all banks," and had counseled a return to "our former habits of industry and simplicity" as the best prescription for the Panic of 1819. He was a friend of slave owners and hell on the Indians, whose appointed role in the Jacksonian vision was to get swept across the continent before a tide of white settlers. Unsurprisingly, Jackson found his political base in the South and the West,* although his support was by no means limited to those places. His supporters became pioneers in how to appeal to and mobilize ordinary voters in an incipient mass democracy, at a time when their rivals still practiced a dated, top-down politics.

---

*What we call the Midwest. For the sake of clarity I occasionally use the term "Midwest," although it wasn't a contemporary usage.

In Adams, the Jackson forces had a perfect foil. The book-ish Yankee had a résumé that would scream "elitist" in any era. Besides being a son of a president, he was a Harvard professor, a Massachusetts senator, a diplomat—a French speaker *and* incipient supporter of the metric system. He lacked the common touch, or really any touch at all. The Jacksonians mustered opposition to his support for high tariffs, internal improvements, and the general expansion of central power, although initiatives like a bankruptcy law (authorized by the Constitution) and a national university and astronomical observatory hardly heralded the arrival of un-checked Leviathan.

In 1828, Jackson brought down the electoral hammer on Ad-ams in a contest, as a cheeky ditty had it, "Between J. Q. Adams, who can write / And Andy Jackson, who can fight." Jackson won the largest percentage of the popular vote of any president up to the twentieth century and both houses of Congress. Despite his theoretical hatred of executive privilege, he imposed an un-precedented mass firing of federal officials for patronage reasons. Jackson established his personal dominance of American politics for the next decade. He became the sun, Henry Clay the moon. There's a reason no one speaks of the "Age of Clay."

As the National Republican presidential nominee in 1832, Clay hoped that a fight over rechartering the Bank of the United States would open up a powerful new avenue of attack for him. The Second Bank of the United States—the first had been the baby of Alexander Hamilton—acted as an incipient central bank. Its notes were the country's best paper currency and it provided some regulatory check on regional and local banks. A mixed public-private corporation, it also held potential for abuse by the well connected—imagine the Federal Reserve run by people seeking to make a profit. The headstrong president of the bank, Nicholas Biddle, pushed for a recharter four years early to force the issue. If in his zeal to kill the bank Jackson vetoed the measure after it passed Congress, Clay and his allies thought it would backfire on him. They calculated that it would turn off all the people in the South and the West who were dependent on access to cheap credit and reliable currency, and that Jackson's highhandedness would alienate congressional leaders.

Instead, Jackson famously executed one of the most punishing acts of political jujitsu in American history. He hated the bank—as a bank, as an issuer of invidious paper currency, as a fount of privilege, and as a competing center of power. He issued a rousing veto message inveighing against it as an unconstitutional excrescence on the body politic tending toward its corruption: "Many of our rich men have not been content with equal protection and equal benefits, but have besought us to make them richer by act of Congress." Biddle sniffed that the message had "all the fury of a chained panther biting the bars of his cage." But it worked. Clay got crushed. He won fewer electoral votes than Adams in 1828 and got no votes at all in Georgia, Alabama, or Mississippi. "The election of 1832," Holt writes, "clearly stamped the National Republican party as a loser and as the tool of the northeastern elite."

From the ashes of the National Republicans, the Whigs gradually arose. States' righters alienated by Jackson's robust nationalism in the nullification crisis of 1832–33 (South Carolina defied the federal government over the tariff) provided the seedbed of Whig parties in the South. Jackson's insistence on withdrawing deposits from the Bank of the United States (still in business until 1837, although not rechartered) in defiance of the law gave his opponents another hook to portray him as dangerous King

Andrew the First and galvanized his adversaries in the Congress. Jackson ran through two Treasury secretaries before settling on the redoubtable Roger Taney—long before his star turn in *Dred Scott*—to work his will as interim secretary. The Senate censured Jackson, who fumed that he wanted to duel Clay over it, and Clay's allies took over key Senate committees in a victory for the inchoate party.

It managed to unite the wildly divergent strands of the anti-Jacksonian forces under the banner "Whig," a hallowed name borrowed from the American Revolution and first promoted by a newspaper editor. At its core was opposition to executive usurpation, exemplified by Jackson with his willful temperament and authoritarian style. "The Whigs of the present day," Clay said in 1834, were heirs of the Whigs who rose up against George III. He vowed to extend "the campaign of 1777." But the revival of the spirit of the revolution got off to a bumpy start. In 1836, the Whigs didn't manage to hold a national convention, nominate a unified candidate for president, or beat Jackson's chosen successor, Martin Van Buren, who lacked all the animal political power of Old Hickory.

This is the motley, politically pressed crew to whom Lincoln hitched his political fortunes. "Always a whig in politics," Lincoln attested to Jesse Fell in 1859, although this might not have been quite right (and, as a technical matter, the Whigs didn't formally organize in Illinois until 1838). Dennis Hanks told Herndon, "I opposed Abe in Politics when he became whig—was till 20 years of age a Jackson Democrat—turned whig—or whiggish about 1828–9." Nathaniel Grigsby, a neighbor and schoolmate of Lincoln's, remembered: "Lincoln in Early years—say from 1820 to 25 was tending towards Democracy—He afterwards Changed."

This was right around the time Jackson was crushing John Adams nationally, and of course in Indiana (by double digits) and in Illinois (by a 2–1 margin). In the next presidential election, in 1832, Henry Clay got all of 31 percent of the vote in Illinois. Lincoln proudly noted years later that even though he lost his first legislative race, he won his own precinct 227–7. "And this too," he wrote of himself, "while he was an avowed Clay man, and the precinct the autumn afterwards, giving a majority of 115 to Genl. Jackson over Mr. Clay."

What attracted Lincoln to the Whigs? Why did he gravitate to the party that would never quite live down the idea that it was the heir to the defunct, aristocratic-friendly Federalists, that it was the party—in the abusive terms of the Democrats—of the "British-bought, bank-Federal-Whig gentry who wear ruffle shirts, silk stockings and Kid gloves"? Why did he associate himself, even before he had left home, even before he was out of Indiana, even before he made any money or had a profession, with the party of the snobs and the elitists, the moralists and the do-gooders? Because he wanted to be one of them. And because he wanted *others* to be like them, too.

Lincoln's Whiggery was a statement of distinctiveness from his surroundings, and the assumptions and behaviors that came with them. It qualifies as one of what historian William Miller calls his "refusals, rejections, and disengagements."

Lincoln grew up among Democrats. They were his neighbors and his family. They loved Andrew Jackson, the Mars of the backwoods, the vindicator of the West and the South and of the common farmer. "We were all Jackson boys & men at this time in Indiana," recalled Nathaniel Grigsby. Having suffered enough of agricultural life, Lincoln didn't look kindly on the agrarian romanticism of the Jacksonians. In a typical sentiment, the Jacksonian journalist William Leggett contrasted "ploughmen" with "merchants." He preferred "hardy rustics" to "lank and sallow accountants, worn out with the sordid anxieties of traffic and the calculations of gain."

Lincoln didn't mind the accountants. It is telling that an early Whig influence on Lincoln was William Jones—a storekeeper. Lincoln worked for him in Indiana and, in the words of one contemporary, "young Abe was warmly attached to Jones." The merchant was such a party stalwart that when Whig standard-bearer Henry Clay lost the presidential election in 1844, he supposedly took it so hard he couldn't work for days. The store would have been a locus for political discussion and newspaper reading. Dennis Hanks said, "[I] think Col Jones made him [Lincoln] a whig." Nathaniel Grigsby thought Jones was Lincoln's "guide & teacher in Politics." Another contemporary recalled, "Col Jones told me that Lincoln read all his books," and "often said that Lincoln would make a great man one of these days."

If the party's typical adherents in Lincoln's early life were represented by his farmer father, probably a Democrat in Indiana (although there is contention over it), and a merchant like Jones, Lincoln would take the storekeeper every time. Those two men fit within the broad demographic schema of the two parties.

Lincoln's father matched the profile of a non-immigrant, non-Catholic Democrat. "Throughout the nation," Michael Holt explains, "Democratic voting strength was concentrated among subsistence farmers in the most remote and economically underdeveloped regions of states—among voters, that is, who feared becoming ensnared in precisely the kind of commercial-monetary network Whigs wanted to foster. In addition, Democrats drew votes heavily from immigrants, Catholics, and others who resented the self-righteous moral imperialism of the dominant Protestant groups they associated with the Whigs."

Jones, on the other hand, was a standard-issue Whig: "Repelled by strident Democratic rhetoric about class conflict, appalled by the consequences of the negative state, and attracted by what they perceived as the economic benefits of the Whig program, the vast majority of wealthy businessmen, professionals, and planters supported the Whig party. So did most people in those areas most deeply involved in the commercial economy— farmers who grew cash crops, miners, manufacturers and their workers, artisans, merchants, and tradesmen."

These were Lincoln's types. Andrew Jackson himself must have had limited appeal to him, even if their backgrounds were similar. Jackson, too, was born in a log cabin. They both fought in Indian wars, although Jackson obviously with much more consequence than Lincoln, who bragged of his mock exploits in the Black Hawk War ("I had a good many bloody struggles with the musquetoes; and, although I never fainted from loss of blood, I can truly say I was often very hungry"). Jackson also made himself a lawyer, a politician, and an up-from-the-bootstraps success story. Yet these were superficialities on top of yawning differences of character and worldview.

Surely Lincoln recoiled from Jackson the duelist, the slave owner and gambler, the high-living plantation owner, the unreflective man of action, the emotional volcano. Jackson exemplified what the Whigs scorned as the "passions." He nearly got entangled in an affair of honor with John Quincy Adams's secretary of the navy *during the 1828 presidential campaign*. He was reputed to have staked his slaves in bets on horse races. He once offered a fifty-dollar reward for a runaway, stipulating "ten dollars extra for every hundred lashes a person will give to the amount of three hundred." All this would have been anathema to a Lincoln who worshipped lawfulness, the careful cultivation of talent, and self-control.

As a young man, Clay wasn't so different from Jackson. He, too, was an impulsive gambler and duelist. But he sought to overcome it. The British writer Harriet Martineau, who chronicled her travels in the United States, thought him "a man of an irritable and impetuous nature, over which he has obtained a truly noble mastery." Most of the time. When Senator John Randolph of Virginia called him a "blackleg," or a gambler who cheats, Clay challenged him to a duel despite his personal vow two years earlier not to participate in such so-called affairs of honor. The stand-off ended harmlessly enough because Clay—then serving as secretary of state—couldn't aim and Randolph didn't want to kill him. Clay articulated the standard that he tried to uphold as a general matter thusly: "All legislation, all government, all society, is formed upon the principle of mutual concession, politeness, comity, courtesy."

The Whig program of economic development and cultural uplift suited Lincoln the practitioner and apostle of self-improvement. Lincoln fashioned himself into an almost perfectly archetypal Whig. It wasn't just that he was ambitious. Plenty of people were ambitious. It was how he was ambitious and for what. His ambition was refracted through a quest for order. Historian Robert Kelley writes that Lincoln joined the party "because he preferred what Whigs believed to be a more civilized way of life." The words "more civilized" are apt. Life on the frontier could be nasty, brutish, and extraordinarily drunken. Lincoln made himself into a sort of countercultural figure. He stood aloof from all that was degrading or prone to check his advancement.

Liquor lubricated everyday life for men and women alike. People considered it an aid to labor, a great tool of medicine, and a guarantee of health. Lincoln himself stated its pervasiveness in an 1842 address to the Springfield Washington Temperance Society: "When all such of us, as have now reached the years of maturity, first opened our eyes upon the stage of existence, we found intoxicating liquor, recognized by every body, used by every body and repudiated by nobody. It commonly entered into the first draught of the infant, and the last draught of the dying man. From the sideboard of the parson, down to the ragged pocket of the houseless loafer, it was constantly found. Physicians prescribed it in this, that, and the other disease. Government provided it for its soldiers and sailors; and to have a rolling or raising, a husking or hoe-down, any where without it, was *positively insufferable.*"

Lincoln didn't drink. Alcohol made him feel "flabby and undone." His stepmother said, "He never drank whiskey or other strong drink—was temperate in all things—too much so I thought sometimes." In a tobacco-soaked environment worthy of a smoking lounge at a European airport or a major-league dugout, Lincoln didn't smoke or chew tobacco, either. He loved to tell the story of sharing a trip on the railroad with a friendly gentleman from Kentucky who offered him sequentially a plug of tobacco, a cigar, and a glass of brandy. After Lincoln refused each offer, the Kentuckian commented, "See here, my jolly companion, I have gone through the world a great deal and have had much experience with men and women of all classes, and in all climes, and I have noticed one thing." What was it? "Those who have no vices have d—d few virtues."

Lincoln didn't gamble, at horse races or cards, and despite his off-color stories, he didn't swear. Reportedly, he once tossed a man out of his store for swearing in front of ladies. As president, he used the phrase "by jings" in the telegraph office and apologized: "By jings is swearing, for my good old mother taught me that anything that had a *by* before it is swearing."

On the frontier, coarse language or a plug of tobacco was the least of it. Fighting constituted a rite of passage, and a matter of honor. Lincoln would eventually get a reputation as a peacemaker, although his record wasn't spotless. Back in Indiana, one family thought that he, "like all his Indiana cronies, was pretty much of a rowdy, and certainly, was not of a saintly nature." When he was nineteen years old, his stepbrother John Johnston fought an adversary named William Grigsby. The son of one of the farmers Lincoln worked for told Herndon: "Wm Grigsby was too much for Lincoln's man—Johnson [*sic*]. After they had fought a long time—and it having been agreed not break the ring, Abe burst through, caught Grigsby—threw him off some feet—stood up and swore he was the big buck at the lick. . . . After Abe did this—it being a general invitation for a general fight they all pitched in and had quite a general fight."

A friend of Lincoln's in New Salem recalled another brawl. Two neighbors, Henry Clark and Ben Wilcox, were embroiled in a lawsuit. Clark lost the suit but averred that nonetheless "he could whip his opponent." Lincoln was Clark's second, and a man named John Brewer the second for Wilcox. The friend recounts, "The parties met, stripped themselves all but their breeches, went in and Mr Lincoln's principal was beautifully whipped. These combats were conducted with as much ceremony and punctiliousness as ever graced the duelling ground. After the conflict the seconds conducted their respective principals to the river washed off the blood, and assisted them to dress."

Then came another provocation: "During this performance, the second of the party opposed to Mr Lincoln remarked—'Well Abe, my man has whipped yours, and I can whip you.' Now this challenge came from a man who was very small in size. Mr Lincoln agreed to fight provided he would 'chalk out his size on Mr Lincoln's person, and every blow struck outside of that mark should be counted foul.' After this sally there was the best possible humor and all parties were as orderly as if they had been engaged in the most harmless amusement."

By the standards of the time and place, Lincoln was practically Gandhi. In Indiana, he had supposedly acted as the mediator in a fierce dispute over ownership of a goose. An acquaintance in Illinois recalled, "When a fight was on hand Abe used to Say to me 'Lets go and Stop it—tell a joke—a Story—Say Something humorous and End the fight in a good laugh.'" He kept his men during the Black Hawk War from killing an old Indian who had wandered into their camp. William Greene, who served with Lincoln, recalled: "Some of the men said to Mr Lincoln—'This is cowardly on your part Lincoln.' Lincoln remarked if any man thinks I am a coward let him test it."

Lincoln's consideration extended to animals, in a frontier environment that would have appalled the ASPCA. After shooting a turkey from the family's cabin as a kid, Lincoln noted in the autobiographical account for Scripps, "He has never since pulled a trigger on any larger game." As a boy he led a little personal crusade against the mistreatment of animals. Nathaniel Grigsby told Herndon: Lincoln "would write short sentences against cruelty to animals. We were in the habit of catching Turrapins—a Kind of turtle and put fire on their back and Lincoln would Chide us—tell us it was wrong—would write against it." He said that Lincoln's injunctions reached all the way down to "crawling insects." His stepsister remembered him giving a mini-sermon, "Contending that an ants life was to it, as sweet as ours to us." Stories of his sometimes inconvenient, sometimes even embarrassing, kindness to animals abound.

There was the story of the hog. One day as Lincoln was crossing the prairie he saw a hog mired in the mud. Mary Owens, whom Lincoln courted, remembered him telling her that "he resolved that he would pass on without looking towards the shoat, after he had gone by, he said, the feeling was eresistable and he had to look back, and the poor thing seemed to say so wistfully—*There now! my last hope is gone*; that he deliberately got down and relieved it from its difficulty." "In many things," she said, "he was sensitive almost to a fault."

And the baby birds. Joshua Speed told Herndon of Lincoln traveling on a country road by horseback, returning to Springfield from a court about thirty miles away. When the party of lawyers stopped to water its horses, Lincoln was nowhere to be seen. John Hardin had been riding back with Lincoln. Asked where he was, Hardin replied, "Oh, when I saw him last he had caught two little birds in his hand, which the wind had blown from their nest, and he was hunting for the nest." Speed said that Lincoln "finally found the nest, and placed the birds, to use his own words, 'in the home provided for them by their mother.' When he came up with the party they laughed at him. Said he, earnestly, 'I could not have slept tonight if I had not given those two little birds to their mother.'"

And the cat. Nathaniel Grigsby remembered staying over with Lincoln in the house of William Jones after a Lincoln speech in the vicinity in 1844: "When we had gone to bed and way in the night a Cat Commenced mewing and scratching—making a fuss generally—Lincoln got up in the dark and Said—Kitty—Kitty—Pussy—Pussy. The cat Knew the voice & manner Kind—went to Lincoln—L rubbed it down—Saw the Sparkling—L took up the Cat—Carried it to the door & gently rubbed it again and again Saying Kitty—Kitty &c—then gently put it down closed the doors."

Lincoln, an acquaintance recalled, "Was fond of cats—would take one & turn it on its back & talk to it for half an hour at a time." At dinner once in the White House, using official flatware, Lincoln fed one of the family's cats, which was sitting on a chair next to him. Mrs. Lincoln asked a guest, "Don't you think it is shameful for Mr. Lincoln to feed tabby with a gold fork?" The president replied, "If the gold fork was good enough for Buchanan I think it is good enough for Tabby."

If these were Lincoln's rejections, his affirmations were the law, reason, and personal and collective reform. In January 1838, he gave a speech at the Young Men's Lyceum of Springfield called "The Perpetuation of Our Political Institutions." In occasionally grandiloquent terms, Lincoln expounded on lawfulness as the foundation of our institutions and of liberty. Citing the fearful work of lynch mobs, he warned of "the increasing disregard for law which pervades the country; the growing disposition to substitute the wild and furious passions, in lieu of the sober judgement of Courts; and the worse than savage mobs, for the executive ministers of justice." In cataloging recent atrocities, he mentioned those who "throw printing presses into rivers" and "shoot editors," an unmistakable reference to the martyred abolitionist publisher Elijah Lovejoy. Mobs in Alton, Illinois, destroyed Lovejoy's presses and dumped them into the Mississippi, and then he was killed trying to defend another press from a rabble.

The answer to this threat to the "fair fabric" of our republic is enshrining the law in an exalted place in our consciousness. "Let reverence for the laws," Lincoln counseled, "be breathed by every American mother, to the lisping babe, that prattles on her lap— let it be taught in schools, in seminaries, and in colleges;—let it be written in Primmers, spelling books, and in Almanacs;—let it be preached from the pulpit, proclaimed in legislative halls, and enforced in courts of justice. And, in short, let it become the *political religion* of the nation."

Lincoln mused how during the American Revolution the basest passions of the people were suppressed or turned against the British rather than inward. That could no longer be the case, as memories of the revolution faded and the people who fought it passed away. Americans would inevitably lose their emotional connection to the event. "Passion has helped us," Lincoln concluded, "but can do so no more. It will in future be our enemy. Reason, cold, calculating, unimpassioned reason, must furnish all the materials for our future support and defence. Let those [materials] be moulded into *general intelligence, [sound] morality* and in particular, *a reverence for the constitution and laws.*"

In his 1842 temperance address, Lincoln was just as high-flying. In it, he warned the foes of drinking against a denunciatory self-righteousness liable to repel rather than persuade. As the great Lincoln scholar Harry Jaffa notes, it is a *temperate* temperance address. By the end, Lincoln swung around again to the American Revolution and praised it as "a solution of that long mooted problem, as to the capability of man to govern himself." Lincoln favored self-government both as a political system and as a personal ideal. The temperance movement brings a freedom of its own: "In *it*, we shall find stronger bondage broken; a viler slavery, manumitted; a greater tyrant deposed."

He called temperance "a noble ally" to the cause of political freedom. Then he launched into a prose poem on freedom's hand-in-hand advance with temperance: "With such an aid, its march cannot fail to be on and on, till every son of earth shall drink in rich fruition, the sorrow quenching draughts of perfect liberty. Happy day, when, all appetites controled, all passions subdued, all matters subjected, *mind*, all conquering *mind*, shall live and move the monarch of the world. Glorious consummation! Hail fall of Fury! Reign of Reason, all hail!"

"His preoccupations with self-control, order, rationality, industriousness," Daniel Walker Howe writes, made Lincoln the prototypical Whig character type. The last quality—industriousness—wasn't merely a personal ethic with Lincoln; it was his touchstone and his gospel. Success for him was a matter of work and of will.

In 1855, Lincoln wrote back to Isham Reavis, who had inquired about studying law with him. Lincoln told him he was away from the office too often to take him on as a student, but he offered this advice: "If you are resolutely determined to make a lawyer of yourself, the thing is more than half done already. It is but a small matter whether you read *with* any body or not. I did not read with any one. Get the books, and read and study them till, you understand them in their principal features; and that is the main thing. It is of no consequence to be in a large town while you are reading. I read at New-Salem, which never had three hundred people living in it. The *books*, and your *capacity* for understanding them, are just the same in all places." Before signing off he urged: "Always bear in mind that your own resolution to succeed, is more important than any other one thing." (Reavis went on to become a judge.)

A few years later, in September 1860, he answered a young man named John Brockman, who asked him "the best mode of obtaining a thorough knowledge of the law": "The mode is very simple, though laborious, and tedious. It is only to get the books, and read, and study them carefully. Begin with Blackstone's Commentaries, and after reading it carefully through, say twice, take up Chitty's Pleading, Greenleaf's Evidence, & Story's Equity &c. in succession. Work, work, work, is the main thing." The emphasis on reading, though obviously necessary for the study of law, also jibed with the Whig emphasis on concerted self-improvement.

His words of comfort in 1860 for a young man from Springfield rejected by Harvard amount to a hymn of praise to willpower: "It is a *certain* truth, that you *can* enter, and graduate in, Harvard University; and having made the attempt, you *must* succeed in it. '*Must*' is the word. I know not how to aid you, save in the assurance of one of mature age, and much severe experience, that you *can* not fail, if you resolutely determine, that you *will* not. . . . In your temporary failure there is no evidence that you may not yet be a better scholar, and a more successful man in the great struggle of life, than many others, who have entered college more easily."

Writing from Washington in 1848, where he was serving in Congress, Lincoln advised Herndon to get over his complaints that the elders in the party were treating the younger Whigs unfairly. Much better to concentrate on what was important: "The way for a young man to rise, is to improve himself every way he can, never suspecting that any body wishes to hinder him. Allow me to assure you, that suspicion and jealousy never did help any man in any situation. There may sometimes be ungenerous attempts to keep a young man down; and they will succeed too, if he allows his mind to be diverted from its true channel to brood over the attempted injury." He added, "You can not fail in any laudable object, unless you allow your mind to be improperly directed."

The point was the same, if the tone harsh and unsparing, in his letters to his stepbrother John Johnston, a pleasant sort, but not a go-getter. In 1848, Lincoln upbraided Johnston in reply to his request for eighty dollars: "At the various times when I have helped you a little, you have said to me 'We can get along very well now' but in a very short time I find you in the same difficulty again. Now this can only happen by some defect in your *conduct*. What that defect is I think I know. You are not *lazy*, and still you *are* an *idler*. I doubt whether since I saw you, you have done a good whole day's work, in any one day. You do not very much dislike to work; and still you do not work much, merely because it does not seem to you that you could get much for it. This habit of uselessly wasting time, is the whole difficulty; and it is vastly important to you, and still more so to your children that you should break this habit."

He came up with an offer to entice Johnston into the cash economy. He suggested that Johnston let Lincoln's father—who lived with him—and his children tend to the farm, while "you go to work for the best money wages, or in discharge of any debt you owe, that you can get." Lincoln said he would match whatever he made, dollar for dollar. "Now if you will do this," he continued, "you will soon be out of debt, and what is better, you will have a habit that will keep you from getting in debt again."

When Johnston said in 1851 that he wanted to sell his Illinois farm and move to Missouri, Lincoln rebuked him again: "What can you do in Missouri, better than here? Is the land any richer? Can you there, any more than here, raise corn, & wheat & oats, without work? Will any body there, any more than here, do your work for you? If you intend to go to work, there is no better place than right where you are; if you do not intend to go to work, you can get along any where. Squirming & crawling about from place to place can do no good." He professed no unkindness, just a desire to get Johnston "to *face* the truth—which truth is, you are destitute because you have *idled* away all your time. Your thousand pretences for not getting along better, are all nonsense—they deceive no body but yourself. *Go to work* is the only cure for your case." Johnston can't have appreciated the hectoring stepbrotherly advice.

For all Lincoln's tenderheartedness and his homespun charm, the Johnston letters hint at a chill in his character. He could be remote. Lost in thought, he would sometimes pass friends on the street without acknowledging them. Herndon described him, when he was studying law, as "often walking unconscious, his head on one side, thinking and talking, to himself." Mary Todd's sister Elizabeth Edwards called him "not Social—was abstracted—thoughtful." She said she had "seen him Sit down at the table and never unless recalled to his Senses, would he think of food."

He ultimately remained a closed book to his acquaintances. His friend and supporter David Davis said that "Lincoln had no spontaneity—nor Emotional Nature—no Strong Emotional feelings for any person—Mankind or thing." He "was not a social man by any means: his Stories—jokes &c. which were done to whistle off sadness are no evidences of sociality." Davis called him "the most reticent—Secretive man I Ever Saw—or Expect to See." Herndon wrote of one of his interviews with John Stuart, "Stuart says he has been at L's house a hundred times, never was asked to dinner." The way Lincoln's close political ally Joseph Gillespie put it is that "he loved the masses but was not strikingly partial to any particular individual." His secretaries in the White House, John G. Nicolay and John Milton Hay, said that when it came to familiarity with Lincoln "there was a line beyond which no one ever thought of passing."

Lincoln fortified himself behind a sense of his own dignity. Michael Burlingame points out that people began calling him "old" when he was still in his thirties. He never liked the nickname Abe. At his law office, according to David Herbert Donald, he called his younger partner William Herndon "Billy"; Herndon called him "Mr. Lincoln." His wife, too, called him "Mr. Lincoln"; before they had children and he began calling her "Mother," he addressed her as "Puss," "little woman," or "child wife." Mary said that Lincoln "was *not* a demonstrative man, when he felt most deeply, he expressed the least."

His marriage to her, despite its famous trials over the years, was another act of self-improvement. Lincoln arrived in Springfield not exactly a ladies' man. Years later he said, "Women are the only things that cannot hurt me that I am afraid of." He never looked like much. One girl in Illinois declared him as "thin as a beanpole and as ugly as a scarecrow!" Nor was he inclined to finery. William Butler, who boarded him in Springfield, recalled: "In all the time he stayed at my house, he never bought a hat or a pair of socks, or a coat. Whenever he needed them, my wife went and bought them for him, and put them in the drawer where he would find them." The sartorial carelessness stayed with him in the White House and drove Mary Todd to distraction. She couldn't stand, among other offenses, that his shirt cuffs were frayed and he never learned to remove his hat properly.

Lincoln hardly made up these deficiencies with an effortless social grace. Elizabeth Edwards said he "Could not hold a lengthy Conversation with a lady—was not sufficiently Educated & intelligent in the female line to do so." His courtship with Mary Owen in the late 1830s ended badly. Her sister, a friend of Lincoln, proposed bringing her from Kentucky so the two could get engaged. Lincoln agreed, having met Mary years before and finding her quite pleasing. When he saw her again, he changed his mind. "I knew she was over-size," Lincoln wrote in a letter to a friend afterward, "but now she appeared a fair match for Falstaff." Out of a sense of obligation, he proposed anyway, and was shocked and "mortified" to be rejected. "Mr. Lincoln was deficient in those little links," she explained later in a letter to Herndon, "which make up the great chain of womans happiness."

In Mary Todd, he "married up," as male politicians always like to say. The uneducated, penniless boy married a woman who had learned French at Madame Charlotte Mentelle's academy in Lexington, Kentucky. From a prosperous Kentucky family, she once showed off her new pony at Henry Clay's mansion. A highly desirable catch, Mary was "quick, lively, gay—frivalous it may be, Social and loved glitter Show & pomp & power," in her sister Elizabeth's description. For her, marrying Lincoln was a come-down in social status. She grew up in a household with personal servants and slaves, then went to living in a four-dollar-a-week room in the Globe Tavern in Springfield, where the couple stayed after their marriage. For him, the marriage was a step up. Lincoln joked of the family that once might have seemed impossibly august to him, "One 'd' was good enough for God, but not the Todds."

Mary's sister Elizabeth had married Ninian Edwards, a Whig politician and son of the former territorial governor of Illinois. The two lived in a Springfield mansion where they entertained the great and good of Illinois politics. Lincoln met Mary there. Through the marriage, he had allied himself to one of the most prominent Whig families in the state, and his wife took an active interest in politics. "She was an Extremely Ambitious woman," Elizabeth Edwards said. Elizabeth initially supported the union, on grounds that Lincoln "was a rising man," before doubting the couple's personal compatibility. John Stuart called the marriage a "policy Match all around." He told Herndon, "His wife made him Presdt. . . . She had the fire—will and ambition—Lincolns talent and his wifes Ambition did the deed."

I n her ambition for her husband, Mary was of course pushing on an open door. William Miller sets out the impressive catalogue of Lincoln's office-seeking: in 1832, 1834, 1836, 1838, 1840, and 1854 (for the Illinois House); in 1843, 1845, and 1846 (for his party's nomination to Congress and for the congressional seat itself); in 1855 and 1858 (for the U.S. Senate). He took a leading role in the presidential campaigns in the state for Henry Clay in 1844 and Zachary Taylor in 1848, as well as laboring on the hustings for William Henry Harrison in 1840 and Winfield Scott in 1852. Herndon said politics was "his life and newspapers his food."

The politics of the day was robustly participatory; in 1840 turnout was 80 percent. It made a great spectacle, with some gladiatorial combat occasionally mixed in. Lincoln's triumph of reason, hoped for in the most soaring passages of his addresses, would have to wait—a good long time. Thomas Ford, a chronicler of Illinois and former governor, described the trajectory of the typical raucous political event: "The stump speeches being over, then commenced the drinking of liquor, and long before night a large portion of the voters would be drunk and staggering about town, cursing, swearing, hallooing, yelling, huzzaing for their favorite candidates, throwing their arms up and around, threatening to fight, and fighting."

In 1840, the Whigs put up William Harrison as their counter to Andrew Jackson, a general and a man of the people. His hard-cider-and-log-cabin campaign ran on hoopla and revelry. Songs and parades, freely dispensed hard cider, and joyfully blatant symbols—coonskins, log-cabin raisings, whiskey in bottles shaped like log cabins—were the order of the day. A Whig rally in Springfield in June was like the Macy's Thanksgiving Day Parade and a July Fourth celebration wrapped into one, with a barbecue for fifteen thousand people and a "flood" of oratory. A Springfield merchant described the party when the Whigs won the election: "I do not believe there has ever been such a jollification since then. The center of the celebration was a big saloon, and there champagne flowed like water. It was a favorite trick to knock the neck off the bottle by striking it on the stove. Lincoln was present and made a great deal of sport with his speeches, witty sayings and stories. He even played leap-frog." (But, the merchant added, "he did not drink a thing.")

In this rollicking environment, Lincoln's physicality served him well. One Springfieldite recalled an 1836 Lincoln speech in Mechanicsburg: "[John] Neal had a fight at the time—the roughs got on him and Lincoln jumped in and Saw fair play." He also remembered Lincoln debating someone at the court house:

"The whigs & democrats had a general quarrel then & there. N. W. Edwards [Lincoln's brother-in-law] drew a pistol on Achilles Morris." In a debate that turned into a tussle with the Whig candidate John Todd Stuart when Stephen Douglas was running against him for Congress, Douglas bit Stuart's thumb. Douglas tried to cane Simeon Francis, the editor of the *Sangamo Journal*, a prominent Whig newspaper in Springfield, for an offending article. Douglas failed after the editor, in Lincoln's words, caught him "by the hair and jammed him back against a market-cart." Lincoln added, "The whole affair was so ludicrous that Francis and everybody else (Douglas excepted) have been laughing about it ever since."

Lincoln wielded his verbal acuity and his wit as his weapons. His particularly merciless take-downs of opponents were called "skinnings," like the famous "skinning of Thomas." During the 1840 campaign, Lincoln got entangled in a controversy with Jesse B. Thomas Jr., a young lawyer from a prominent family who was a Whig but not a reliable one. At an event in Springfield, Thomas accused—correctly, it seems—Lincoln and his confederates of writing an anonymous political letter and falsely attributing it to him. Lincoln responded savagely. "He imitated Thomas in gesture and voice," Herndon reported, "at times caricaturing his walk and the very motion of his body. Thomas, like everybody else, had some peculiarities of expression and gesture, and these Lincoln succeeded in rendering more prominent than ever. The crowd yelled and cheered as he continued. Encouraged by these demonstrations, the ludicrous features of the speaker's performance gave way to intense and scathing ridicule." Thomas left the platform in tears, and Lincoln eventually apologized.

Lincoln's taste for ridiculing the opposition led to his own scrape with an affair of honor. He had to admit to writing a pseudonymous article viciously lampooning the state's prickly state auditor, a Democrat, James Shields. The offended official issued a challenge. Even though dueling was illegal in Illinois, with his honor at stake, Lincoln accepted. The episode now reads like farce, yet no one treated it as one at the time.

As the challenged party, Lincoln had the choice of weapons and picked "Cavalry broad swords of the largest size, precisely equal in all respects." He further stipulated that the clash would take place in a box set out on the ground and divided in two, with the penalty of death for overstepping the center line and surrender of the contest for overstepping the back line. Lincoln had fashioned a fight depending largely on who had the longer and strong arms. Shields was five-eight or nine, and Lincoln was about half a foot taller. As his colleague in the legislature Robert L. Wilson attested, Lincoln had arms "longer than any man I ever knew, when standing Straiht, and letting his arms fall down his Sides, the points of his fingers would touch a point lower on his legs by nearly three inches than was usual with other persons."

Later, the lawyer and politician Usher Linder asked Lincoln why the choice of such odd weapons: "To tell you the truth, Linder, I did not want to kill Shields, and felt sure that I could disarm him, having had about a month to learn the broadsword exercise; and furthermore, I didn't want the d—d fellow to kill me, which I rather think he would have done if we had selected pistols." Once the parties arrived at the designated dueling ground, a spot known as "Bloody Island" in the middle of the Mississippi River, the dispute was "adjusted" and the swordplay avoided. Embarrassed by the imbroglio, Lincoln never liked to talk about it afterward.

(On the way to meet Shields, Lincoln had seen a family mired in the mud and in typical fashion simply couldn't bear to pass by, despite presumably having other things on his mind. A witness recalled: "Lincoln was about to stop when one of his Company— 'Now Lincoln don't make a d—d fool of yourself—Come— Come along—' Lincoln didn't pay no attention to what the man said—got off his horse—L took my horse & his own & tied them to the strangers waggon by ropes—Straps & strings—pulled the man with his family—When we got through scarcely any man Could have told what or who we were.")

Lincoln's forensic and intellectual talents—misapplied in the anonymous and pseudonymous articles he ceased writing after the Shields affair—made him a natural political leader. As soon as he joined the Illinois legislature, his colleagues looked to him for assistance writing speeches and legislation, just as his family and neighbors had with letters when he was a boy. Joseph Gillespie said that "as early [as] 1834, 5, he was put forward as the spokesman of the whig party, and he never disappointed them or fell below their expectation."

Robert Wilson explained the keys to his persuasive force. "He was, on the stump, and in the Halls of Legislation a ready Debater, manifesting extraordinary ability in his peculiar manner of presenting his subject," he wrote in a letter to Herndon. "He did not follow the beaten track of other Speakers, and Thinkers, but appeared to comprehend the whole situation of the Subject, and take hold of its first principles; He had a remarkable faculty for concentration, enabling him to present his subject in such a manner as nothing but conclusions were presented." According to Wilson, Lincoln's memory gave him a store of material to illustrate "every Subject however complicated with annecdotes drawn from all classes of Society, accomplishing the double purpose, of not only proving his Subject by the annecdote, But the annecdote itself possessing so much point and force, that no one ever forgets, after hearing Mr Lincoln tell a Story, either the argument of the Story, the Story itself, or the author."

Lincoln thrilled to the nitty-gritty of elections and legislative mechanics and ladled out partisan invective with relish, but underneath his politics rested a foundation of substance. John Stuart said Lincoln "felt no special interest in any man or thing—Save & Except politics—loved principles and such like large political & national ones."

Consider the hoopla campaign for William Harrison in 1840. It demonstrated both Lincoln's occasional low-down practicality and his high seriousness. He favored the nomination of Harrison over his sainted Henry Clay for purely pragmatic reasons—Harrison seemed more electable. The Whigs proceeded to unleash just the sort of onslaught on President Van Buren that President Adams had suffered at the hands of the Jacksonians. They dubbed the president, caught presiding over a depression, "Martin van Ruin" and portrayed him living in champagne-soaked luxury at the White House, where he hired French chefs to sate his epicurean tastes. Lincoln eagerly partook of the demagoguery. He denounced Van Buren as "in feeling and principle an Aristocrat." He excoriated him in hair-raisingly scurrilous terms for supposedly advancing black suffrage back in New York in 1821. When a Whig friend complained of the unedifying tone of the campaign for Harrison, Lincoln supposedly replied, "It is all right; *we must fight the devil with fire.*"

Yet the campaign wasn't as substance-less as legend has it, or as the Whig ditty "without a why or a wherefore we'll go for Harrison therefore" suggested. The clashing positions of the parties were clear enough, and Lincoln enunciated them with great force.

Harrison came up just short in Illinois, even as he swept to victory nationally. But Lincoln may have begun to feel a calling to something greater at this time. "I think it grew and bloomed and developed into beauty, etc., in the year *1840 exactly*," Herndon said of his aspiration for higher office. "Mr. Lincoln told me that his ideas of something burst in him in 1840."

From immature politico to budding statesman, his touchstone remained Henry Clay. He eulogized his hero after his death in 1852. In Lincoln's telling, "Mr. Clay's predominant sentiment, from first to last, was a deep devotion to the cause of human liberty—a strong sympathy with the oppressed every where, and an ardent wish for their elevation. With him, this was a primary and all controlling passion." As for his country, Lincoln continued, Clay "burned with a zeal for its advancement, prosperity and glory, because he saw in such, the advancement, prosperity and glory, of human liberty, human right and human nature. He desired the prosperity of his countrymen partly because they were his countrymen, but chiefly to show to the world that freemen could be prosperous."

Lincoln burned with the zeal he attributed to Clay. Until the issue of slavery arose to loom over all else, Lincoln devoted his career chiefly to economics. He sought the prosperity of his countrymen through Whig principles and Whig policies, and made the cause of canals, railroads, banks, and industry his own. The railsplitter became, in the argot of a later era, a "capitalist tool."

Chapter 3

"The True System": The Genius of American Capitalism

Man is not the only animal who labors; but he is the only one who improves his workmanship.
— ABRAHAM LINCOLN, FIRST LECTURE ON DISCOVERIES AND INVENTIONS, 1858

In December 1840, the Illinois legislature fought desperately over the fate of the Bank of Illinois. Democrats hated the institution as a tool of the powerful and sought to kill it. With the bank tottering in the midst of an economic crisis, they had their opportunity. The bank couldn't redeem its notes in specie—in other words, gold and silver—as required by its charter. But the legislature had given it a reprieve. It wouldn't have to start such payments again until the legislature's next session.

That created an opening for enemies of the bank. The governor had called the legislature back into session two weeks early. The Democrats realized that they could vote to adjourn at the end of the two weeks and formally make that period a distinct session. Then the bank would be forced to resume specie payments immediately, at great risk to the institution.

The Whigs did their own maneuvering. The legislature couldn't adjourn if it didn't have a quorum. The Whigs didn't show up for the proceedings, held in a church in the new capital city of Springfield while the capitol building was still under construction. Lincoln and his Whig colleague Joseph Gillespie monitored the situation from the floor. According to Gillespie, the sergeant-at-arms was ordered to round up members. "We soon discovered," he recalled, "that several Whigs had been caught and brought in and that the plan had been spoiled and we (Lincoln & I) determined to leave the Hall and going to the door found it locked and then raised a window & jumped out but not untill the democrats had succeeded in adjourning."

The sergeant-at-arms supposedly refused orders to chase the retreating members: "My God! gentlemen, do you know what you ask? Think of the length of Abe's legs, and then tell me how I am to catch him."

After the ludicrous exit, Democrats chanted, "He who fights and runs away, lives to fight another day." A Democratic newspaper delighted in lampooning Lincoln for his retreat out the first-floor window: "We have not learned whether these flying members got hurt in the adventure, and we think it probable that at least one of them came off without damage, as it was noticed that his legs reached nearly from the window to the ground! . . . We learn that a resolution will probably be introduced into the House this week to inquire into the expedience of raising the State House one story higher, in order to set in the third story so as to prevent members from jumping out windows! If such a resolution passes, Mr. Lincoln in future will have to climb down the spout."

Afterward, Lincoln didn't like to be reminded of what he called "that jumping scrape." Gillespie said, "I think Mr Lincoln always regretted that he entered into the arrangement as he deprecated everything that Savored of revolutionary." The incident nonetheless speaks to his priorities. What kind of politician was Lincoln? The kind that might jump out of a window to save a bank.

Lincoln believed that if we acted on sound economic principles, and stayed true to the philosophical foundations of America, the prospects for the country's growth were boundless. To say he had an expansive vision of the country's ability to forge material progress understates it. In a lecture on discoveries and inventions in the late 1850s, he spoke of how man could "dig out his destiny." He could find riches as yet unimaginable, so long as he was diligent and inquisitive enough and operated in an environment that protected property and encouraged its acquisition. He noted (rather indelicately) that "yankees" had almost instantly discovered gold in California that "had been trodden upon, and overlooked by indians and Mexican greasers, for centuries."

He spun the discovery of gold into a larger metaphor. "There are more mines above the Earth's surface than below it," Lincoln said. "All nature—the whole world, material, moral, and intellectual—is a mine." It is our work "to develope, by discoveries, inventions, and improvements, the hidden treasures of this mine." If the metaphor is overdone, the depth of feeling is clear. Lincoln thrilled to the world-changing imagination and enterprise of a Whitney or a McCormick, a Fulton or a Colt, a Goodyear or a Morse.

For all Lincoln's clear-eyed realism about human nature, he had a deep faith in the generative capacities of man. "Lincoln was possessed by the optimism of Western Civilization," Gabor Boritt writes in his definitive *Lincoln and the Economics of the American Dream*, "reborn in the Renaissance, grown to maturity in the Enlightenment, and triumphant in nineteenth century America, which saw man as the master of his own destiny. Perhaps nowhere was this world view stronger than in American conceptions about economics, particularly among Whigs."

Lincoln devoted himself to the question of how to make free men prosperous. He took his economic principles into the public square fearlessly and unyieldingly. He leavened them with his own personal experience and his zeal for economic mobility— matching capitalist rigor with bottom-up populism. This combination runs throughout Lincoln's career and came to define his new Republican Party.

He and other Whigs—and then Republicans—relied heavily on the contemporary work of Francis Wayland and Henry Charles Carey. In 1837, Wayland published the widely read *The Elements of Political Economy* and Carey the highly influential *Principles of Political Economy*. Herndon said Lincoln "ate up, digested, and assimilated" Wayland's *Elements*.

The president of Brown University, as well as a moral philosopher, Wayland gave pride of place to private property and to labor. He argued "that every man be allowed to gain all that he can," and "to use it as he will." He maintained that property "lays at the foundation of all accumulation of wealth, and of all progress in civilization." If government fails to protect it, "capital emigrates, production ceases, and a nation . . . sinks down in hopeless despondence." He embraced the labor theory of value and wrote, in a passage that Lincoln could have cut-and-pasted into his speeches, "Labor has been made necessary to our happiness. No valuable object of desire can be produced without it. . . . The Universal law of our existence, is, 'In the sweat of thy face shalt thou eat thy bread, until thou return to the ground.'"

Wayland saw no conflict between capital and labor: "One who owns the capital, unites in production with another or others, who perform the labor. . . and there are just proportions to be observed between the wages of labor and the wages of capital." He denounced as "robbery" any coercion in the exchange of labor and capital.

He defended the Bank of the United States, as well as paper currency. He made the case for his economics in terms of facilitating the rise of workers. Lincoln absorbed it all. Boritt writes of Lincoln's views: "The importance of property and capitalism; their virtues for the man who wished to 'make' something of himself; the benefits of industrialization, credit, and paper money; and hostility toward slavery—these were basic elements of his thinking that received systematic support from his study of Wayland."

Henry Carey thought in a similar key. He maintained that there is a "harmony of all real interests" in the country (one of his books was titled *The Harmony of Interests: Agricultural, Manufacturing, and Commercial*). The era's most prominent protectionist thinker, he favored industrialization to diversify the economy and drive up wages, and a protective tariff to promote it. He wrapped it all in a profound optimism, resting on the assumption of "a tendency to equality of physical and intellectual condition, and to the general ownership of wealth."

These arguments accorded with Lincoln's deep-set personal tendencies. He wasn't any more romantic about farms when he left them behind than he had been when living on one. In the

White House in 1864, he told a story about an early memory. It captured the inevitable vicissitudes of agriculture. The Knob Creek farm in Kentucky rested in a valley. Lincoln remembered planting pumpkin seed in a big field on a Saturday afternoon, while other boys planted corn: "The next Sunday morning there came a big rain in the hills, it did not rain a drop in the valley, but the water coming down through the gorges washed ground, corn, pumpkin seeds and all clear off the field." All that work for naught.

He never pandered to farmers. In an 1859 address to the Wisconsin State Agricultural Society in Milwaukee, he prefaced his remarks by saying he wouldn't "employ the time assigned me, in the mere flattery of the farmers, as a class. My opinion of them is that, in proportion to numbers, they are neither better nor worse than other people."

The rest of the address is a splendidly Lincolnian performance. He talked of the importance of more efficient agriculture and mused in detail about how a "Steam Plow" might work. He recommended "book-learning" and science—botany, chemistry, and "the mechanical branches of Natural Philosophy," "especially in reference to implements and machinery." He related how he loved invention: "I know of nothing so pleasant to the mind, as the discovery of anything which is at once *new* and *valuable*—nothing which so lightens and sweetens toil, as the hopeful pursuit of such discovery."

Lincoln had the taste for machinery of a frustrated engineer. As president, he was a booster of an early version of the machine gun and promoted the breech-loading rifle. He tested new rifles for himself in an area behind the White House, in violation of a rule that guns shouldn't be fired in the District. Once, the tinkerer-in-chief whittled a wooden gun sight for the new breech-loading Spencer rifle.

William Herndon said "he was causative; his mind, apparently with an automatic movement, ran back behind facts, principles, and all things to their origin and first cause—to that point where forces act at once as effect and cause. He would stop in the street and analyze a machine. He would whittle a thing to a point, and then count the numberless inclined planes and their pitch making the point. Mastering and defining this, he would then cut that point back and get a broad traverse section of his pine-stick, and peel and define that. Clocks, omnibuses, language, paddle-wheels, and idioms never escaped his observation and analysis."

Returning from a campaign swing for Zachary Taylor in 1848, Lincoln saw a steamboat on the Detroit River that had run aground, and he got an idea. He devised and sought a patent for a mechanism for "a new and improved manner of combining adjustable buoyant air chambers with a steam boat or other vessel for the purpose of enabling their draught of water to be readily lessened to enable them to pass over bars, or through shallow water."

His application with the patent office included enumerated drawings with the various parts of the device marked with letters, and a detailed explanation of how it would work, to wit: "The ropes f.f. are connected to the vertical shafts at i.i. as shown in Figs. 1. & 2." On it went in that vein. He obtained Patent Number 6,469.

Lincoln's knack for mastering and explaining the workings of machines served him well in his patent cases as a lawyer. One of his fellow lawyers, Grant Goodrich, recounted to Herndon a patent infringement case involving a water wheel, tried in Chicago in 1850. Lincoln represented the defense. "He had tended a saw-mill for some time," Goodrich wrote, "& was able in his arguments to explain the action of the water upon the wheel, in a manner so clear & inteligable, that the jury was enabled to comprehend the points and the line of defense." Lincoln won. As a general matter, Goodrich recalled, "He had a great deal of Mechanical genius, could understand readily the principles & mechanical action of machinery, & had the power, in his clear, simple illustrations & Style to make the jury comprehend them."

Lincoln considered patents a boon to mankind. In his lecture on discoveries and inventions, he included patent laws among the great innovations of history, along with printing and the discovery of America. Before their introduction, "any man might instantly use what another had invented; so that the inventor had no special advantage from his own invention." The patent laws "secured to the inventor, for a limited time, the exclusive use of his invention; and thereby added the fuel of *interest* to the *fire* of genius, in the discovery and production of new and useful things."

Property was another Lincoln enthusiasm that, like patent law, might seem arid to someone less attuned than he was to its foundational value. For him, property was "a positive good in the world," as he told workingmen from New York in 1864. Daniel Walker Howe writes that Lincoln believed, as the nineteenth-century theologian Horace Bushnell put it, a "grand moral struggle centers in the holding and use and transmission of property."

He had seen that process impaired in his youth. An antiquated system of land titles in Kentucky had blighted his father's attempts to hold and improve property. The state originally belonged to Virginia, which passed along laws it had inherited from English land tenure wholly inappropriate in the frontier context. On top of this, Virginia sold off more land than actually existed in Kentucky. Thomas Cooper, an early-nineteenth-century political philosopher, said that "a purchaser in Kentucky buys a law-suit with every plot of unoccupied land he pays for there."

Thomas Lincoln lost money on two properties thanks to flawed titles, and then got chased off his last farm in the state by a lawsuit. He moved to Indiana, where the federal Land Ordinance of 1785 imposed more order and reliability on surveys and land titles. A British lawyer who visited Lincoln in the White House in 1864 said that the president talked to him about "queer" features of English land law. He then complained that "in the State of Kentucky, where he was raised, they used to be so troubled with the same mysterious relics of feudalism, and titles got into an almighty mess with these pettifoggin' incumbrances turnin' up at every fresh tradin' with the land, and no one knowin' how to get rid of 'em."

Lincoln the devotee of economic growth, the mechanically inclined amateur inventor, the defender of property and patent law applied himself first to realizing the potential of Illinois. In 1839, a resolution of the legislature written in his hand declared that Illinois "surpasses every other spot of equal extent upon the face of the globe, in *fertility* of soil," and argued that it could sustain "a greater amount of agricultural wealth and population than any other equal extent of territory in the world." The resolution urged "that all our energies should be exerted to bring that wealth and population among us as speedily as possible."

How? First of all: improvements.

Arguments over infrastructure, and especially the constitutionality of federal projects, played an outsize role in early American politics. In the Federalist Papers, Alexander Hamilton and James Madison celebrated the Constitution for creating the predicate for new links of transportation. As George Washington's Treasury secretary, Hamilton celebrated transportation improvements in his justly famous Report on Manufactures. He wrote that the new interest in "improvement of inland navigation" could only "fill with pleasure every breast, warmed with a true zeal for the prosperity of the country." He then quoted Adam Smith for the proposition, "Good roads, canals, and navigable rivers, by diminishing the expense of carriage, put the remote parts of a country more nearly upon a level with those in the neighborhood of the town. They are, upon that account, the greatest of all improvements."

Such projects became one of the grounds for the epic contention between Hamilton and Jefferson. The Virginian supported infrastructure, too, but objected to what he considered Hamilton's overly expansive interpretation of the Constitution. Hamilton thought the Constitution granted the government "implied powers" to act on its specifically enumerated ones. Jefferson thought an extensive federal infrastructure program required a constitutional amendment.

The debate dragged on over the decades, with the constitutional amendment never forthcoming. Amid presidential vetoes of various proposed projects, federal funding nonetheless increased, although in a haphazard fashion. As Adam J. White points out in an essay on the history of infrastructure, Jefferson himself didn't let his constitutional scruples stop him from signing a plan for the National Road connecting the Potomac and Ohio rivers. So it went. Andrew Jackson vetoed the Maysville Road, which would have connected the National Road to other major arteries, yet he spent twice as much on transportation as all previous presidents and showered the country with pork-barrel projects.

As presidents and Congress argued over constitutional interpretation, much of the action was at the state level, where Lincoln was eager to pick up the baton. Transportation difficulties loomed large in his early life. His family's Indiana farm had been a full sixteen miles from the thoroughfare of the Ohio River. As we have seen, his first venture with Denton Offutt was beset by poor roads and a barely navigable river. The mud of central Illinois was called "prairie gumbo" and made life in Springfield a miserable mess.

The eighth circuit that Lincoln rode for so many years as a lawyer was known as the "mud circuit." As the circuit-riding Judge David Davis complained, "[b]ad roads, broken bridges, swimming of horses, & constant wettings, are the main incidents in Western travel." Lincoln apparently took the lead in checking out the river fords on account of his height. He pranked his lawyerly entourage once by telling them a stream was so deep they had better strip before riding across and watched in amusement as the unnecessarily naked party forded the shallow water.

From the first, Lincoln the politician fixated on improving transportation. By the second paragraph of his announcement of his initial candidacy for the legislature in March 1832, he was pronouncing on "the public utility of internal improvements." When he made it to the legislature, he immediately introduced a proposal for a bridge: "That Samuel Musick his heirs and his assigns be and they are hereby authorized to erect a toll bridge across Salt creek in Sangamon county at or near the place where the said Musick is now authorized to keep a ferry." At first, the legislature focused on chartering private transportation companies, but they couldn't raise the necessary capital for projects at a time when small savers not interested in risky investments controlled much of the nation's savings.

Illinois decided it had to act directly. The state created a massive program of public works, and what might have been a prudential effort to fill a public need became a frenzy, fueled by a speculative mania.

Everyone looked to New York State's Erie Canal for inspiration. New Yorkers had conceived of it as a connection to the hinterlands farther west that would make New York, in the words of Governor DeWitt Clinton, "the great depot and warehouse of the western world." When federal funding wasn't forthcoming, New York determined to finance the project itself, a canal of more than three hundred miles connecting the Hudson River to Lake Erie. Begun in 1817 and completed in 1825, "Clinton's Big Ditch" was truly grandiose. As recently as 1816, there had only been about one hundred miles of canal in the entire country, and only three of them longer than two miles.

In its conception and execution, it represented the spirit of a fearlessly enterprising people in a hurry to meet the future. In the absence of trained professionals, lawyers and other talented amateurs acted as engineers. All told, the canal cost $7 million and proved worth every penny. Toll revenue on the Erie and the related Champlain canal hit half a million dollars in 1825, and rose from there. New York's manmade waterway quickly outpaced the Mighty Mississippi as a commercial thoroughfare. The project paid off its construction debt in eleven years, and sent shipping costs between Lake Erie and New York City plummeting.

The canal was an exuberant leap into the future, and seemed a cost-effective one at that. No wonder it fired imaginations. A couple of Illinois counties were named after DeWitt Clinton, and Joshua Speed recalled how Lincoln told him how "in reference to Internal improvements & the best interest and advancement of this State, that his highest ambition was to become the De Witt

Clinton of Ills." Illinois wanted to keep up with the neighboring states of Ohio and Indiana, which were reaching for the glories of the new era of transportation, Indiana with what was called "the Mammoth Internal Improvement Bill."

Passed in early 1837, the resulting Illinois infrastructure program ran to about $10 million. It came to be known as the System, a statewide extravaganza encompassing 1,300 miles of railroad, including two trunk lines running north-to-south and east-to-west, and sundry other projects, from new roads to river improvements. For counties somehow not touched by this inescapable net of infrastructure, the legislature thoughtfully appropriated two hundred thousand dollars for areas that might otherwise feel left out. This was on top of the Illinois & Michigan Canal, funded separately.

"Work on all these gigantic enterprises," Herndon explained, "was to begin at the earliest practicable moment; cities were to spring up everywhere; capital from abroad was to come pouring in; attracted by the glowing reports of marvelous progress and great internal wealth, people were to come swarming in by colonies, until in the end Illinois was to outstrip all others, and herself become the Empire State of the union." All of it was to be financed through borrowing. Illinois learned the lesson of the Erie Canal, that great ventures could be financed through state bonds, all too well.

The scope of the Illinois program seems so fantastical in retrospect that a widely accepted explanation for its passage is gross log-rolling undertaken by Lincoln and his colleagues from Sangamon County. Exceptionally tall, they were known as "the Long Nine," a derisive moniker drawn from the name of a lousy cigar. The Long Nine supposedly traded their votes for the improvement scheme in exchange for support for moving the capital from Vandalia to Springfield, in Sangamon. There is no doubt that Lincoln and his Sangamon colleagues fought hard for the move in legislative trench warfare, and that Lincoln was nobody's naïf. During his first term in the legislature, he learned at the knee of John Stuart, or "Jerry Sly." Stuart later described how, in one instance, "Lincoln and I made a trade with [fellow legislator Sidney] Breese to the effect that we would help pass his railroad bill if he would help us secure the appointment of the Canal Comrs. [commissioners] by the Governor."

But at the end of the day the System passed because, in a classic bubble mindset, nearly everyone wanted it and nearly everyone believed in it. Members of both parties supported it, and the public welcomed it as a vehicle for increasing population and raising land values. One lawmaker predicted that the bonds "would go like hotcakes." Such was the presumed glory of the legislature's work that once it was completed, in the words of one anonymous witness who may have been Lincoln himself, "All Vandalia was illuminated. Bonfires were built, and fire balls were thrown, in every direction."

That was the high point. The Panic of 1837 and a subsequent depression crushed all the state's vaulting hopes. Never a fan, Governor Joseph Duncan advocated repealing the System almost immediately. Lincoln persisted in his support, even as things began to unravel. He wanted to come up with the additional funds necessary to keep the System alive by having Illinois buy all the public lands in the state—with the federal government's cooperation—and resell them at a profit. The scheme required borrowing another $5 million. It was a nonstarter. Washington wasn't interested.

Democrats took to calling the projects "Infernal Improve-ments." At first, Lincoln refused even to rank projects in the Sys-tem by their merit, lest it undermine political support for the plan in the areas with projects slated to get axed first. Stingy about other appropriations, he was willing to spend more money to try to get over the hump to better times. He thought, "We had gone too far to recede, even if we were disposed to do so." If Illinois simply quit, it would incur massive losses with nothing to show for them. A Democrat mocked him in Lincolnian fashion for pro-posing more of the disease as a cure. "A drunkard in Arkansas," he related, "took so much of the *cretur*, that he lost his reason and remained for some time in a state of insensibility. His wife tried every experiment to cure him; but it was of no avail, until a neighbor came to the house and recommended some *brandy toddy*. The insensible man rose at the word *toddy*, and said 'that is the stuff.'"

Lincoln realized what was going to happen. He wrote to John Stuart, then a congressman, at the beginning of 1840 that the "In-ternal Improvement System will be put down in a lump, without benefit of clergy." He supported raising taxes rather than repudi-ating the state's debt, and it didn't help the cause of the System that it became associated with taxation. There was an awful lot of debt not to repudiate. The state ran up more than $10 million of it, without completing anything except a fifty-nine-mile stretch of railroad between Springfield and Meredosia that proved use-less.

In 1841, the state defaulted on its interest payments. Former governor Thomas Ford wrote in his history of Illinois that the state "became a stench in the nostrils of the civilized world." It sold off the property on which it had planned to build the system and its railroad iron and timber. The Springfield and Meredosia line, which cost $900,000 to build, was sold for all of $21,100. Illinois didn't manage to pay off its debt until 1881 (it still outpaced Ohio, which didn't pay off its own improvement debt until 1902).

The disaster didn't shake Lincoln's faith in the correctness of his ultimate goal. When he made it to Congress in 1847, he argued for transportation projects on a national scale. In a speech responding to Democratic criticisms in 1848, he acknowledged that when a legislature takes up such projects there is a tendency toward—ahem—"undue expansion." But he was unconvinced by the objection that Congress would necessarily end up approving projects with benefits too localized to justify their funding by the nation. Consider the navy. It indisputably benefits the nation, yet "is of some peculiar advantage to Charleston, Baltimore, Philadelphia, New-York, and Boston, beyond what it is to the interior towns of Illinois." Conversely, consider the Illinois & Michigan Canal, which, when it was eventually completed, had become a conduit for sugar to get more cheaply from New Orleans to Buffalo—"a benefit resulting *from* the canal, not to Illinois where the canal *is*, but to Louisiana and New-York where it is *not*."

He advocated determining through statistical analysis the worthiest projects. In his conclusion, neatly summarizing his lifelong attitude to improvements, he said: "Let the nation take hold of the larger works, and the states the smaller ones; and thus, working in a meeting direction, discreetly, but steadily and firmly, what is to be made unequal in one place may be equalized in another, extravagance avoided, and the whole country put on that career of prosperity, which shall correspond with it's extent of teritory, it's natural resources and the intelligence and enterprize of it's people."

As central to Lincoln as infrastructure was banking, particularly federally controlled banking to produce a sound paper currency and widespread availability of credit. He could deliver "a very sensible speech" in opposition to specie currency—money coined from gold or silver—as early as 1832, according to his early law partner Stephen T. Logan. In his first published speech in January 1837, Lincoln vigorously defended his views on banking and cheekily praised his adversary for his *decided superiority*"—especially in "the faculty of entangling a subject, so that neither himself, or any other man, can find head or tail to it."

Illinois replicated the national drama of the Bank War on a smaller scale. The legislature created a state bank in 1835, and chartered two others. The state bought bank stock and figured, wishfully, that it could fund improvements with the inevitable dividends. Intertwined in other ways, the banks and the improvements were fated to meet the same bad end. The state bank itself became the occasion for partisan war and a proxy for clashing economic visions. The Jacksonians attacked, Gabor Boritt writes, "not only the most blatant symbol, but also one of the most effective instruments, of the undesirable new world of growing commercial-industrial capitalism." Characteristically, Lincoln rallied to its defense.

The bank's stockholders were supposed to be residents of the state, but Eastern financiers ended up with much of the stock, opening the bank up to populist attack. In that January 1837 speech, Lincoln worked to forestall an investigation by opponents of the bank. He brushed off the question of stock ownership as a dispute among capitalists who "have got into a quarrel with themselves." The controversy had been stirred up by politicians, who "are, taken as a mass, at least one long step removed from honest men." "I say this," he added, "with the greater freedom because, being a politician myself, none can regard it as personal." Laying it on thick at the end, he argued that the legislature lacked the authority to launch the investigation. "I am opposed," he said, stretching his case well beyond the point of credulity, "to encouraging that lawless and mobocratic spirit, whether in relation to the bank or any thing else, which is already abroad in the land."

The core of Lincoln's argument for the bank came down to economics. Ordinary, enterprising people needed credit and a safe, widely available currency (and specie alone wasn't adequate). In short, you can't have a cash economy without reliable cash. To this end, the state bank issued notes, backed by specie, that circulated as currency. "By injuring the credit of the Bank," Lincoln argued, "you will depreciate the value of its paper in the hands of the honest and unsuspecting farmer and mechanic." If the enemies of the institution could go all the way and "wipe the Bank from existence," he warned, they would "annihilate the currency of the State" and "render valueless in the hands of our people that reward of their former labors."

This is the line that would consistently run throughout Lincoln's advocacy on banking. Prior to the Civil War, currency in the United States was a riot of confusion. All around the country, state banks issued notes as paper currency of widely varying quality. The notes in the East tended to be reliable, but elsewhere it was a crapshoot. In the West, wildcat banks were situated in remote locations "out among the wildcats," so no one could find them to try to redeem their notes for specie.

As many as seven thousand different kinds of bank notes circulated. A contemporary observer complained that "the frequently worthless issues of the State of Maine, the shinplasters of Michigan, the wildcats of Georgia, of Canada and Pennsylvania, the red dogs of Indiana and Nebraska, the miserably engraved notes of North Carolina, Kentucky, Missouri and Virginia and the not-to-be-forgotten stumptails of Illinois and Wisconsin are mixed indiscriminately with the par currency of New York and Boston."

Lincoln wanted to move toward something more uniform and sensible, while pushing back against the simplistic and impractical hard-money gospel of the Jacksonians. He excoriated President Martin Van Buren's "independent treasury" plan, which was the latest iteration in the Bank Wars at the national level. After Andrew Jackson had pulled funds out of the Bank of the United States, he deposited them in what were dubbed "pet banks" around the country. This ironically contributed to the rising speculative spirit in the land. It gave states even more incentive to charter banks in the hope of getting federal deposits and pumped the banks with money. Van Buren proposed to remain true to the Jacksonian antibanking faith by severing the government's relationship with banks altogether and keeping federal funds in an independent treasury.

Lincoln thought this was tantamount to ensuring that "the money is performing no nobler office than that of rusting in iron boxes." He insisted that "money is only valuable while in circulation." This is why the country needed a national bank of the sort the Democrats had just destroyed. "We do not pretend," he said, getting to the crux of the matter, "that a National Bank can establish and maintain a sound and uniform state of currency in the country, in *spite* of the National Government; but we do say, that it has established and maintained such a currency, and can do so again, by the *aid* of that Government; and we further say, that no duty is more imperative on that Government, than the duty it owes the people, of furnishing them a sound and uniform currency."

Such a currency was another logical step in forging a unified commercial network in the country. It wasn't going to happen, though—not yet. Lincoln kept at it anyway, even if not all his points hit home. At one campaign stop in 1840, he said he had witnessed a constable selling a horse for just twenty-seven dollars that very morning, in an unmistakable sign of the ravages of the deflation wrought by the Democrats. The constable happened to be listening and objected that the horse sold for that amount only because . . . it was blind in one eye.

In Illinois, he was going to lose the fight over the state bank. The battle went through various permutations, including "the jumping scrape," until finally, in 1842 the state bank gave up the ghost. Governor Ford, along with many others, concluded of banks, "we must be satisfied, that we in the State of Illinois, are better off without them than with them." Everything Lincoln had fought for had collapsed in a heap, at least for the time being.

The tariff constituted a third mainstay of Lincoln's economics. It was, of course, the subject of deep contention. The South had felt aggrieved by the "Tariff of Abominations" of 1828. Martin Van Buren crafted it to elect Andrew Jackson by disregarding the interests of people who wouldn't be or didn't need to be won over to Old Hickory, including the Cotton South. Lots of heavy breathing and a nullification crisis later, the tariff was revised in 1833 as a gesture to that region. It was scheduled to fall over the next decade, but it wasn't changed fundamentally. In 1842 it went up again, in a victory for the Whigs, and then was reduced in 1846, in a victory for the Democrats.

Southerners had good economic reason to oppose the tariff. It meant they had to pay higher prices for manufactured goods, and they didn't like the idea of the federal government accumulating more funds that could then be spent on a Whig agenda of improvements. (In the absence of an income tax, the tariff was far and away the nation's main source of revenue.) Lincoln went to pains to try to prove that the tariff reduced the price for goods, although not persuasively. The price of protection is borne by the consumer, both in higher prices for imports and for the protected domestic products. Lincoln's best case for protection came down to their role in a nationalistic vision of an industrializing America fostering its own internal market on the way to taking its place among the world's foremost nations.

The tariff gave American industry the space to robustly grow despite the competition of a far more advanced industrial behemoth in Britain. In a fragment written for himself in 1847 while working out his thinking, Lincoln waxed poetic about an allegorical blacksmith whose operations were devastated by the end of the protective tariff: "all is cold and still as death—no [sm]oke rises, no furnace roars, no anvil rings." In the story, a farmer wants to sell flour to the blacksmith ("Vulcan"), but can't because of his reduced state. For Lincoln, the point is the tariff's contribution to an economy with a diverse internal market that ultimately isn't merely a commodity producer for Britain. A Whig campaign circular that he signed in 1843 deemed the tariff "indispensably necessary to the prosperity of the American People." "Give us a protective tariff," he said, according to one recollection of a speech around this time, "and we will have the greatest country on earth."

Lincoln's policies aimed to create a thriving commercial republic. His work as a lawyer, though much more varied, leaned in the same direction. The offices of Lincoln & Herndon didn't look like much. One lawyer said they appeared "innocent of water and the scrub-man since creation's dawn." Upstairs in a building near the capitol in Springfield, they had smudged windows and run-down furniture, including a large, cluttered pine table and a couch on which Lincoln would lounge and read.

Disorganization ruled the day. Lincoln apologized to Richard Thomas in 1850 for not replying to a letter from him in a timely manner, but "when I received the letter I put it in my old hat, and buying a new one the next day, the old one was set aside, and so, the letter lost sight of for a time." Herndon recalled one feature of the office filing system, a bundle of papers in which Lincoln would slip anything he wanted to refer back to: "Some years ago, on removing the furniture from the office, I took down the bundle and blew from the top the liberal coat of dust that had accumulated thereon. Immediately underneath the string was a slip bearing this endorsement, in his hand: 'When you can't find it anywhere else, look in this.'" It only got more chaotic when Lincoln brought his boys to the office. Herndon complained that they "would tear up the office, scatter the books, smash up pens, spill the ink, and [piss] all over the floor."

John H. Littlefield wanted to study law with Lincoln & Herndon. When he met Lincoln in the office, the lawyer said he hoped Littlefield wouldn't be as zealous in his study of Blackstone and Kent as two prior students had been. He pointed to an ink stain on the wall: "Well, one of these young men got so enthusiastic in his pursuit of legal lore that he fired an inkstand at the other one's head." Immediately upon his acceptance, Littlefield began tidying up a bit. He found that some seeds Lincoln as a congressman had for distributing to constituents had fallen out and sprouted in dirt collected on the floor.

Life out on the circuit wasn't any more glamorous or comfortable. Lincoln rode in a buggy pulled by his horse Old Buck, with books and a change of underwear in a green carpetbag. He could be out for three-month stretches, getting good business. Lawyers tended to share beds, although Judge David Davis—weighing some three hundred pounds—got one all to himself (and needed a two-horse buggy). Discomforts didn't bother Lincoln. "If every other fellow grumbled at the bill-of-fare which greeted us at many of the dingy taverns," Davis recalled, "Lincoln said nothing." Still, Davis did remember that "He once Said at a table—'Well—in the absence of anything to Eat I will jump into this Cabbage.'"

Circuit life was a festival of storytelling and joshing male camaraderie. Henry Whitney, a fellow lawyer who wrote a book on circuit life with Lincoln, recounted how another lawyer got a rip in his pants that exposed his underwear when he gestured during his arguments before the court. His colleagues started a penny subscription to patch his pants. Lincoln refused: "I can't contribute anything to *the end in view*."

Lincoln's cases often weren't worthy of a budding statesman. In 1851, there was the case of *McKinley v. Watkins* that arose after a horse trade between Joseph Watkins and William McKinley went bad (the horse received by Watkins died within two months). There was the case of *Rarey v. Swords* arising from the failure of Samuel Swords to follow through on building a house for William Rarey in payment of a debt. The case of *Watkins v. Gale* began when Hankerson Watkins sued Jonas Gale for cutting down one hundred swamp oak trees and four burr oak trees on his property without permission. And *Walker v. Morrison* concerned a $5.76 promissory note John Morrison gave William Walker.

Most of the time, Lincoln made a point of his affordability. In 1856, when a client sent Lincoln twenty-five dollars for his work drawing up some papers, Lincoln wrote back, "You must think I am a high-priced man. You are too liberal with your money. Fifteen dollars is enough for the job. I send you a receipt for fifteen dollars, and return to you a ten-dollar bill." (For context, this was about year after Lincoln's first attempt at winning a seat in the U.S. Senate.) In one instance, he took only twenty-five dollars after winning a large judgment for his client. In another, when the recipient of his legal advice wanted to pay him, or failing that, give him something, Lincoln recommended that "when you go down stairs just stop at the stationers, and send me up a bottle of ink."

For all that, Lincoln was an accomplished but by no means great lawyer, with a notable practice before the Illinois Supreme Court and in the federal courts. He became a key advocate for the railroads, which became more and more important in the state despite the collapse of the System. The Illinois Central arose from the ashes of that fiasco after Congress granted Illinois land to give to the railroad, making it the first of the land-grant roads. It was incorporated by the state in 1851. By 1856, it ran more than seven hundred miles from north-to-south and was the longest railroad in the country. People now fought to take credit for it. Illinois politician Sidney Breese, an advocate of the railroad, had inscribed on his tombstone, HE WHO SLEEPS BENEATH THIS STONE PROJECTED THE ILLINOIS CENTRAL RAILROAD.

Lincoln lobbied for the railroad's incorporation and it put him on a retainer. He represented it, far and away the foremost corporation in the state, in dozens of cases in the mid to late 1850s. The growth of the railroads was a boon to lawyers, involving an area that was new and murky and therefore held great potential for litigation. The fees involved could be substantial. "Billy," Herndon recalled Lincoln saying of the Illinois Central, "it seems to me that it will be bad taste on your part to keep on saying the severe things I have heard from you about railroads and other corporations. The truth is, instead of criticizing them, you and I ought to thank God for letting this one fall into our hands."

Although he also took up cases on the other side, in keeping with his lawyer's ethic of taking whatever business he could get, in his most notable cases Lincoln eased the way for the transportation revolution he had done so much to promote in office. He represented the Alton & Sangamon Railroad in an important 1851 case. A few years earlier he was a signatory on a report promoting the railroad "as a link in a great chain of rail road communication which shall unite Boston and New York with the Mississippi." Now, one James Barret, who had subscribed to thirty shares of stock of the railroad to be paid in installments, wanted to renege. When the route of the railroad was shortened to bypass his property, it made the project less lucrative and appealing to him. But if Barret could back out, it would encourage others to stop payment, too, and deplete the railroad's capital. It would make it more difficult for railroads in the future to change and improve their routes. The case went up to the Illinois Supreme Court, where Lincoln prevailed in a decision that relied on his reasoning and became widely cited.

In another case in 1853 involving a threat to the interests of the railroads, McLean County tried to levy taxes on the Illinois Central's 118 acres in the county. It sought to do this despite the exemption the state had granted to the railroad from exactly such local taxes. The railroad had to contemplate, in addition to its state tax, getting taxed by every county it touched. As Lincoln put it in a (not entirely grammatical) note spelling out the potential magnitude of the additional tax liability, "*The Company own* near two million acres; & their road runs through twentysix counties." The case also went to the state supreme court and Lincoln won, in another victory for the march of the roads. (He had to sue the Illinois Central to get his five-thousand-dollar fee—an astronomical payment for that time that led Stephen Douglas later to attack him for "taking the side of the company against the people.")

Still another consequential case involved a spur off the Illinois Central, run by the Rock Island Railroad, that headed west to the Mississippi. It built the first railroad bridge over the river, from Rock Island, Illinois, to Davenport, Iowa, a significant opening of the farmland west of the Mississippi to market forces from the East. When two weeks after its opening the steamboat *Effie Afton* crashed against the bridge and destroyed it, the steamboat's owners sued to remove the bridge. In a lawsuit pregnant with economic and sectional implications, Lincoln represented the railroad.

The steamboat operators hated the bridge as an obstacle to navigation and as a herald of a new world. When it was destroyed in the wake of the crash, steamboat captains blew their whistles in joy, "a greater celebration than follows an excited election," as Lincoln would put it before the jury. If there couldn't be bridges across the Mississippi, the railroad network would have a premature Western terminus and stunt the growing railroad network. Would the Mississippi remain the main artery of commercial traffic, with its inevitable connection with Southern interests, or would the railroad create an opening to the East? Or put another way, would St. Louis and the river, or Chicago and the railroad, win out as transit hubs?

Lincoln dove into the details of the crash, the current, the wind, the speed and condition of the boat, the depth and width of the channel, the angles involved, and so on. But before the jury he also addressed the larger question. He said that he "had no prejudice against steamboats or steamboatmen, nor any against St. Louis, for he supposed they went about as other people would do in their situation. St. Louis as a commercial place, may desire that this bridge should not stand, as it is adverse to her commerce, diverting a portion of it from the river." That couldn't be the overarching consideration, though. "There is a travel from East to West," he continued, "whose demands are not less important than that of the river. It is growing larger and larger, building up new countries with a rapidity never before seen in the history of the world." Eventually, in a drawn-out case, Lincoln and the bridge prevailed.

Lincoln the lawyer for railroad interests doesn't jibe with his image as the tribune of the common man—at least it doesn't on the surface. Historian Mark Neely notes Lincoln's association "with stock-jobbers and note-shavers, boosters and developers." The early twentieth century poet and Lincoln biographer Edgar Lee Masters complained of his identification with "lawyers and bankers and traders and merchants." As early as 1840, Lincoln had to defend himself from charges of elitism with invocations of his humble origins that once would have gone without saying.

Ninian Edwards told Herndon of a campaign stop in 1840. One Colonel E. D. Taylor charged Lincoln "with belonging to the aristocracy." Lincoln replied that "whilst Col. Taylor had his stores over the country, and was riding in a fine carriage, wore his kid cloves and had a gold headed cane, he [Lincoln] was a poor boy hired on a flat boat at eight dollars a month." That wasn't all. As Edwards continued to relate (rendered in run-on fashion by Herndon), Lincoln said back then he "had only one pair of breeches and they were of buckskin now . . . if you know the nature of buckskin when wet and dried by the sun, they would shrink and mine kept shrinking until they left for several inches my legs bare between the top of my Socks and the lower part of my breeches—and whilst I was growing taller they were becoming shorter: and so much tighter, that they left a blue streak around my leg which you can be seen to this day—If you call this aristocracy I plead guilty to the charge."

If his agenda was vulnerable to attack as favoring the well-off, Lincoln conceived of it entirely differently. It wasn't for—as he wrote dismissively in 1858 of the Whigs whom he couldn't win over in his Senate contest with Stephen Douglas—the "exclusive silk-stocking whiggery," "the nice exclusive sort." It was for the man on the rise. In the 1830s, the *Sangamo Journal*, with which Lincoln was closely associated, put the argument for improvements and banks in terms of aspiration. Without them, the poor would have no prospects except working as "hewers of wood and drawers of water" for the rich. Without access to capital, the "industrious poor" had no hope of lifting themselves up onto a higher economic plane.

The Whig polemicist Calvin Colton developed the argument at greater length in his *Junius Tracts* making the case for his party in 1844. He defined the country as one of mobility and striving: "Ours is a country, where men start from an humble origin, and from small beginnings rise gradually in the world, as the reward of merit and industry, and where they can attain to the most elevated positions, or acquire a large amount of wealth, according to the pursuits they elect for themselves. No exclusive privileges of birth, no entailment of estates, no civil or political disqualifications, stand in their path; but one has as good a chance as another, according to his talents, prudence, and personal exertions. This is a country of *self-made men*, than which nothing better could be said of any state of society."

This state of society can't apply, though, if foolish anticapitalist policies suppress economic vitality. "It has been a prevalent and fatal doctrine in this country," he wrote, "with a certain class of statesmen, that it is always a safe policy and a duty in the government, to fight against moneyed capitalists, in whatever place or shape they lift up their heads, whether in banks, or in manufactories, or in any and all other forms and enterprises requiring associated capital." This is so foolish because "it is not considered, that the employment and thriving of the people depend on the profitable investment of the moneyed capital of the country." Therefore, "that policy which destroys the profit of money, destroys the profit of labor. Let government strike at the rich, and the blow falls on the heads of the poor."

Lincoln would make this case with great power, especially as his emphasis on aspiration dovetailed with his case against slavery and as he transitioned from Whig to Republican. "So while we do not propose any war upon capital," he explained in a stirring riff in a speech in New Haven, Connecticut, in March 1860, "we do wish to allow the humblest man an equal chance to get rich with everybody else. When one starts poor, as most do in the race of life, free society is such that he knows he can better his condition; he knows that there is no fixed condition of labor, for his whole life."

He continued in a personal mode, "I am not ashamed to confess that twenty five years ago I was a hired laborer, mauling rails, at work on a flat-boat—just what might happen to any poor man's son! I want every man to have the chance—and I believe a black man is entitled to it—in which he *can* better his condition—when he may look forward and hope to be a hired laborer this year and the next, work for himself afterward, and finally to hire men to work for him! That is the true system." He wanted a country where "you can better your condition, and so it may go on and on in one ceaseless round so long as man exists on the face of the earth!"

Lincoln—and his like-minded Whigs and Republicans—engineered a momentous shift. He democratized Whiggish economics. He took an economic point of view descended from Alexander Hamilton—with all the elitist baggage that implies—and baptized it in the great, rolling Jordan River of American democracy. In Lincoln, the banks and the log cabin met. In Lincoln, the laboring man became the master of his own economic destiny. The storied political scientist Louis Hartz explained that economic power came to be defined "as within the reach, within the legitimate ambition, of all. The old gentilities are gone, and by an ironic paradox, the Hamiltonian Whig economic goal is attained amid enthusiasms wholly un-Whig in character."

For all the frustrations and fits and starts of Lincoln's policy initiatives, his broad economic vision was steadily vindicated in Illinois, and in the country—improved transportation and commercial networks, more people and more innovation, a spiraling upward economic rush. The improvements eventually came in the state. The Illinois & Michigan Canal had never been completely abandoned. It opened its locks in 1848, twelve years after construction began, and traffic boomed throughout the 1850s. But canals were no longer the future. The amount of railroad track jumped a hundredfold in the state—from 26 to 2,799—in the two decades after 1840. By 1860, Illinois had the second-largest amount of track of any state in the country.

Illinois reflected national trends. The country went through a canal-building boom that saw more than three thousand miles constructed by 1840. But then cost overruns and disappointing toll revenues on many routes and the dawning of the age of the railroad sent canals into retreat. The railroads were more reliable and practical than even the best canals. Americans embraced them with a fervor. At more than three thousand miles, the United States already had more railroad track than the entirety of Europe in 1840. New England and New York led the way in the 1840s, when another five thousand miles were added nationally, and then the Midwest rapidly began to catch up in the 1850s, when another twenty-two thousand miles were added.

Through the new, cheaper means of east-west transit, the Atlantic Ocean reached out and touched the rivers and lakes of the Midwest. Technology conquered distance. To use Lincoln's term from his lectures on discoveries and inventions, the "mines" of the middle of the country—the land capable of producing a stupendous agricultural bounty—were unlocked to markets on the East Coast and beyond.

Previously, dragging goods over land by horse had been incredibly cumbersome and expensive. Historian George Rogers Taylor quotes a United State Senate committee report from 1816: "A coal mine may exist in the United States not more than ten miles from valuable ores of iron and other materials, and both of them be useless until a canal is established between them, as the price of land carriage is too great to be borne by either." According to the report, getting a ton of goods across the ocean from Europe to the United States cost $9. The cost of getting a ton of goods thirty miles within the United States on the ground? Also $9.

The Allegheny Mountains had been a nearly insuperable obstacle to the development of an extended market. As Taylor relates, to get to Eastern markets, bulky Western goods had to circumvent the mountains by moving in a great arc, down the Mississippi, then up along the coast to Philadelphia, Boston, or New York. To get to the West, Eastern goods had to make it across the mountains or come upriver from New Orleans (a trip facilitated by the advent of the steamboat). The rise of the canals made a direct East–West route possible. Eastern manufactured goods headed directly west, and agricultural products in the opposite direction in great abundance.

The railroads instantly made ground transportation cheaper, and as they improved, it got cheaper still. From around 1815 to the Civil War, the cost of shipping bulky freight on land dropped 95 percent (some of this drop could be attributed to an economy-wide decline in prices). And it got there faster. Whereas earlier in the century it had taken more than fifty days to get goods from Cincinnati to New York, the railroad could get them there in as few as six days. Commerce on the Mississippi continued to grow, but Eastern manufactured and Western agricultural goods made up a smaller proportion of it. Human ingenuity was trumping sheer geography. The North increasingly cemented the Midwest to itself and its economic system, and effectively detached the region from the South.

The South noticed. In 1852, *DeBow's Review*, a proslavery journal that advocated Southern economic independence, blamed the Northern "enemy" for the decline of New Orleans: "Armed with energy, enterprise, and an indomitable spirit, that enemy, by a system of bold, vigorous, and sustained efforts, has succeeded in reversing the very laws of nature and of nature's God—rolled back the mighty tide of the Mississippi and its thousand tributary streams, until their mouth, practically and commercially, is more at New York or Boston than at New Orleans."

The railroads had a revolutionary impact not just by connecting markets but through their very operation. They needed more capital than had any business venture before, and therefore drove innovations in finance. They had to oversee vast, highly complex operations spanning greater distances and involving more workers than in any business venture before, and therefore led the way in new methods of corporate management. They had a hunger for iron, and therefore contributed to advances in iron-making. They reliably fed factories with raw materials and carried their finished products to the wide market, and therefore supported the development of mass-production manufacturing.

If Thoreau warned that "we do not ride on the railroad; it rides upon us," Lincoln saw in the railroad the heroic extension of human potential. He might have agreed with the poet Joaquin Miller, who maintained that "there is more poetry in the rush of a single railroad across the continent than in all the gory story of the burning of Troy." Or with the economist Joseph Nimmo, who later in the century noted that "the railroad with its vast possibilities for the advancement of the commercial, industrial, and social interests of the world ran directly counter to the pre-existing order of things."

The nature of farming changed. To buy the goods now coming from the East, farmers needed cash and to get cash they had to grow for the market. Subsistence farming gave way to commercial farming, and specialization. The population of the free states west of the Alleghenies boomed and by 1850, the Midwest had caught the Northeast in population. To feed ever-increasing demand, manufacturing grew and the factory system took hold. Productivity soared. According to historian Bruce Levine, from 1840 to 1860 value added in agriculture grew by 90 percent and in manufacturing by 350 percent. Urbanization proceeded at an astonishing clip.

In Illinois, Chicago exploded. The Illinois & Michigan Canal and the railroads fed its growth. Within four years of its incorporation in 1833, it was the largest town in the state. The city went from one minor railroad line in 1849 to an intricate and far-reaching network just a few years later. Travel time getting there from New York collapsed to three days whereas it had previously taken more than three weeks. Chicago was on its way to surpassing St. Louis as a transportation hub. The extensive countryside connected to it became one of the greatest breadbaskets on earth, and Illinois produced more corn and wheat than anywhere else in the country. Exports of grain jumped from 10,000 bushels prior to 1840 to 31 million twenty years later. On top of this, the city was a rapidly industrializing juggernaut.

It used to be that settlement had to be concentrated near rivers, but the railroads cleared the way for more people to live in the state's interior. As Eric Foner notes, Illinois boomed, becoming the fourth largest state in the country after its population doubled in a decade, to 1.7 million by 1860. The urban population increased three-fold, rising to almost a quarter of a million from 64,000. Immigrants from eastern states and from abroad settled at a rapid clip, overwhelming settlers from the south. The Republican stronghold of the North benefited most from the economic and demographic transformation. Illinois was becoming an ever more thoroughly Lincolnian state.

Changes that many deemed impossible had come to his adopted home. It hadn't been long ago that Jacksonians could insist: "The West is agricultural; it has no manufactures, and it never will have any of importance." To the contrary, by the 1850s Illinois was a rising manufacturing power. Gabor Boritt notes that Lincoln must have had contempt for the argument that inherent economic constraints would preserve the status quo in Illinois. Lincoln might call to mind, he writes, "the old British free trade argument that Americans could no more have complex manufactures than orange crops. Within his lifetime the United States had not only developed complex industries but, after acquiring new territories, was producing oranges. The lessons of the first half of the nineteenth century were plain. Natural limits could both be surmounted and outflanked."

Milton Hay, uncle of John Hay, Lincoln's White House secretary, described the epochal changes in life brought by the railroads. It was, he maintained, the "dividing line in point of time between the old and the new. Not only our homemade manufactures, but our homemade life and habits to a great measure disappeared. . . . We farmed not only with different implements but in a different mode. Then we began to inquire what the markets were and what product of the farm we could raise and sell to the best advantage. The farmer enlarged his farm and no longer contented himself with the land that himself or his boys could cultivate, but he must have hired hands and hired help to cultivate his large possessions."

Lincoln knew the homemade world all too well and exulted in its eclipse. Returning in 1859 to Indiana, near where he had been raised, he elicited laughter when he said "he grew up to his present enormous height on our own good soil of Indiana." But he noted that the former "unbroken wilderness" had given way to "wonderfully different" conditions. In his New Haven speech in 1860, he celebrated development in the Northeast: "Up here in New England, you have a soil that scarcely sprouts black-eyed beans, and yet where will you find wealthy men so wealthy, and poverty so rarely in extremity? There is not another such place on earth!" In an undated fragment for himself perhaps composed circa 1858 or 1859, he wrote: "We proposed to give *all* a chance; and we expected the weak to grow stronger, the ignorant, wiser; and all better, and happier together. We made the experiment; and the fruit is before us. Look at it—think of it. Look at it, in it's aggregate grandeur, of extent of country, and numbers of population—of ship, and steamboat, and rail."

Lincoln didn't just thirst for his country's glory; he also sought his own. Joshua Speed told Herndon that after Lincoln issued the Emancipation Proclamation, they had a conversation where "he alluded to an incident in his life, long passed, when he was so much deppressed that he almost contemplated suicide—At the time of his deep deppression—He said to me that he had done nothing to make any human being remember that he had lived—and that to connect his name with the events transpiring in his day & generation and so impress himself upon them as to link his name with something that would redound to the interest of his fellow man was what he desired to live for."

Linking his name to something great must have seemed a far-off prospect when he returned to Springfield in 1849 from his single term in Congress, having failed to secure a patronage appointment from the incoming administration of Zachary Taylor.

According to Herndon, Lincoln "despaired of ever rising again in the political world." He had been the lone Whig in the state's seven-person congressional delegation, and he couldn't attain any higher office given the partisan terrain in Illinois. His restless upward march had been checked.

Lincoln had been left far behind by his political rival, Stephen Douglas. In the mid-1850s, Lincoln wrote a private note about Douglas that was unsparing in its honesty and its envy: "Twenty-two years ago Judge Douglas and I first became acquainted. We were both young then; he a trifle younger than I. Even then, we were both ambitious; I, perhaps, quite as much so as he. With *me*, the race of ambition has been a failure—a flat failure; with *him* it has been one of splendid success. His name fills the nation; and is not unknown, even, in foreign lands. I affect no contempt for the high eminence he has reached. So reached, that the oppressed of my species, might have shared with me in the elevation, I would rather stand on that eminence, than wear the richest crown that ever pressed a monarch's brow."

The final sentence makes reference to the intrusion of slavery in a central, unavoidable place in the nation's politics. It raised questions much deeper than economic development, questions about the country's meaning and its very survival. Douglas had an outsize role in the coming crisis. He became the inadvertent architect of, and foil for, Lincoln's rise to destiny.

Chapter 4

"Our Fathers": The Lincoln-Douglas Debates and the Purpose of America

They meant to set up a standard maxim for free society,
which should be familiar to all, and revered by all; constantly
looked to, constantly labored for, and even though never
perfectly attained, constantly approximated, and thereby
constantly spreading and deepening its influence. . . .
—ABRAHAM LINCOLN, SPEECH IN SPRINGFIELD,
ILLINOIS, 1857

I n June 1858, Lincoln was about to accept the Republican
nomination for Senate. Parties usually didn't endorse candidates until after the election of state legislators, who, in the days
before the Seventeenth Amendment provided for direct election
of senators, decided who would represent their state in the U.S.
Senate. But Illinois Republicans wanted to make a point. The
party's power brokers back east had been flirting with Stephen
Douglas after he broke with Southern Democrats. The state party
made its zeal for Lincoln unmistakable at an enthusiastic convention in Springfield. It declared him "the first and only choice of

the Republicans of Illinois for the U.S. Senate, as the successor of Stephen A. Douglas."

Lincoln knew this moment was coming, since support had been steadily building for him in county conventions. He spent a month preparing his speech, according to Herndon. He wrote notes on "slips, put these slips in his hat, numbering them, and when he was done with the ideas, he gathered up the scraps, put them in the right order, and wrote out his speech." A few days before the event, Springfield Republican John Armstrong recalled, Lincoln gathered some friends "in the Library Room in the State house in the city of Springfield, for the purpose of getting their opinion of the policy of delivering that Speech."

Eight or twelve of them sat at a round table and Lincoln read what would become its immortal House Divided opening passage: "'A house divided against itself cannot stand.' I believe this government cannot endure, permanently half *slave* and half *free*." He read the beginning "slowly & cautiously so as to let Each man fully understand it." The reaction around the table was cool, to say the least. "Every Man among them," Armstrong told Herndon later, "Condemned the speech in Substance & Spirit," and the House Divided language "as unwise & impolitic, if not false."

About it being impolitic, they were indisputably correct. Stephen Douglas came back to Lincoln's House Divided language again and again during the campaign as proof Lincoln was a radical bent on disunion.

One interpretation of the speech is that Lincoln was playing chess when everyone else was playing checkers, and already had his eye on the presidential race in 1860 rather than the lowly Senate race in 1858. Historian Don Fehrenbacher notes how fanciful it is to believe Lincoln was anything but deadly intent on beating

Douglas in the race at hand. He points to a campaign strategy memo Lincoln wrote categorizing and breaking down the 1856 vote by each legislative district. After pages of tabulation, Lincoln writes:

> By this, it is seen, we give up the districts numbered 1.2.3. 4.5.7.8.10.11.15.16.17.18.19.20.23.28.29.&30, with 22 representatives—
>
> We take to ourselves, without question 37.40.42.43.44.45. 46.47.48.49.50.51.52.53.54.55.56.57.& 58. with 27 representatives—
>
> Put as doubtful, and to be struggled for, 6.9.12.13.14.21. 22.24.25.26.27.31.32.33.34.35.36.38.39& 41. with 26 representatives"

These aren't the calculations of someone blithely unconcerned with victory.

Lincoln delivered the House Divided speech because he wanted to accentuate his difference with Douglas, but more fundamentally because he believed it. The sentiment wasn't new for him. In a scorching 1855 letter to the Kentuckian George Robertson, Lincoln vented his despair over achieving the peaceful extinction of slavery. He concluded, "Our political problem now is 'Can we, as a nation, continue together permanently—forever—half slave, and half free?' The problem is too mighty for me." T. Lyle Dickey, an Illinois lawyer and politico, recalled hearing Lincoln say much the same thing at a political meeting in the fall of 1856. Dickey told Herndon, "After the Meeting was over—Mr Lincoln & I returned to Pike House—where we occupied the Same room—Immediately on reaching the room I said to Mr

Lincoln—'What in God's name could induce you to promulgate such an opinion.'"

In Lincoln's view, at stake in the debate with Douglas and with apologists for slavery was what he called our "central idea," upon which our government ultimately depends. We could either stay true to the idea bequeathed to us by 1776, or resort to a new one accommodating slavery's spread and its permanent place in our national life. That was the choice. For his part, Lincoln planted his flag firmly in the Declaration of Independence.

"I believe the declara[tion] that 'all men are created equal' is the great fundamental principle upon which our free institutions rest," Lincoln wrote in an 1858 letter. It had made America a land of individual effort and advancement and, therefore, of stupendous abundance. "We are a great empire," Lincoln said in a speech at Kalamazoo, Michigan, in 1856. "We are eighty years old. We stand at once the wonder and admiration of the whole world, and we must enquire what it is that has given us so much prosperity, and we shall understand that to give up that one thing, would be to give up all future prosperity. This cause is that every man can make himself."

In the Senate contest in 1858, Lincoln waged a fight to preserve and to extend that "one thing." He happened to be doing it in a campaign against the man he had debated, envied, and scorned throughout his career. This latest iteration of the Lincoln-Douglas struggle implicated the deepest ideals of the republic. Douglas, too, was a railroad man. He shepherded the bill to passage granting Illinois the land for the Illinois Central. Douglas, too, wanted to see the country grow, and in fact was more enthusiastic about its westward expansion than was Lincoln. Douglas agitated for a transcontinental railroad and a tide of settlers sweeping toward the

Pacific. He sounded just like Lincoln when, shortly after his arrival in Illinois, he wrote back east, in fulsome praise of the state's potential: "Illinois possesses more natural advantages, and is destined to possess greater artificial and acquired advantages, than any other state in the union or on the globe."

The question between the two wasn't the country's economic policies or its extent, so much as its very nature, the basis on which the House Divided would be made whole. Lincoln insisted that it be on the ground of the Declaration, which he considered the acid test for the American Dream, the Great Writ of American aspiration, the timeless guarantor of the equality of opportunity that would elevate all through the workings of commercial enterprise. In the ensuing existential crisis of the union, Lincoln translated into national gospel his vision of a republic of striving.

Stephen Douglas's background made him more natural Whig material than did Lincoln's. Douglas came from Vermont, and was the son of a doctor. He had been educated in a preparatory school in a pedagogical splendor unknown to Lincoln. But he, too, had to struggle to rise and found his way upward through the law and politics. His father died when he was an infant. When his mother moved in with her brother, Douglas had to work for his uncle as a laborer and didn't appreciate the arrangement any more than Lincoln would have. As a young man, he headed west and arrived in Illinois via Cleveland and St. Louis not too long after Lincoln, with just a couple of bucks in his pocket. When he left home, he supposedly told his mother, who was curious when he would be back to visit, "On my way to Congress, Mother."

Despite his New England roots, Douglas embraced the hero of the West, Andrew Jackson, and the populism of his Democratic Party. He had fallen for Jackson back in Vermont during the campaign of 1828. "From this moment," he remembered, "my politics became fixed, and all subsequent reading, reflection and observation have but confirmed my early attachment to the cause of Democracy." In the 1830s, he declared, "in this country there are two opposing parties," on one side "the advocates of the rights of the people" and on the other "the advocates of the privileges of Property."

At five feet, four inches tall, with remarkably short legs, Douglas was all energy and aggression, "a perfect steam engine in breeches," as one fellow lawyer put it. Reckless and risk-taking by nature, Douglas was ferociously ambitious. He got himself selected as a state's attorney within about a year of becoming a lawyer.

The paths of the two young politicians in a hurry constantly intersected. Mary Todd had flirted with Douglas back when she was single. Ninian Edwards told Herndon how Lincoln at one point fell for his comely young cousin, Matilda Edwards. She fielded a score of entreaties for marriage, including, according to Edwards, from Douglas, whom "she refused . . . on the grounds of his bad morals."

Lincoln and Douglas served in the state legislature together. By that time, Douglas was already known as the "Little Giant," although his opponents mocked him as the "Peoria Bantling." In a sly reference to his diminutive stature, Lincoln wrote to a fellow Whig legislator in 1837: "We have adopted it as part of our policy here, to never speak of Douglass at all. Is'nt that the best mode of treating so small a matter?" (Missouri senator Thomas Hart Benton would once say of Douglas that "his legs are too short, sir. That part of his body, sire, which men wish to kick, is too near the ground!")

The two met often on the rhetorical battlefield. Before there were *the* Lincoln-Douglas Debates, there were Lincoln-Douglas debates. A newspaper report recorded a Lincoln stop in Tremont, Illinois, during the 1858 campaign: "He went through with a rapid account of the times when he had advocated the doctrines of the Whig party in Tazewell County during the successive campaigns of 1840–'44–'48 and '52, and alluded to the fact that he had often met Douglas upon the very steps upon which he was speaking, before as now to oppose his political doctrines."

When Lincoln's law partner John Stuart ran against Douglas for Congress in 1838 (beating him by all of thirty-six votes), Lincoln berated the Democrat in anonymous letters in the *Sangamo Journal* that Douglas denounced for their "vindictive, fiendish spirit." Lincoln did all he could to get Stuart over the top and may even have taken his place at a debate in Bloomington when his friend was ill.

In late 1839, in the run-up to the presidential campaign in the coming year, the political banter between the Whigs and Democrats hanging around the Springfield store owned by Joshua Speed became particularly heated. According to Herndon, Douglas "sprang up and abruptly made a challenge to those who differed with him to discuss the whole matter publicly, remarking that, 'This store is no place to talk politics.'" Lincoln participated in the ensuing debates. In an initial contest, Douglas beat him badly. Lincoln "left the stump literally whipped off of it," a Democratic newspaper happily related, "even in the estimation of his own friends."

Joseph Gillespie wrote Herndon about the episode: "He was very sensitive where he thought he had failed to come up to the expectations of his friends. I remember a case. He was pitted by the Whigs in 1840 to debate with Mr Douglass the Democratic champion. Lincoln did not come up to the requirements of the occasion. He was conscious of his failure and I never saw any man so much distressed. He begged to be permitted to try it again and was reluctantly indulged and in the next effort he transcended our highest expectations."

This was Lincoln's widely praised and reproduced speech filleting the Van Buren independent Treasury plan. He began by noting the small audience present. "I am, indeed, apprehensive," he said, "that the few who have attended, have done so, more to spare me of mortification, than in the hope of being interested in any thing I may be able to say. This circumstance casts a damp upon my spirits, which I am sure I shall be unable to overcome during the evening. But enough of preface."

After lashing the Van Buren proposal, Lincoln reserved some of his firepower for Douglas at the end. He recalled a Douglas speech on an earlier night justifying the expenditures of the Van Buren administration: "Those who heard Mr. Douglass, recollect that he indulged himself in a contemptuous expression of pity for me. 'Now he's got me,' thought I." Then, Lincoln said he realized that the reasons proffered by Douglas for the spending were "untrue" or even "supremely ridiculous." He said he then realized that he had nothing to worry about: "when I saw that he was stupid enough to hope, that I would permit such groundless and audacious assertions to go unexposed, I readily consented, that on the score both of veracity and sagacity, the audience should judge whether he or I were the more deserving of the world's contempt."

A minor triumph for Lincoln, but nothing to compare to the continual rise of Stephen Douglas, who was prodigiously talented

and unbelievably successful. He became the state's youngest secretary of state in 1840, right before being named to the state's
supreme court. (He liked to be called "judge" ever after.) He arrived in the House of Representatives four years before Lincoln
and got promoted to the Senate in 1846 at the same time Lincoln
was elected to his one unremarkable and unsatisfying term in
the House, where he languished as a freshman in the back of the
chamber on "Cherokee Strip." Such was Lincoln's obscurity that
the Republican politician John Wentworth wrote to Herndon
that when Lincoln was nominated for president, "few of his old
[congressional] colleagues remembered him," and "Speaker Win-
throp, of his own party, is said to have asserted . . . that he would
not recognize [him] if he should meet him in the street."

By 1852, Douglas was a serious contender for the Democratic
presidential nomination, finishing third at the convention. Lincoln was out of office back in Illinois, lamenting of Douglas,
"time was when I was in his way some." Now, he commented,
"such small men as I, can hardly be considered as worthy of his
notice; & I may have to dodge & get between his legs."

When the Kansas–Nebraska Act passed in 1854, repealing the
Missouri Compromise, Douglas was in the midst of the national
debate, indeed driving the national debate, while Lincoln was
practicing law. He hadn't quit politics, but was relatively inactive.
Lincoln later recalled in his autobiographical statement for John
Scripps that "his profession had almost superseded the thought of
politics in his mind, when the repeal of the Missouri compromise
aroused him as he had never been before."

The Kansas–Nebraska Act had begun as an effort by Douglas
to establish a government for the unorganized territory west of
Iowa and Missouri, a parcel of the northern portion of the Louisi-

ana Purchase including what would eventually become the states of Kansas and Nebraska. The Missouri Compromise had banned slavery in the Louisiana Purchase north of the 36'30" parallel. The Kansas-Nebraska Act would efface the Missouri Compromise prohibition and let the people in the territory decide the status of slavery "under the doctrine of popular sovereignty."

With a keen eye for the main chance, Douglas didn't lack for reasons to push the act. He wanted a transcontinental railroad and wanted a route benefiting Illinois (and making his own real estate holdings more valuable). That was impossible so long as Southerners blocked legislation to organize the Kansas-Nebraska territory. They considered the Missouri Compromise's prohibition on slavery in the Northern territories an affront. If Douglas could get them on board, it would have the additional benefit of enhancing his standing in the South and increasing his odds as a presidential candidate. Popular sovereignty would in theory cool national passions on the issue by making it a matter of democratic choice by voters in each locale. In any case, climate and soil would naturally check the spread of slavery into new territory in the north. For Douglas, it looked like a win-win several times over.

At first, the repeal of the Missouri Compromise was left implicit in the act. Under pressure from Southerners, though, Douglas added language declaring it "inoperative and void." He knew that the proposal, disturbing a long-standing dispensation at the behest of the South, would "raise a hell of a storm." So it did. But Douglas was nothing if not a genius legislative mechanic. It was he, not the "Great Compromiser" Henry Clay, who had figured out how to get the Compromise of 1850 through Congress, settling what had been the prior major sectional flare-up over the country's new territory. With the support of the administration of President Franklin Pierce, and a healthy helping of patronage to bring around reluctant Northern Democrats, Douglas cajoled, argued, and strategized his way to victory in the spring of 1854. "I had the authority and power of a dictator throughout the whole controversy in both houses," he boasted.

Douglas reaped the whirlwind, and so did the country. The South's prospective expansion into what had been considered territory locked away for freedom outraged and galvanized antislavery forces in the North. Douglas said burning effigies of him could light his way "from Boston to Chicago." When he showed up in the latter city to defend the act, he got hooted at and lashed back, "Abolitionists of Chicago! It is now Sunday morning. I'll go to church and you may go to Hell." The law soon enough issued in a low-simmering civil war between pro- and antislavery forces fighting over the status of "bloody Kansas." "I look upon that enactment not as a *law*," Lincoln wrote of Kansas-Nebraska in an 1855 letter to Joshua Speed, "but as *violence* from the beginning. It was conceived in violence, passed in violence, is maintained in violence, and is being executed in violence."

The forces unleashed by Kansas-Nebraska buffeted both parties, but destroyed Lincoln's Whigs. For a time it seemed that the nativist Know-Nothing party would emerge ascendant. It, too, was torn apart by sectional conflict, though, and a significant drop in immigration sapped some of its energy. After a period of partisan chaos, with every state embarking on its own path, the anti-Nebraska forces coalesced into the new Republican Party. Lincoln wrote in that same letter to Speed, "You enquire where I now stand. That is a disputed point. I think I am a whig; but others say there are no whigs, and that I am an abolitionist."

He made a gradual transition into the new Republican Party

that channeled the natural anti-aristocratic feelings of the public
into its attacks on the slave South, or "the Slave Power," capital-
ized. It enjoyed the protection of a South that overawed American
government for much of its early existence. Slaveholders won most
of the country's first sixteen presidential elections. Through 1861,
twenty-three of the thirty-six speakers of the House had been
Southerners. Supreme Court justices had been disproportionately
from the South. The federal government had a distinctively
Southern flavor that benefited the region intensely protective of
its peculiar institution.

From the first, slavery was overwhelmingly, although not entirely, a Southern phenomenon. In 1790, New York had more
slaves than any other city besides Charleston, South Carolina.
Even then, though, fewer than 6 percent of all slaves were in the
North. In the latter half of the eighteenth century, slave labor
tended to be concentrated in tobacco, rice, and indigo, grown in
the Chesapeake area and the Carolinas and Georgia. The revolution in cotton production with the advent of Eli Whitney's gin
greased its spread throughout the westward-expanding south.

By 1850, about two-thirds of slaves worked on cotton plantations. Altogether, about a fourth of Southern whites owned slaves
as of 1860. They ranged from owners of five to six slaves who
worked alongside their chattel, to a better-off group of about a
quarter of all slaveholders who owned up to fifty slaves, to the
top three thousand families, who alone owned about a tenth of
all the slaves.

Slavery was quite simply the cornerstone of the South, to borrow the phrase of the vice president of the Confederacy, Alexander Stephens. In 1860, the South's nearly 4 million slaves were
collectively worth about $3 billion, or more than all the nation's

banks, railroads, and factories put together, according to historian Eric Foner. As the rest of the world experienced a wave of emancipations, the South stood with the likes of Brazil, Cuba, and Puerto Rico on the ramparts of slavery. Even Russia was emancipating the serfs.

The South craved more territory. It wanted to spread slavery and to forge new slave states to maintain the balance between North and South in the Senate. It eagerly supported the annexation of Texas in 1845 and the ensuing war with Mexico. The most aggressive Southerners coveted additional ground even farther south, in Cuba and elsewhere in Latin America. This push fed the tragicomic Southern tradition of filibustering, whereby a rogue's gallery of Southern politicians and adventurers sought to take Latin American territory through their private exertions for the glory of Southern empire.

For his part, Lincoln had always opposed slavery, but with cat's feet, cautiously, moderately. "I am naturally anti-slavery," Lincoln averred in April 1864. "If slavery is not wrong, nothing is wrong. I can not remember when I did not so think, and feel."

He didn't have much direct experience of it. Lincoln remembered "a tedious low-water trip, on a Steam Boat from Louisville to St. Louis" with Joshua Speed in 1841. About a dozen slaves were on board, "shackled together with irons." He told Speed in a letter years later that the "sight was a continual torment to me." Such a spectacle, repeated whenever he touched a slave state, "has, and continually exercises, the power of making me miserable."

His family had lived on the borderlands of slavery. His native Kentucky was a slave state, although a somewhat attenuated one. Still, out of 7,500 people in Hardin County, where Lincoln spent his earliest years, more than 1,000 were slaves. At one point, Lincoln's father worked on a milldam alongside slaves. His parents belonged to South Fork Baptist Church. When the church split over the issue of slavery, they joined the antislavery faction at Little Mount Baptist Church. Lincoln told Scripps that his father took the family across the Ohio River and into Indiana "partly on account of slavery."

"Slave States," Lincoln would say much later, perhaps speaking from experience, "are places for poor white people to remove FROM; not to remove TO. New free States are the places for poor people to go to and better their condition."

He wasn't often called on to legislate on the matter. In 1837, he was one of just six votes opposing resolutions in the Illinois legislature that excoriated abolitionism and declared that "the right of property in slaves is sacred." Lincoln could manage to get only one other legislator, who wasn't running for reelection, to sign onto a statement of dissent. It argued "that the institution of slavery is founded on both injustice and bad policy," although it included the caveat that "the promulgation of abolition doctrines tends rather to increase than abate its evils."

As a congressman, he offered a plan for Washington, D.C., of gradual, compensated emancipation—always his preference—if approved by the District's voters; it didn't go anywhere. He opposed the Mexican War, offering his "spot" resolutions demanding to know the precise location of the alleged Mexican invasion of American soil that justified the war. This opened him to attack back home where the war was popular, as "Spotty Lincoln" or "Ranchero Spotty," with his "pathetic lamentation over the fate of those Mexicans." When Congressman David Wilmot of Pennsylvania offered an amendment, the famous Wilmot Proviso, excluding slavery from land acquired from Mexico, Lincoln voted for it "as good as forty times," he later claimed.

Even after Kansas-Nebraska, he never swung into the camp of the abolitionists. He favored the nonextension of slavery as a means toward its eventual extinction, with the endgame never exactly clear. He didn't believe that natural conditions would stop its spread, as Douglas maintained. He pointed out that Illinois and Missouri were side by side, separated only by the Mississippi. Yet only Illinois was a free state, its status secured by a federal prohibition from the beginning. Nonextension had the political advantage of sidestepping or playing into anti-black sentiment—keeping slavery out of the West was indistinguishable from keeping out blacks. Taking this tendency a step further, Lincoln remained an advocate of the voluntary colonization of blacks years into the Civil War.

Kansas-Nebraska radicalized him, nonetheless. He staked his reputation and tethered his ambition to the cause of antislavery. In a fragment he wrote for himself in July 1858, he opened by noting, "I have never professed an indifference to the honors of official station." Then he mused on all the opponents of abolishing the slave trade in Great Britain and how long they had succeeded in preserving the trade. "Though they blazed," he wrote, "like tallow-candles for a century, at last they flickered in the socket, died out, stank in the dark for a brief season, and were remembered no more, even by the smell. School-boys know that Wilbeforce [sic], and Granville Sharpe [sic], helped that cause forward; but who can now name a single man who labored to retard it?"

As the contest over slavery became the focus of his public advocacy, Lincoln's rhetoric took on the majesty with which we now associate it. Beginning in August 1854, he made the case publicly against the Kansas-Nebraska Act, several times directly in reply to Douglas. We have the record of his speech in Peoria in October 1854. The Whig paper in Springfield, the *Illinois State Journal*, took seven issues to print the speech's nearly seventeen thousand words, carefully edited by Lincoln himself. As Lewis Lehrman points out, the speech is the urtext of Lincoln's advocacy for the next decade, with nearly everything else an elaboration.

Prior to the passage of the Kansas-Nebraska Act, Lincoln referred to the Declaration only twice in public. Thereafter, it became a staple of his rhetoric and worldview, "his political chart and inspiration" in the words of his secretary John G. Nicolay. The Declaration had become a field of battle in the fight over slavery. Opponents of slavery brandished the glorious sentence from its preamble: "We hold these truths to be self-evident, that all men are created equal, that they are endowed by their Creator with certain unalienable Rights, that among these are Life, Liberty and the pursuit of Happiness." The Chicago abolitionist newspaper the *Western Citizen* published the preamble on the front of every edition.

Lincoln may have first read the Declaration in the law book *The Statutes of Indiana*. Betraying his logical cast of mind, Lincoln referred to it as containing "the definitions and axioms of free society." For the South, it was a pernicious invitation to error. John C. Calhoun in 1848 called the idea that "all men are born free and equal" nothing less than "the most false and dangerous of all political error." Southern extremist George Fitzhugh agreed. "Liberty and equality are new things under the sun," he wrote disapprovingly. Indiana senator John Pettit called the central contention of the Declaration "a self-evident lie"—a line that became a constant target for Lincoln.

In his 1852 eulogy for Henry Clay, Lincoln already remarked on "an increasing number of men, who, for the sake of perpetuating slavery, are beginning to assail and ridicule the white-man's charter of freedom—the declaration that 'all men are created free and equal.' So far as I have learned, the first American, of any note, to do or attempt this, was the late John C. Calhoun." From there, Lincoln jabbed, "it soon after found its way into some of the messages of the Governors of South Carolina. We, however, look for, and are not much shocked by, political eccentricities and heresies in South Carolina."

Lincoln cited a Virginia clergyman who had noted dismissively that the Declaration's statement of universal equality is not found in the Bible but comes "from Saint Voltaire, and was baptized by Thomas Jefferson." The man of the cloth went on to argue that he had never seen two men who were actually equal, although he admitted—he must have styled himself a wit—that "he never saw the Siamese twins." Lincoln observed archly, "This sounds strangely in republican America," and insisted that "the like was not heard in the fresher days of the Republic."

Distant from his own father, Lincoln felt a deep patriotic filial piety to "the fathers." In the Lyceum address, he declared: "Let every man remember that to violate the law, is to trample on the blood of his father." It is our duty to transmit "undecayed" our inheritance of constitutional liberty, out of "gratitude to our fathers, justice to ourselves, duty to posterity, and love for our species in general." At Peoria, he said, "I love the sentiments of those old time men." In a stirring Chicago speech in 1858, he spoke of the "iron men" of the past, of "those old men," and "that old Declaration of Independence."

A sense of loss suffuses his statements in the 1850s. At Peoria, he lamented that "Little by little, but steadily as a man's march to the grave, we have been giving up the OLD for the NEW faith." He imagined what would have happened had Senator Pettit denigrated the Declaration during the Founding generation: "If it had been said in old Independence Hall, seventy-eight years ago, the very door-keeper would have throttled the man and thrust him into the street."

Lincoln sought to recapture what seemed to be slipping away, to catch the falling flag of our patriotic patrimony. "He endeavored to bring back things to the old land marks," Joseph Gillespie wrote Herndon, "but he never would have attempted to invent and compose new systems. He had boldness enough when he found the building racked and going to decay to restore it to its original design but not to contrive a new & distinct edifice." Lincoln wanted to "re-adopt," as he said at Peoria, the Declaration. The road to salvation ran through 1776, he argued in a gorgeous passage: "Our republican robe is soiled, and trailed in the dust. Let us re-purify it. Let us turn and wash it white, in the spirit, if not the blood, of the Revolution."

Lincoln believed that this renewal is exactly the purpose for which the Declaration had been intended. He had complicated feelings about Thomas Jefferson even though he categorized him as one of "those noble fathers—Washington, Jefferson, and Madison." Henry Clay argued that his was the party that truly continued in the tradition of Jefferson, and so did Lincoln. But Lincoln had no use for Jefferson the aristocrat, the hypocritical slaveholder and celebrant—like Andrew Jackson—of yeoman agriculture. It was Jefferson's Declaration that he adored.

Lincoln practically gushed in a 1859 letter to a Republican festival in Boston marking the anniversary of Jefferson's birth: "All honor to Jefferson—to the man who, in the concrete pressure of a struggle for national independence by a single people, had the coolness, forecast, and capacity to introduce into a merely revolutionary document, an abstract truth, applicable to all men and all times, and so to embalm it there, that to-day, and in all coming days, it shall be a rebuke and a stumbling-block to the very harbingers of re-appearing tyranny and oppression."

For Lincoln, the Declaration laid the philosophical foundation for the liberal capitalism he wanted to spread and vindicate. It made the case for human dignity and created the predicate for a system that endlessly developed human potential. It undergirded what Republicans extolled as "free-labor civilization."

Lincoln saw a biblical warrant for the natural rights the Declaration enunciated. As far back as roughly 1847, he wrote in notes for himself about tariff policy, "In the early days of the world, the Almighty said to the first of our race 'In the sweat of thy face shalt thou eat bread.'" It follows that all good things come from labor and "such things belong to those whose labour has produced them." Except that "it has so happened in all ages of the world, that *some* have laboured, and *others* have, without labour, enjoyed a large proportion of the fruits. This is wrong, and should not continue. To [secure] each labourer the whole product of his labour, or as nearly as possible, is a most worthy object of any good government."

In those notes, Lincoln ruminated on what he considered the wasted cost of transportation of bringing goods here from overseas. In the much more consequential debate over slavery, he returned again and again to the biblical injunction to live from your own sweat. He denounced "the same old serpent that says you work and I eat, you toil and I will enjoy the fruits of it." In contrast, Lincoln defended the principle that "each individual is naturally entitled to do as he pleases with himself and the fruit of his labor." Or in more down-to-earth terms, "I always thought that the man who made the corn should eat the corn."

The truth of this proposition was obvious enough to be itself self-evident. In a fragment written for himself probably in the late 1850s, Lincoln said it had been "made so plain by our good Father in Heaven, that all *feel* and *understand* it, even down to brutes and creeping insects. The ant, who has toiled and dragged a crumb to his nest, will furiously defend the fruit of his labor, against whatever robber assails him. So plain, that the most dumb and stupid slave that ever toiled for a master, does constantly *know* that he is wronged. So plain that no one, high or low, ever does mistake it, except in a plainly *selfish* way."

This view accorded with the thought of the philosophical inspirer of the Declaration, John Locke. The late-seventeenth-century English philosopher posited an inalienable right to life and liberty that extended to a right to property. Most fundamentally, we all have an equal and natural right to the inalienable possession of ourselves. "For men being all the workmanship of one omnipotent, and infinitely wise maker," Locke wrote, "they are his property, whose workmanship they are, made to last during his, not one another's pleasure." We extend ourselves to the outside world through work, and therefore acquire the right to property in particular things: "Whatsoever then he removes out of the state that nature hath provided, and left it in, he hath mixed his labour with, and joined to it something that is his own, and thereby makes it his property."

It is this short chain of reasoning, legal scholar Bradford William Short argues, that binds the natural-rights philosophy of the

Declaration to the economic premises of Lincoln and his allies: "Free labor ideology *is* the theory of the inalienable right to life and liberty," Short writes. "It is more than that too, of course, but it necessarily always includes the theory at least at its core, as one of its first premises."

Lincoln and his allies believed they had seen this view of the world play out in the North, "a dynamic, expanding capitalist society, whose achievements and destiny were almost wholly the result of the dignity and opportunities which it offered the average laboring man," as Eric Foner puts it.

The South begged to differ.

Historian John McCardell traces the development of proslavery thought from an emphasis on a biblical, paternalistic foundation to a frankly racist argument, as the leadership of the South shifted from the old seaboard to the rapidly growing interior. In 1845, South Carolina governor James Hammond wrote letters defending slavery to a British abolitionist. Referring to the Bible and history, he maintained that slavery was "a moral and humane institution, productive of the greatest political and social advantages," including free people who were "higher toned and more deeply interested in preserving a stable and well ordered Government." The argument had a distinctly antidemocratic key. Hammond boasted that in the South, "intelligence and wealth" didn't give way to the "reckless and unenlightened numbers."

Soon there arose a more "scientific" defense of slavery. Alabama doctor Josiah Nott championed a version of it that he charmingly deemed "niggerology." He dispensed with the Bible to argue that blacks and whites were two different species, and published a collection of ethnological writing called *Types of Mankind*. In an essay directed to "The Non-Slaveholders of the South," influential journalist James De Bow underlined the implications: the white man "can look down at those who are beneath him, at an infinite remove." Alabama's William Lowndes Yancey said the South elevated the white man "amongst the master race and put the negro race to do this dirty work which God designed they should do."

The South boasted of the benefits of its system of racial hierarchy. In *Slavery Justified*, George Fitzhugh boasted how in the South "all is peace, quiet, plenty and contentment. We have no mobs, no trades unions, no strikes for higher wages, no armed resistance to law, but little jealousy of the rich by the poor."

In their indictment of Northern capitalism, the Southern ideologists focused on the rise of wage labor, or "wage slavery," as they deemed it. It had begun to supplant independent proprietorship as the dominant form of economic activity. According to Foner, by 1850 there were more wage earners than slaves, and by 1860, possibly more wage earners than self-employed workers. Fitzhugh insisted that wage earners, rather than experiencing the beneficence of one master, were "slaves of the *community*." He located the source of the North's inhumanity in the remorseless ethic of "every man for himself," the "whole moral code of Free Society."

The attack on wage labor relied on a zero-sum, class-conflict analysis of the economy. The labor movement maintained this view even after the Civil War, and Jacksonians in the North could be just as fierce in their denunciations. The New England intellectual Orestes Brownson, a Democrat, denounced wages as a mere salve for those "tender consciences who would retain all the advantages of the slave system without the expense, trouble, and odium of being slaveholders."

No matter what the North told itself, according to this critique, the workers at the bottom of society couldn't possibly escape their lot, any more than could field hands toiling in the cotton fields. They were doomed forever to remain the victims of Northern capitalism's soulless individualism. South Carolina's James Hammond deemed these workers the "mud sills," part of the class in any society fated "to do the mean duties, to perform the drudgeries of life." Only hypocrisy and self-delusion keep the North from admitting, he thundered, that "[y]our whole class of manual laborers and operatives, as you call them, are slaves."

Lincoln had no patience for arguments in favor of a benevolent hierarchy made by the people who happened to live comfortably atop that hierarchy. Circa 1858, he wrote a spirited fragment for himself punctuated like a schoolgirl's text message. He lampooned apologists for the South: "But, slavery is good for some people!!! As a *good* thing, slavery is strikingly peculiar, in this, that it is the only good thing which no man ever seeks the good of, *for himself.* Nonsense! Wolves devouring lambs, not because it is good for their own greedy maws, but because it [is] good for the lambs!!!"

He took particular aim at one Frederick A. Ross, an Alabama minister and author of *Slavery Ordained by God.* In deciding whether or not a hypothetical slave (called Sambo by Lincoln) should be free or not, Dr. Ross doesn't think to consult his slave. "While he consider[s] it," Lincoln writes, "he sits in the shade, with gloves on his hands, and subsists on the bread that Sambo is earning in the burning sun." Perhaps, Lincoln concludes, Ross might not be "actuated by that perfect impartiality, which has ever been considered most favorable to correct decisions."

Lincoln's critique of the Slave South is inseparable from his view of the free economy as the field for self-improvement. He wrote in a note for a speech in the late 1850s: "Advancement—improvement of condition—is the order of things in a society of equals." In his 1859 address to the Wisconsin State Agricultural Society, he evoked the America of upward mobility as "the just, and generous, and prosperous system, which opens the way to all—gives hope to all, and energy, and progress, and improvement of condition to all." The South's ideal worker, in contrast, was "a blind horse upon a tread-mill."

Defenders of free labor fiercely resisted the "mud sill" view of society and the imputation that the North reduced its workers to "wage slaves." They believed in an essential identification between labor and capital. And however dire conditions might be in the industrializing cities of the North (overcrowded and unsanitary), they knew that the free laborer (obviously) had much more opportunity to exercise his autonomy and to better his condition than his alleged counterpart in bondage in the South.

"I have noticed in Southern newspapers," Lincoln said in Kalamazoo in 1856, "the Southern view of the Free States." He noted how they "insist that their slaves are far better off than Northern freemen. What a mistaken view do these men have of Northern laborers! They think that men are always to remain laborers here—but there is no such class. The man who labored for another last year, this year labors for himself, and next year he will hire others to labor for him."

This is a highly schematic portrayal, but it captures the essence of the matter. Free workers did tend to get better jobs over time, and to become better off than their fathers. If they felt stymied, they could always pick up and move elsewhere.

As for the South, the free-soil image of it was of a sink of backwardness wrought by slavery. Its romantic image of itself was of a bastion of high-minded paternalism above the money-grubbing of the degraded North. Neither was quite right, as the economic historian Robert Fogel demonstrates. Whatever justifications were thrown on the top of the slave system, it was basically a business proposition, a racket. What made it distinctive was the coercion and theft of labor, not separation from the market or absence of the profit motive.

Feeding overseas demand for cotton, plantations fully partook of the international economy, more so than any other sector of the nation's economy. They were, in the context of the time, enormous economic enterprises whose owners were enormously wealthy, and in fact made up the lion's share of the richest people in the country. The point of the gang labor of the cotton plantations was to regiment and maximize the efficiency of slave workers. Planters were very sensitive to the change in prices for crops, and so adjusted what they grew accordingly.

The system worked—up to a point. If the South were a country in 1860, according to Fogel, it would have been the fourth richest in the world. Per capita income grew at an impressive clip, and from 1840 to 1860, faster than that of the North. Driven by their slave gangs, the large plantations were more productive than free and slave small farms.

Nonetheless, the South was a society dominated by a planter elite upholding a twisted aristocratic ideal, largely dependent on one crop and on human bondage to produce it, unable to keep pace with a North leaping into modernity.

The population in the South was too dispersed to support Northern-style urbanization and industrialization, and the planters had no interest in either. Commercial conventions met constantly in the 1840s and 1850s to promote the idea of a more diversified economy to compete with that of the North. The likes of James De Bow called for action, as he put it, "in the busy hum of mechanism, and in the thrifty operations of the hammer and anvil." To no avail. The entire system leaned the other way. Planters wanted to protect their power from any competitors or disruptive forces; cotton was so productive that there was little incentive to invest in anything else; and slavery made labor-saving technology less important.

The Southern transportation network, compared to that of the North, was rudimentary. The planters just had to export their crop and so long as there was enough of a network to get it to market and exported, that was enough. Southern states built railroads, but they usually didn't reach beyond the state line. The only railway connecting Memphis to Charleston, east to west, was built with a multitude of different gauges.

The South couldn't attract or hold on to people the way the North could. Fogel notes that the relatively new Southern states farther West—places like Mississippi and Arkansas—lost more native-born whites than they gained during the 1850s. And foreign immigrants overwhelmingly settled in the North, feeding factories with cheap labor. Education lagged. Planters didn't have reason to invest in human capital outside the plantation system. According to economic historian Douglass North, with a little less than half of the white population of the North in 1850, the South had one-third as many public schools, one-fourth as many students, and one-twentieth as many libraries.

Above all, the South was committed to slavery. Slave-owning was the avenue to wealth and to prestige. A way of life was built upon it, and the region's self-regard depended on it. The South considered the criticisms from the North ignorant and insulting.

The South felt defensive, because it had so much to be defensive about. It had lashed itself to a system that was profoundly unjust and left it grossly underdeveloped compared to the North.

This was the backdrop to Lincoln's combat with Douglas. The legendary affair between the two raged much more widely than the immortal seven debates. The two traveled a collective ten thousand miles. Lincoln gave sixty-three speeches, usually about two hours in length. Douglas gave 130, in a count that included shorter improvised remarks, and had almost lost his voice by the end. Lincoln wasn't as well-known, of course. Papers outside of Illinois were liable to spell his name Abram. But Douglas knew what he was up against. "I shall have my hands full," he predicted.

Lincoln's friend Joseph Gillespie wrote Herndon about what he considered the respective appeals of the candidates: "Douglass was idolized by his followers. Lincoln was loved by his. Douglass was the representative of his partisans. Lincoln was the representative man of the unsophisticated People. Douglass was great in the estimation of his followers. Lincoln was good in the opinion of his supporters. Douglass headed a party. Lincoln stood upon a principle."

At the beginning of the campaign, Lincoln followed Douglas around and replied after his speeches in a strategy of calculated self-abasement. Lincoln considered it "the very thing" because it allowed him "to make a concluding speech on him." Embarrassed that its candidate seemed an afterthought, the Republican state committee insisted that Lincoln request the joint debates. Lincoln's initial proposal would have meant about 50; Douglas agreed to 7. They ranged up and down the state, with Lincoln's most favorable territory in the northern part of the state (Ottawa, Freeport, Galesburg), Douglas's in the south (Jonesboro), and the most contested areas in the middle (Charleston, Quincy, Alton).

At the time of the debates, Senator Douglas looked every bit a man of his station. He dressed, Michael Burlingame writes, "in the so-called plantation style, with a ruffled shirt, dark blue coat with shiny buttons, light-colored trousers, well-polished shoes, and a wide brimmed hat." Lincoln looked as disheveled as ever, dressed in a black alpaca outfit and ill-fitting stovepipe hat and toting an old carpetbag. Illinois lawyer Jonathan Birch recalled to Jesse Weik (Herndon's fellow researcher) that he "carried with him a faded cotton umbrella which became almost as famous in the canvass as Lincoln himself."

Douglas crisscrossed Illinois in style, in the "palace car" of the directors of the Illinois Central Railroad. His traveling companions included his second wife, Adele, who was twenty-two years old and a grand-niece of Dolley Madison (Douglas had lost his first wife a few years earlier, in 1853); a sculptor working on his bust; and a collection of stenographers and loyal editors. He smoked cigars at his whistle-stops, and as the campaign progressed, drank more and more. In one version of his lecture on discoveries and inventions, Lincoln went out of his way to slyly tweak Douglas, a champion of an expansionistic movement calling itself "Young America." "If there be anything old which he can endure," Lincoln said of the characteristic Young American, "it is only old whiskey and old tobacco."

Festooned with a banner declaring S.A. DOUGLAS, THE CHAMPION OF POPULAR SOVEREIGNTY, the Douglas train came outfitted with a cannon dubbed "Popular Sovereignty," or "Little Doug." It boomed the arrival of the exalted statesman. Lincoln commented sardonically of the cannon, "There is a passage, I think, in the Book of Koran, which reads: 'To him that bloweth not his own horn—to such a man it is forever decreed that . . . his horn shall not be blowe-ed!'"

Lincoln flew coach. He traveled in ordinary passenger cars on trains with, the *Chicago Press & Tribune* observed, "no cannon and powder monkeys before him." Once he rode on the caboose of a freight train that had to make way for the flag-bedecked Douglas conveyance. "Boys," Lincoln remarked, "the gentleman in that car evidently smelt no royalty in our carriage." Compared to Douglas, he was practically a hobo. The Illinois lawyer Birch described to Jesse Weik seeing Lincoln board a train during the campaign in his usual outfit, including "the inevitable umbrella." According to Birch, "On his arm was the cloak that he was said to have worn when he was in Congress nine years before." Lincoln chatted with acquaintances until nighttime. Then he found a seat by himself. "Presently he arose," Birch said, "spread the cloak over the seat, lay down, somehow folded himself up till his long legs and arms were no longer in view, then drew the cloak about him and went to sleep. Beyond what I have mentioned he had no baggage, no secretary, no companion even."

The two were impressive debaters in their own way. Lincoln was blessed with a verbal acuity that Douglas, whom Don Fehrenbacher calls "among the least quoted of major American statesmen," couldn't match. But Douglas was magnetic and lively. He had none of Lincoln's lawyerly respect for the facts and careful argumentation. Lincoln complained of his "audacity in maintaining an untenable position." Their styles, as Allen Guelzo points out, reflected the different sensibilities of their parties—Douglas blustery and passionate, Lincoln logical and precise.

The events made for rollicking, open pageants of democracy.

They drew thousands, straining to hear the two men declaiming from the same platforms, with people jockeying for position near the candidates and some clambering up with them. Douglas's voice was booming, Lincoln's high-pitched—making it easy to hear. The partisans of the rivals faced off with competing parades, brass bands, banners, hecklers, and salutes by cannon. "The prairies," wrote a New York journalist, "are on fire."

After the first debate at Ottawa, Illinois, Lincoln's supporters carried him off on their shoulders as a band played, "Hail, Columbia!" At the next debate, in Freeport, a small boy got up on the platform and sat on Douglas's lap, then on Lincoln's. Someone in the crowd at that encounter threw a piece of melon that hit Douglas when he got up to speak—perhaps less of an indignity than one visited upon him at a campaign stop in Danville, where his carriage was befouled with what was delicately referred to as "loathsome dirt."

At the town of Charleston, Illinois, the Douglas demonstration was graced by thirty-two young women on horseback. Each lady represented a state of the union. Half carried sticks of ash in homage to Henry Clay (his estate was Ashland); half sticks of hickory in honor of Andrew Jackson ("Old Hickory"). Lincoln countered with a wagon full of thirty-two lasses of his own. The candidates' supporters tussled over whether a pro-Lincoln or pro-Douglas banner would grace the platform. That of the Lincoln partisans declared, LINCOLN WORRYING DOUGLAS AT FREEPORT, illustrated by a depiction of Lincoln as a dog going for Douglas's throat. Douglas supporters hauled up a derisive banner depicting a white man and black woman, NEGRO EQUALITY. (To mark one Lincoln campaign stop in Rushville, Douglas supporters simply hoisted a black flag on top of the courthouse.)

Douglas sought to portray Lincoln as an extremist. Lincoln wanted to blunt the charge, but also—somewhat at cross-purposes with this goal—get the debate on the higher plane of the House Divided speech to condemn Douglas for his moral indifference to slavery.

Douglas certainly wasn't where the South was. In fact, he had thrilled and impressed Republicans by breaking with the administration of his fellow Democrat James Buchanan over its embrace of the fraudulent proslavery Lecompton Constitution in Kansas. He was by no means a rabid supporter of slavery. But he held a dim view of the humanity of blacks and wanted to get on with what he considered the more important matter of settling the rest of the continent and perhaps taking territory farther south.

He had a ferocious opening debate in Ottawa, but Lincoln picked up in the final clashes as he reached for the moral high ground and Douglas began to get worn down. Amid much that was petty, repetitive, and forgettable, the basic argument went like this:

Douglas rejected Lincoln's House Divided speech as a call for sectional conflict and for national uniformity. At Ottawa, he said the House Divided doctrine was "revolutionary and destructive of the existence of this Government." The Founders knew, Douglas argued, "when they framed the Constitution that in a country as wide and broad as this, with such a variety of climate, production and interest, the people necessarily required different laws and institutions in different localities." That included slavery.

Douglas didn't feel the slightest bit defensive about the Founders. "Washington and his compeers in the convention that framed the constitution," he said at Jonesboro, "made this government divided into free and slave State." The Declaration of Independence had nothing to do with it.

He sneered at Lincoln's use of the Declaration. At Galesburg, he called Lincoln's belief "that the negro and the white man are made equal by the Declaration of Independence and by Divine Providence" nothing less than "a monstrous heresy." How could Jefferson possibly have meant to say that "his negro slaves, which he held and treated as property, were created his equals by Divine law, and that he was violating the law of God every day of his life by holding them as slaves?"

The Founders didn't literally mean all men were created equal. "They desired to express by that phrase," Douglas said at Jonesboro, "white men, men of European birth and European descent, and had no reference either to the negro, the savage Indians, the Fejee, the Malay, or any other inferior and degraded race, when they spoke of the equality of men." No, as Douglas said at Charleston and elsewhere, "I say that this government was established on the white basis. It was made by white men, for the benefit of white men and their posterity forever, and never should be administered by any except white men."

Douglas thought it a travesty that the country's march across the continent and perhaps farther south should be checked by agitation over slavery. Douglas said at Freeport, "I answer that whenever it becomes necessary, in our growth and progress to acquire more territory, that I am in favor of it, without reference to the question of slavery." This process of acquisition might take us far afield. "The time may come, indeed has now come," Douglas explained at Jonesboro, "when our interests would be advanced by the acquisition of the island of Cuba. When we get Cuba we must take it as we find it, leaving the people to decide the question of slavery for themselves, without interference on the part of the federal government, or of any State of this Union." So, too, with "any portion of Mexico or Canada, or of this continent or the adjoining islands."

Lincoln countered that, like it or not, we were indeed a House Divided. The difference between slavery and freedom wasn't a matter of a pleasing diversity among the states. "I shall very readily agree with him that it would be foolish for us to insist upon having a cranberry law here, in Illinois, where we have no cranberries, because they have a cranberry law in Indiana, where they have cranberries," Lincoln said in Alton. "I should insist that it would be exceedingly wrong in us to deny to Virginia the right to enact oyster laws where they have oyster, because we want no such laws here." But slavery was, obviously, a more consequential matter: "When have we had any difficulty or quarrel amongst ourselves about the cranberry laws of Indiana, or the oyster laws of Virginia, or the pine lumber laws of Maine, or the fact that Louisiana produces sugar, and Illinois flour?"

Lincoln charged that Douglas wanted the peace of surrender on slavery. "To be sure if we will all stop and allow Judge Douglas and his friends to march on in their present career until they plant the institution all over the nation, here and wherever else our flag waves, and we acquiesce in it, there will be peace. But let me ask Judge Douglas how he is going to get the people to do that?" The senator's position, Lincoln argued at Alton, was "that we are to care nothing about it! I ask you if it is not a false philosophy? Is it not a false statesmanship that undertakes to build up a system of policy upon the basis of caring nothing about *the very thing that every body does care the most about?*"

He objected to Douglas's contention that the Founders "made" the country half-slave and half-free. "The exact truth," he said of slavery at Alton, "is that they found the institution existing among us, and they left it as they found it. But in making the government they left this institution with many clear marks of disapprobation upon it."

As for Jefferson, Lincoln said at Galesburg, "that while Mr. Jefferson was the owner of slaves, as undoubtedly he was, in speaking upon this very subject, he used the strong language that 'he trembled for his country when he remembered that God was just'; and I will offer the highest premium in my power to Judge Douglas if he will show that he, in all his life, ever uttered a sentiment at all akin to that of Jefferson."

Lincoln returned repeatedly to arguments about the Founders that were staples of his throughout the 1850s. They had set a date, 1808, for when the slave trade could be prohibited, and promptly prohibited it as soon as the day arrived. They excluded it from the Northwest territory—the chunk of territory that would become the states of Ohio, Indiana, Illinois, Michigan, Wisconsin, and Minnesota (in part)—in the Northwest Ordinance of 1787. "Why stop its spread in one direction," he asked at Alton, "and cut off its source in another, if they did not look to its being placed in the course of ultimate extinction?"

Lincoln gave the Founders a favorable gloss. The federal government was happy to see slavery expand into the Gulf states in the first part of the nineteenth century. Eric Foner points out that between the ratification of the Constitution and 1854, nine slave states entered the union and the slave population grew from 700,000 to more than 3 million. But Lincoln was right that we had regressed since the Founding. In percentage terms, there were fewer free blacks in the South in 1860 than half a century earlier, both because free blacks left and the South had made it even harder for blacks to earn their freedom. From 1830 on, the South tightened its legal grip, seeking to deny any light of hope from shining through cracks in the system. States made it illegal even for masters to teach slaves to read. In a wave of restriction in the late 1850s, Louisiana generously passed a law called "An Act to Permit Free Persons of African Descent to Select a Master and Become Slaves for Life." Arkansas gave free blacks the choice of leaving or getting enslaved.

Lincoln wanted the mark of disapprobation back on slavery. This was the crux of the matter: the morality of human bondage. "When Judge Douglas says that whoever, or whatever community, wants slaves, they have a right to have them," Lincoln explained at Quincy, "he is perfectly logical if there is nothing wrong in the institution; but if you admit that it is wrong, he cannot logically say that anybody has a right to do wrong." Douglas met the question with an evasion. "He has the high distinction," Lincoln said, "so far as I know, of never having said slavery is either right or wrong. Almost everybody else says one or the other, but the Judge never does."

Lincoln obviously didn't have this problem. In the debates, he called slavery "a moral, social and political wrong." It follows that, he continued in Quincy, "We deal with it as with any other wrong, in so far as we can prevent its growing any larger, and so deal with it that in the run of time there may be some promise of an end to it."

He argued that the Douglas view opened the way for two potential developments favorable to the entrenchment and spread of slavery. The first was further Southern expansionism, which Douglas himself cited as a benefit of his approach. "If Judge

Douglas' policy upon this question succeeds," Lincoln said at Galesburg, "and gets fairly settled down, until all opposition is crushed out, the next thing will be a grab for the territory of poor Mexico, an invasion of the rich lands of South America, then the adjoining islands will follow, each one of which promises additional slave fields." The second, another *Dred Scott* decision, built upon the country's moral indifference to slavery.

The first decision had been bad enough. The Supreme Court held in 1857 that blacks couldn't be citizens and there was no power under the Constitution to prohibit slavery in the territories. The Court did Douglas one better, and ruled the Missouri Compromise unconstitutional. In his decision, Chief Justice Roger Taney spoke of the Negro as an "ordinary article of merchandise and traffic," "so far inferior that [he] had no rights which the white man was bound to respect." The Radical Republican congressman Thaddeus Stevens said of that line that it "damned [Taney] to everlasting fame; and, I fear, to everlasting fire."

Among other things, *Dred Scott* made a mockery of popular sovereignty. Douglas had constructed his entire edifice upon people freely choosing whether or not to open their territories to slavery. Then the Supreme Court said it couldn't be done. Lincoln pressed Douglas on this point with his famous questions at Freeport, which Douglas answered with his Freeport Doctrine—as a practical matter, slavery could be excluded by "unfriendly legislation," no matter what the high court said. Lincoln ridiculed the idea that local laws could override the Supreme Court. And he feared the next easy step to the nationalization of slavery: "It is merely," he said at Ottawa, "for the Supreme Court to decide that no State under the Constitution can exclude it, just as they have already decided that under the Constitution neither Congress nor the Territorial Legislature can do it."

Throughout the debates, Douglas spoke of blacks in the same key as Taney. One of his most reliable arguments was the low-down, unembarrassed pander to negrophobia, in his struggle with what he constantly referred to as the Black Republicans.

At the first debate in Ottawa, he put it to listeners this way: "Do you desire to turn this beautiful State into a free negro colony, in order that when Missouri abolishes slavery she can send one hundred thousand emancipated slaves into Illinois, to become citizens and voters, on an equality with yourselves?" In the final debate at Alton, he made this ringing affirmation: "I would not blot out the great inalienable rights of the white men for all the negroes that ever existed."

In Freeport, he scraped bottom when he referred to the great black abolitionist Frederick Douglass as one of Lincoln's advisers. He told the story of how the last time he had been in town, "I saw a carriage and a magnificent one it was, drive up and take a position on the outside of the crowd; a beautiful young lady was sitting on the box seat, whilst Fred. Douglass and her mother reclined inside." He generously allowed how "if you, Black Republicans, think that the negro ought to be on a social equality with your wives and daughters, and ride in a carriage with your wife, whilst you drive the team, you have a perfect right to do so." George Wallace called this putting the hay down low where the goats can get it. This riff was met with a cry of "Down with the negro."

For his part Lincoln drew a distinction between natural rights, which he believed extended to everyone, and political and social rights, which he thought should be circumscribed depending on circumstance. In the first debate in Ottawa, he quoted from his speech at Peoria when he had considered the possibility of freeing blacks and making them "politically and socially, our equals." He had said, "My own feelings will not admit of this; and if mine would, we well know that those of the great mass of white people will not. Whether this feeling accords with justice and sound judgment, is not the sole question, if indeed, it is any part of it. A universal feeling, whether well or ill-founded, can not be safely disregarded."

In Charleston, located in the middle of the state and heavily populated by conservative Whigs, Lincoln opened his presentation with a disclaimer: "I will say then that I am not, nor ever have been in favor of bringing about in any way the social and political equality of the white and black races." He added "that there is a physical difference between the white and black races which I believe will for ever forbid the two races living together on terms of social and political equality. And inasmuch as they cannot so live, while they do remain together there must be the position of superior and inferior, and I as much as any other man am in favor of having the superior position assigned to the white race."

"I do not understand," he added, "that because I do not want a negro woman for a slave I must necessarily want her for a wife. My understanding is that I can just let her alone. I am now in my fiftieth year, and I certainly never have had a black woman for either a slave or a wife. So it seems to me quite possible for us to get along without making either slaves or wives of negroes."

To our ears all this sounds damnable, but context matters. Lincoln never had the luxury of addressing a Vassar College faculty meeting. All of the states where Lincoln had resided—Kentucky, Indiana, and Illinois—at one point banned blacks. Any black person coming into Illinois had to post a one-thousand-dollar bond.

A referendum in 1848 to allow the state legislature to prohibit free blacks from entering the state got 70 percent of the vote.

Lincoln's opposition to the full panoply of rights for blacks is less remarkable than his forthright defenses of their humanity. In Chicago in 1858, at the beginning of the campaign, he gave Douglas yet more fodder when he said, "Let us discard all this quibbling about this man and the other man—this race and that race and the other race being inferior, and therefore they must be placed in an inferior position. . . . Let us discard all these things, and unite as one people throughout this land, until we shall once more stand up declaring that all men are created equal."

Lincoln himself so "quibbled" during the debates, but only under constant racist attack and only under the pressure of a close-fought election where winning over anti-black voters was imperative. It is Lincoln's high points that are most extraordinary. And it was to them that he would prove true in the coming years of great testing.

In the final debate at Alton, Lincoln cast the choice over slavery as another battle in "the eternal struggle between these two principles—right and wrong—throughout the world. They are the two principles that have stood face to face from the beginning of time; and will ever continue to struggle. The one is the common right of humanity and the other the divine right of kings. It is the same principle in whatever shape it develops itself. It is the same spirit that says, 'You work and toil and earn bread, and I'll eat it.' No matter in what shape it comes, whether from the mouth of a king who seeks to bestride the people of his own nation and live by the fruit of their labor, or from one race of men as an apology for enslaving another race, it is the same tyrannical principle."

That tyrannical principle strikes at the core of who we are not just as *a* people, but as people. At Alton, Lincoln said of the racially exclusive view of the Declaration: "I combat it as having a tendency to dehumanize the negro—to take away from him the right of ever striving to be a man." Appealing to the self interest of his listeners (again, in language jarring to modern sensibilities), Lincoln evoked an American West free of slavery, as a wide-open platform for aspiration: "Now irrespective of the moral aspect of this question as to whether there is a right or wrong in enslaving a negro, I am still in favor of our new Territories being in such a condition that white men may find a home—may find some spot where they can better their condition—where they can settle upon new soil and better their condition in life." He wanted the West as "an outlet for free white people everywhere, the world over—in which Hans and Baptiste and Patrick, and all other men from all the world, may find new homes and better their conditions in life."

Whatever the allure of this vision, it didn't get Lincoln over the top against Douglas, of course. More people voted in Illinois in 1858 than in the presidential election of 1856. Republicans won the popular vote yet the apportionment of legislative districts favored Democrats and allowed Douglas to prevail anyway. Democrats held the south, the Republicans the north, and Lincoln lost the race in the Whig belt in the middle of the state. Henry Whitney recalled in a letter to William Herndon that Lincoln thought he could only count on the loyalty of his law partner: "He said to me on the day Douglas was elected to the U.S. Senate—& bitterly too—'I expect everyone to desert me except Billy.'"

Instead, he ascended to glory. In time, he won the larger argument—at a cost in blood and treasure that would have seemed unimaginable to him standing on those debate platforms with Douglas. After his election to the presidency, on his long trip to Washington in early 1861, making stops and speeches along the way, he addressed the New Jersey Senate. He remembered how "away back in my childhood, the earliest days of my being able to read, I got hold of a small book, such a one as few of the younger members have ever seen, 'Weem's Life of Washington.'" He said the events surrounding the battle at Trenton transfixed him and stayed with him still: "You all know, for you have all been boys, how these early impressions last longer than any others. I recollect thinking then, boy even though I was, that there must have been something more than common that those men struggled for." That something, he continued, "held out a great promise to all the people of the world to all time to come."

He stopped at Independence Hall in Philadelphia to lead a raising of the new flag bearing thirty-four stars, after Kansas had just joined the union and Oregon in 1859. In an impromptu talk, he invoked the deeper promise of the founding generation "that in due time the weights should be lifted from the shoulders of all men, and that all should have an equal chance." With threats to his personal safety in mind, he continued, "But, if this country cannot be saved without giving up that principle—I was about to say I would rather be assassinated on this spot than to surrender it."

He wouldn't be assassinated. Not yet. Not on that spot. Not before he waged and won a war that defeated the Southern system and opened the way for the ascendance of the vision that had motivated him from his very first stirrings as a politician.

Chapter 5

———

"A Great Empire": Lincoln's Vision Realized

I chant the new empire grander than any before . . .
My sail-ships and steam-ships threading the archipelagoes,
My stars and stripes fluttering in the wind.
—WALT WHITMAN, "A BROADWAY PAGEANT," 1860

Right after his reelection in 1864, Lincoln wrote the first draft of his annual message to Congress, on pieces of pasteboard or boxboard.

In a passage of the data-laden document, he evoked the waxing strength of the Union. He noted its increasing population as shown in the higher number of voters than in 1860. "A table is appended showing particulars," he noted, before getting to the larger point: "The important fact remains demonstrated, that we have *more* men *now* than we had when the war *began*; that we are not exhausted, nor in process of exhaustion; that we are *gaining* strength, and may, if need be, maintain the contest indefinitely. This as to men. Material resources are now more complete and abundant than ever. The national resources, then, are unexhausted, and, as we believe, inexhaustible."

He exaggerated only slightly.

In the war, Lincoln's industrializing, rapidly growing capitalist republic overwhelmed the agrarian South partly through sheer demographic and economic muscle. Hamilton trumped Jefferson. Free labor beat slavery. The dynamic North—hustling, innovating, pulling people in from abroad—bested the underdeveloped South. "We began without capital and if we should lose the *greater* part of it before this [war] is over," Secretary of the Treasury Salmon P. Chase boasted in 1863, "labor would bring it back again and with a power hitherto unfelt among us."

The notion that the war itself, a charnel house for America's youth and a great grinding wheel of material destruction, drove the industrialization of the North is a myth. But it represented a victory of Lincoln's style of modernizing capitalism. It wiped out slavery and vindicated his view of the American creed. It decisively broke the South's political power, and the remnants of the South's economic model moldered in a region that became as "peculiar" in the American context as the institution of bound labor that had precipitated the war. The country set out on a path of robust democratic capitalism that made it richer—and better—than if it had chosen any other alternative. In the aftermath, the country emerged a budding world power with, in the words of Herman Melville, "empire in her eyes."

Before General Winfield Scott ever had reason to come up with his Anaconda Plan ("Scott's Great Snake") to subdue the Confederacy, the South felt squeezed. On the cusp of the nineteenth century, the North and the South had similar populations. The immigrants who poured into the country—5 million in the four decades prior to the war—overwhelmingly made their home in the more congenial free North rather than the South. Another 800,000 came during the course of the war. In 1860, the North had 19 million people to the South's 12 million, counting the almost 4 million slaves. In 1800, the South accounted for 46 percent of Congress; in 1860, just 35 percent.

In the early 1850s, the likes of Massachusetts politician Henry Wilson—eventually a senator and a vice president—could already vow to "surround the slave States with a cordon of free States and, in a few years, not withstanding the immense interests combined in the cause of oppression, we shall give liberty to the millions in bondage." The South didn't consider it an idle threat. It feared the creation of more free states in the West, and the chipping away of the protective cocoon it had built around the slave system, from the *Dred Scott* ruling to the prohibitions of abolitionist literature in the mails. Robert Toombs, a senator from Georgia, warned of the pernicious effects of Republican patronage powers alone, predicting their exercise "would abolitionize Maryland in a year, raise a powerful abolition party in Va., Kentucky and Missouri in two years, and foster and rear up a free labour party in [the] whole South in four years."

Slavery suffered from the abrasions inherent in its contact with the free North and with urban civilization. Border states and cities had relatively high populations of free blacks. As of the late 1850s, half of blacks in Maryland were free. Slave owners feared the dangerously subversive effects of urban life and industrial employment, although Southern industry did resort to slave labor. Frederick Law Olmsted, the great landscape designer and journalist, noted how owners hesitated to rent their slaves out to ironmongers and the like for fear the slaves "had too much liberty, and were acquiring bad habits. They earned money by overwork, and spent it for whisky, and got a habit roaming about and taking care of themselves."

With the Republican victory in the 1860 election, the Northern system was certain to wax rather than wane, as its industry continued to grow and it settled a free West. The Southern Democrats and their 1860 presidential nominee, John Breckinridge (destined to become the Confederate secretary of war), wanted a federal government favorable to slavery. They wanted it to take Cuba as another slave state and eschew assistance to industry or the free settlement of the West. Failing that, there was the option of secession. "We must," one planter with 2,000 slaves said, "do it now or never. If we don't secede now the political power of the South is broken." It chose now. As William Lowndes Yancey of Alabama put it, "We propose to do as the Israelites did of old under Divine direction—to withdraw our people from under the power that oppresses them and in doing so, like them to take with us the Ark of the Covenant of our liberties."

With Ark in tow, the South deluded itself that King Cotton, feeding the maw of factories in the North and in England, could force surrender to his regal will. "The slave-holding South is now the controlling power of the world," South Carolina senator Hammond maintained, betraying more Southern patriotism than strategic sense. "The North without us would be a motherless calf, bleating about, and die of mange and starvation."

There is no doubt that the South was the Saudi Arabia of cotton. At a low cost, it produced more cotton than anyplace else on the planet, about two-thirds of the world's crop, accounting for $277 million of the South's $577 million gross farm income by one estimate. Exports went from 83 million pounds in 1815 to roughly 1.8 billion in 1860, with three-quarters of the crop shipped to England. Although never enough to be decisive, the Confederacy had its share of sympathizers in New York (deeply involved in the transatlantic cotton trade) and in England (where so many depended on textile mills for their livelihood) on purely commercial grounds. The abolitionist Wendell Phillips complained in late 1860 of the self-interested sentiment for appeasement in the North: "The saddest thing in the Union meetings of last year was the constant presence, in all of them, of the clink of coin—the whir of spindles—the dust of trade. You would have imagined it was an insurrection of pedlers against honest men."

The newly elected Lincoln arrived in February 1861 in a Washington rife with proposals for sectional compromise. (Lincoln didn't always make a good first impression. The ambassador from Holland sniffed after a fancy dinner with the president-elect and other diplomats that "his conversation consists of vulgar anecdotes at which he himself laughs uproariously.") William E. Dodge, a "merchant prince" of New York who had relinquished his suite at Willard's hotel for the Lincolns, gave voice to the instinct toward accommodation. He warned Lincoln of the economic consequences of violent conflict. "The whole nation shall be plunged into bankruptcy," he told him, and "grass shall grow in the streets of our commercial cities." Lincoln replied that he would defend the Constitution, "let the grass grow where it may."

The grass didn't grow, at least not in the North. It was already too far ahead. In 1860, the South contributed only about a tenth of the country's manufacturing. The North's industrial sector was already more mechanized than Britain's. Most foreign trade passed through Northern ports. The North had much more railroad mileage. Six of ten Northern workers were in nonagricul-

tural occupations; less than 20 percent of Southern workers were. Pennsylvania produced 580,000 tons of pig iron, far more than the entire Confederacy. Financially, the South lagged as badly.

When Southerners quit Congress, they gave Republicans carte blanche to pass their domestic agenda, which had previously foundered on sectional splits. The departed Southerners wrote themselves a new constitution that pointedly banned spending on internal improvements and import duties to protect industry, although these provisions did nothing to restrain the Confederate government's actual intervention in the private economy during the war. Granted a free hand, congressional Republicans effected a program to make old Henry Clay proud.

A restless ambition undergirded the Republican vision. They wanted to see America grow, spreading its system of enterprise and free labor across the continent, to the benefit of all regardless of class and to the ultimate end of realizing the country's inchoate greatness. Historian Walter McDougall calls the goal "a free-labor empire challenging British supremacy." Congressional Republicans laid the foundation with legislation on improvements, banks, the tariff, and the development of the West—"all calculated," in the words of Louis Hacker in his economic history of the United States, "to widen and defend the domestic market and lower production costs."

They voted to create an artery to the West Coast with the Pacific Railroad Acts. Already in 1820, people were talking of a transcontinental railroad. The contention wasn't constitutional but sectional. Whenever a route was proposed through one section, it aroused enough opposition in the other to shut it down. Congress now simply selected a path in the North. Congress created the Union Pacific, the first time it had chartered a corporation since the ill-fated Second Bank of the United States. The Union Pacific started from Omaha, while the Central Pacific began from Sacramento, California, and headed East. The government showered the two companies with millions of acres of federal land and millions in government bonds.

Congress had set the table for a movable feast of corruption. The alternative, though, was no transcontinental railroad at all, at least not anytime soon. Heather Cox Richardson recounts the case for the railroad in her valuable history of Civil War economic legislation. By definition, such a project couldn't be backed by one state, and it ran through Western territories directly controlled by Congress. Purely private financing almost certainly couldn't have been found for it. Besides the sheer size and cost, the project struck out across unsecured land vulnerable to attack by hostile Indians.

Without the railroad, getting to California was an adventure, sometimes a death-defying one. James A. McDougall was a transplant to California via Illinois who eventually became a congressman and senator from his adopted state. According to a former colleague in Illinois, he once got lost in the mountains traveling from Illinois to San Francisco and almost starved. He arrived at his destination "in rags, clothed partly in skins, without money, and not having seen a barber or razor for months. He went to the best hotel in the city, and was at first refused admittance."

Easing the transit would open the West to enterprising Easterners. It would encourage free farmers to settle in the prairie and give them a market back east. It would draw the West closer, lest California get detached by centrifugal forces pulling the country apart. It would facilitate trade with Asia. Finally, it would secure access to the West's newly discovered gold at a time when the country urgently needed the specie. Such was the faith in the ample riches to be had that one newspaper reported that Indians out west shot gold bullets from their guns.

Republicans regularized the nation's banking to finance the war. The country had a financial system appropriate to "an agrarian economy tributary to foreign markets," as Richard Franklin Bensel writes in his brilliant history of this period, *Yankee Leviathan*. When London sneezed, the American financial system tended to get a cold. Obviously, the North lacked the financial architecture for fighting a war of national survival.

At the outset, currency in the West collapsed because it had been backed extensively by Southern state bonds; in Wisconsin, rioters targeted Milwaukee's banks. In late 1861, the government couldn't raise the funds it needed for the war. The banks suspended specie payments and the government abandoned the gold standard for domestic transactions. By the end of 1861, almost all the mercantile houses in New York had gone bust, with only 16 out of 913 still solvent. It was around this time that President Lincoln met with General Montgomery Meigs and lamented, among other things, that "Chase has no money and he tells me he can raise no more." Then Lincoln summed up the situation in his memorably despairing phrase, "The bottom is out of the tub."

Under extreme duress, Congress acted. The Legal Tender Act authorized the Treasury to issue notes, printed with green ink, hence known as "greenbacks," that were legal tender for all public and private debts. Subsequently, Congress taxed the motley notes that were issued by state banks and circulated as currency to push them out of the way. In a step toward a more uniform system, it authorized charters for "national" banks that could issue their own notes, but had to meet a variety of standards for soundness. The number of national banks rose, while the number of state banks collapsed from roughly 1,500 to 300 in the two-year period from 1863 to 1865. It was the advent of a version of the national banking system that had been so bitterly opposed by Jacksonians.

Republicans passed a sweeping protective tariff. In a letter before the Republican convention in May 1860, Lincoln had assured Edward Wallace, who wanted to publicize Lincoln's position on the tariff, that "In the days of Henry Clay, I was a Henry-Clay-tariff-man; and my views have undergone no material change on that subject." The Republicans championed higher tariffs in 1860 with an eye to the electorally significant industrial states of Pennsylvania and New Jersey, although it was ticklish because the party didn't want to offend its new Democratic enlistees who might not be enamored of its economics.

One of Lincoln's awkward moments on his way to Washington after winning the election came in Pittsburgh, where he addressed the issue in front of a rain-soaked crowd of five thousand, in vague and halting terms: "The tariff bill now before Congress may or may not pass at the present session. I confess I do not understand the precise provisions of this bill, and I do not know whether it can be passed by the present Congress or not." He went on in this vein for a while before concluding that he hoped "that all sections may share in common the benefits of a just and equitable tariff." A week later, at Harrisburg, he (charitably) called his earlier remarks "rather carefully worded."

The bill Lincoln danced around was the Morrill Tariff, which was passed by Congress and signed into law by President Buchanan shortly before he took office. Sponsored by Representative Justin Morrill of Vermont, it spread its duties widely across all sectors of the economy to avoid unfairly burdening any one group of consumers. Republicans justified the tariff as an exercise in nationalism that would help laborers by creating a strong domestic economy. "Men of Missouri, men of Michigan," intoned Pennsylvania Congressman James Campbell, "men from all the iron-bearing States, men of the whole land, will you not unite with us in developing the vast resources of the country?" Like St. Augustine praying for chastity, supporters of the tariff said they wanted to be free-traders—but not yet. Campbell maintained that free trade is "the object to which society is tending," yet isn't appropriate "in a new and poor country": "foreign competition would stifle in their bud all those things which it requires in order to prosper—capital, skillful workmen, experienced overseers, easy communication, and a good market; in fact, all the conditions which time alone can give. A transition, consequently, is indispensable; and to preach free trade to a country which does not enjoy all these advantages, is nearly as equitable as to propose that a child contend with a grown man."

The government also needed the revenue. Congress created an income tax during the war, although reluctantly since Republicans were wary of interfering with private wealth creation. The tax paled as a source of funds. During the war, tariffs brought in about $300 million, income taxes about $50 million.

Lincoln repeatedly signed increases in tariffs. Rates on dutiable imports were almost 50 percent by the end of the war. American industry, increasingly technologically proficient, needed protection less than ever before, but the duties did their work. They were a boon to the iron and steel industries, and by the end of the war, basically locked out some foreign goods.

Republicans passed a land-grant college bill. Morrill had been agitating for one for years. He wanted to promote wide access to a college education emphasizing practical instruction. Opposition emanated from the West, which worried about giving Western acreage to states back East, and the South, which attacked the bill as an unconstitutional outrage, "one of the most monstrous, iniquitous and dangerous measures which have been submitted to Congress," in the words of Senator Clement Claiborne Clay Jr., of Alabama. Morrill persisted. Maneuvering around the hostile chairman of the House public lands committee, another Alabaman named Williamson R. W. Cobb who had the "humor of a buffoon and the manner of a tin-peddler" in Morrill's estimation, he got the bill to President Buchanan's desk in 1859. Buchanan vetoed it.

Three years later, Lincoln signed the act into law. States received thirty thousand acres of federal land per congressman and senator to sell and use the proceeds to fund colleges focusing on agriculture and mechanics. Horace Greeley hailed it as promising a "wide and lasting good." It would advance knowledge "of the sciences which underlie and control the chief processes of Productive Labor."

Finally, Republicans passed the Homestead Act. There had long been proposals to give parcels of federal land to farmers to work. But they were controversial and created cross-currents within both the Whig and Democratic parties. Lincoln wasn't all that interested in homestead legislation since he had never particularly wanted to promote agriculture. As a good Whig back in Illinois, he had favored selling the public lands and spending the proceeds on improvements. Originally, some Southerners favored a homestead law. Andrew Johnson of Tennessee, Lincoln's vice president and successor, was a longtime and persistent supporter.

After the Kansas-Nebraska Act, though, the push for a homestead law became caught up in the fight over the character of Westward expansion.

Southerners denounced the proposal as a threat to their political power, yet another tool in the hands of those hoping to exclude slavery from the West and flood it with free farmers. One Virginia congressman attacked it as leading to "the propagation of northern sentiment and the multiplication of northern representatives here and in the Senate." Virginia senator James Mason inveighed against the proposal in 1860, alleging Northern intent to win for itself "command and control of the destinies of the continent." He called it "a political engine and a potent one" against the South, "part of this 'measure of empire'" to connect, as belonging indissolubly to it, the whole slavery question with the homestead policy.

In the 1850s, Southern senators repeatedly killed homestead bills and President Buchanan vetoed one bill that made it to his desk.

Republicans took up the cause. It was another way to demonstrate that they favored the interests of free working people and of immigrants against the Slave Power. The party's 1860 platform endorsed the legislation. Lincoln himself didn't publicly address the homestead issue until after the election. "I have to say that in so far as the Government lands can be disposed of," he said in an 1861 speech to German working men in Cincinnati, on his way to Washington, "I am in favor of cutting up the wild lands into parcels, so that every poor man may have a home."

In making their case, Republicans attacked land speculators who bought large tracts of land from the federal government and then sold them at profit to the little guy. They believed the Homestead Act would break up land monopolies and boost the agricultural potential of the country and therefore the entire economy. It would devote public lands to "the purpose for which their Creator designed them—the assignment of a limited quantity to each head of a family, for the purpose of cultivation and subsistence," in the words of Wisconsin Republican representative John Fox Potter. The act passed in 1862 and gave 160 acres to farmers to improve and to own after five years. Horace Greeley exulted: "Young men! Poor men! Widows! resolve to have a home of your own!"

This was an extraordinary bout of congressional activism, at the same time as the exigencies of war inevitably enhanced the powers of the Northern state. Still, as Richard Franklin Bensel points out, the industrial and agricultural sectors ran free of government controls. The labor force, although tapped for manpower for the war, was relatively unmolested. The government became entangled with the financial system, but that system was also becoming more modern, sophisticated, and free of European influence. Given its vitality and wealth, the North could wage the war without subjecting itself to heavy-handed command-and-control policies. Compared to the overmatched Confederacy, it was a laissez-faire haven.

The Southern political economy came to depend on bureaucratic control and government expropriation. An extensive conscription law effectively subjected the entire labor force to centralized direction. The government had the discretionary power to exempt certain occupations and to detail men to civil duties deemed necessary; private concerns, therefore, depended on the government for workers. Despite the constitution, the government subsidized the construction of railroads and by the end of the war assumed control of them and, by extension, the supply of raw materials. A government bureau undertook the operation of mines. Under the pressure of events, the Confederate government occupied the commanding heights of Southern industry.

It "impressed" property from manufacturers, farmers, and railroads to supply the military. In other words, it forced its owners into exchanging the goods for a price. The system led to wide-ranging price controls. One Confederate congressman complained of the government agents who were "as thick as locusts in Egypt." Under pressure from the Union blockade, the government eventually prohibited the importation of luxuries and took control of a vast array of exports. It imposed a more progressive income tax than the North did, and stifled commerce with various onerous taxes. It distributed the revenues of a tax on slave overseers to states for relief payments; nearly 40 percent of families in Alabama were on relief in 1864, according to Bensel.

In short, the Confederates pioneered a program of a kind of war socialism back when Woodrow Wilson—the progressive president who would run the country's economy on a similar basis during World War I—was still in knee-pants. The Southern stance wasn't opposition to government per se, but opposition to those social and economic forces in the North that threatened the slave system. "One of the great ironies of American political development," Bensel writes, "is that a central state as well organized and powerful as the Confederacy did not emerge until the New Deal and subsequent mobilization for World War II."

It worked as well as could be expected—which is to say, not well at all. The financially feeble Confederacy couldn't pay for the war with bonds or, despite its best efforts, tax revenues. It resorted to churning the printing presses, and reaped a ruinous inflation

that outpaced that of the North. The Confederacy couldn't effi-
ciently move supplies on its inadequate, deteriorating railway network and had trouble keeping the army's horses fed. The civilian
population suffered an abundance of shortages. "At the stroke of
secession," historian Walter McDougall observes, "the South had
a booming economy and no army. By 1864 it had an army and no
economy, unless one counts smuggling, tax evasion, speculation,
hoarding, trading with the enemy, scrounging and subsistence
farming."

Soon enough, it barely even had an army, down to 155,000
troops ready to fight by the beginning of 1865. The war killed
about a quarter of military-age white males in the South. The
United States would have had to suffer more than 6 million
dead in World War II for a comparable loss on a per capita basis.
It liberated some $3 billion worth of slaves. It destroyed more
than half the South's farm machinery. It wiped out about two-
fifths of its livestock. The real estate market cratered. The value
of Confederate bonds and paper currency—tenuous even during the war—disintegrated into nothingness with predictably
cataclysmic consequences for the financial system.

The North's advantages, on the other hand, had only grown
during the conflict. Its production continued to expand, although
at a slower pace than before or after the war. The North exploited
an already extant economic machine. Its factories churned out
roughly 1.5 million rifles. Its railroad network grew, and supplied
and moved Union armies in prodigious feats of logistics. Starting
from nearly nothing, it built a navy of nearly seven hundred ships.
Farms not only kept civilians and the army fed, they replaced
missing Southern produce and *still* exported massive amounts of
goods abroad. Settlement of the West continued, with 5 million

acres passing from government into private hands. At the height of its mobilization, with a million men under arms, the United States had become the world's foremost military power.

The country had avoided getting riven into two, or more if the nation's cohesion had been shattered. In a January 1861 speech, William Seward colorfully invoked what would have been the upshot of a broken United States. He spoke of seeing an American man-of-war entering a foreign port and how "all the people blessed it as a harbinger of hope for their own ultimate freedom." Then he imagined the same ship entering the same port under different auspices: "The flag of thirty-three stars and thirteen stripes has been hauled down, and in its place a signal is run up, which flaunts the device of a lone star or a palmetto tree. Men ask, 'Who is the stranger that thus steals into our waters?' The answer contemptuously given is, 'she comes from one of the obscure republics of North America. Let her pass on.'"

The war slammed the door on an alternative future of a Slave South as international defender of slavery and conqueror of territory in the Caribbean and Latin America, in a Manifest Destiny for the planter set. Any number of counterfactuals are possible assuming that the South had been allowed to peaceably secede or had won its independence by force of arms. None of them are favorable to liberty or the future of an America as we would come to know it.

Instead, the war shattered the South's political power for the next seven decades. After 1860, Midwesterners dominated the presidency in ensuing elections the way Southerners once had. The South couldn't even manage a Senate president or Speaker of the House for a few decades after the war. The country tilted on a different axis.

Kansas senator Samuel Pomeroy expressed the new dispensation when, in a debate over the possibility of colonizing ex-slaves during the war, he said he would prefer to colonize *slaveholders* on grounds that they "are dangerous, and they are not producers." Radical Congressman Thaddeus Stevens said much the same in plugging for thoroughgoing reconstruction of the South in 1865: "If the South is ever to be made a safe republic let her land be cultivated by the toil of its owners, or the free labor of intelligent citizens. This must be done even though it drive the nobility into exile. If they go, all the better. It is easier and more beneficial to exile seventy thousand proud, bloated and defiant rebels than to expatriate four million laborers, native to the soil and loyal to the government."

Southern fire-eaters had wanted the federal government as their tool, an instrument for the protection and expansion of slavery and the suppression of abolition. Rather than abet the slave order, the federal government crushed it and took up the cause of "the producers," in Pomeroy's phrase. In all their different guises, the producers were now in the saddle. The effect of the policies instituted during the war shouldn't be exaggerated— railroads and factories would have been built, and the continent settled, without them. And they had doleful unintended consequences, including the inevitable market distortions and corruption when government entangles itself with business. At the margins, though, federal policy encouraged and protected the interests of the shock troops of free-labor civilization, as their dreams and schemes, sweat and toil, ingenuity and brazenness drove the propulsive growth of a continental colossus.

Lincoln didn't live to see it. But he had envisioned it, or something like it, as far back as New Salem. Lincoln's republic was about to become a world power and the most far-reaching middle-class society the world had ever known—"a great empire," as he had called it in a poetic exaggeration in the 1850s, indeed.

The war had brought a massive growth of government that immediately began to retreat, although never to its antebellum levels. During the war federal spending exceeded $1 billion, before dipping below $250 million in the late 1870's (excluding payments on the debt). When peace came, wartime taxes were liquated. Nearly all manufacturing taxes were abolished by 1868, the income tax in 1872.

Debt had been the main means of financing the war. By the end, the government had accumulated $2.7 billion in debt, from $90 million when Lincoln took office. Mary Todd told Herndon that Lincoln had planned after the end of his presidency to take a trip to Europe and then "return & go to California over the Rocky Mountains and see the prospects of the soldiers &c. &c digging [out] gold to pay the National debt." But the tide of red ink receded. The government enjoyed a long period of budget surpluses and the debt had dwindled below 10 percent of gross domestic product by 1890. Between the flotation of all of those bonds and the deluge of greenbacks, Louis Hacker writes, "the nation's credit base was remarkably extended and manufacturing now had its capital fund with which to build up its plant."

Its industry operating behind a benign protective wall shielding it from competition, America leapt to the head of the class of industrial powers. From 1860 to the turn of the century, investment in manufacturing increased from $1 billion to almost $10 billion. More than half of the country's commodity output was manufacturing, and Illinois, Ohio, and Michigan were among the country's top manufacturing states. Industry employed about a quarter of the nation's workforce. Soon enough, industrial production in the United States matched that of Great Britain, France, and Germany put together.

America's rural and urban populations both grew and provided a consumer base for manufactured products. Total population nearly doubled from 1870 to 1900, hitting 76 million, up from 40 million in 1870. Cities mushroomed—New York at more than 3 million, and Chicago at more than 1 million. By some estimates half of the increase in manufacturing was simply a product of a larger workforce. Accounting for 80 percent of the industrial workers, the foreign-born or the children of the foreign-born constituted the muscle of American industry.

At the same time, the former battlefield of Kansas saw its population jump from 100,000 to a million from 1860 to 1880. Iowa and Michigan's populations doubled. Minnesota's quadrupled. Agricultural output increased vastly from the end of the war to the cusp of the 20th century. Production of wheat and corn leapt by more than 200 percent.

The Homestead Act drew people to the land and out into the Great Plains. In the end, by the 1870s, there would be homestead claims for 270 million acres, equaling about a tenth of the country's territory. The land-grant college act, meanwhile, had a rocky start. Lacking suitable students, many institutions struggled. At one point, Louisiana State University had more professors than students. But the act (and a follow-on in 1890) created more than 70 colleges and universities, many of them of enduring significance in American higher education.

The railroads continued to conquer the continent. Another 20,000 miles were added in the decade from 1860 to 1870, reaching about 50,000 total. Congress authorized another three transcontinentals, also showered with free land. Already in 1868, the United States had the most railroad track per capita on earth. More than a third of U.S. iron went to making rails. By 1890, the railroads were running on some 167,000 miles of track.

The story of this surge in construction is as grubby as it is heroic. It involves feats of construction in conditions and over distances that once would have seemed impossible. It also involved highly creative and brazen acts of theft, aided and abetted by the politicians who supported the ventures. The transcontinental railroad has competing symbols. On the one hand, there's the tableau at Promontory Summit when after some 1,800 miles the Union Pacific and Central Pacific met in 1869 and the last spike was knocked into the final tie, in the nineteenth-century equivalent of the moon landing (the "work of giants," said William Tecumseh Sherman). On the other, there is the Crédit Mobilier construction company, set up to grossly overcharge while building the Union Pacific and enrich insiders, leading to a scandal that erupted publicly during the Grant administration ("the King of Frauds," said the *New York Sun*).

It is hard to grasp the scope of government support for the railroads, in mind-bogglingly generous loans and land giveaways. The historian of the railroads Richard White writes that "railroads received the land equivalent of small countries." All told they got in excess of 130 million acres of federal land, an amount that, if it were made into a state, would be larger than all the others except Alaska and Texas. The lavish subsidies naturally encouraged the building of uneconomical roads. In the aftermath of the Panic of 1893, a quarter of railroad assets were in receivership.

Despite the corruption, waste, and inefficiency, railroads had a large hand in the transformation of American economic life. Together with the telegraph—Lincoln's first inaugural reached the West Coast via pony express; his second via telegraph—they brought the country ever tighter together. They hastened the settlement of the West and connected the settlers with the wider world. They cut the time it took to get from one coast to another from months to less than a week. They drastically reduced the cost of shipping. They gave us standard time, replacing the lunatic patchwork of different local times with a few time zones. By 1890, nearly everyone lived relatively close to a railroad or a canal, on average within ten miles even in sparsely populated areas, according to historian Walter Licht. The backwoods isolation Lincoln had known in his youth was giving way in the new era.

The Census Bureau declared the frontier closed in 1890. "Up to and including 1880," it said, "the country had a frontier of settlement, but at present the unsettled area has been so broken into by isolated bodies of settlement there can hardly be said to be a frontier line." The Civil War had barely ended when the United States acquired Alaska, taking, in the words of Charles and Mary Beard, "the western front out on the Pacific."

A revolution swept American business. Corporate behemoths unimaginable in the previous age of small, family-run businesses dominated the economic landscape by the turn of the century. They didn't need to look abroad to Britain for capital anymore. They could find it on a burgeoning Wall Street. The war had created a class of financiers, mostly in New York, who had been involved in the debt-financing of the conflict and became increasingly influential after it ended. In 1864, according to Bensel, there had been fewer than 200 bankers and brokers in New York City; by 1870, there were nearly 2,000. The country now had a national financial market. Banks in the big cities operated all around the country and the public had gotten a rudimentary education in modern finance through Jay Cooke's great Civil War bond drives.

The captains of this new economic dispensation are known as Robber Barons, a pejorative that doesn't do justice to their contribution, even if their sharp practices, ruthlessness, corruption, and greed are legendary. It was famously said that John D. Rockefeller's Standard Oil could do anything with the Pennsylvania legislature except refine it.

Most of them grew so rich because they were so good at what they did. Bigness didn't guarantee success, or else every American child would know of the exploits of such giants as Great Western Cereal and Consolidated Rubber Tire. If firms weren't well managed they went under, and the transportation and communications revolutions brought intensified competition.

Andrew Carnegie represented the new breed. It tended to consist of men who didn't come from wealth, who had little in the way of education, and who started on the lowliest rungs of the business ladder. They were self-made titans of business.

Carnegie's family left Scotland when it could no longer make a living—in other words, he was exactly the type Lincoln had invoked in his vision of America as an outlet for strivers the world over. Starting as a telegraph clerk at the Pennsylvania Railroad, Carnegie worked his way up and learned business as he went. He developed a passionate attachment to iron, which led him to steel. At the end of the Civil War, the U.S. produced 1,643 tons of Bessemer steel; by 1897, it produced more than 7 million tons. Carnegie poured his profits into innovations to make steel cheaper (and to take more market share). He wrote in a 1900 essay, "If there be in human society one truth clearer and more indisputable than another it is that the cheapening of articles . . .

insures their general distribution." Down and down he drove the costs of production and the price of steel, from about $60 per ton in 1875 to $30 in 1888.

This was a boon to the economy, and to Carnegie. But who would begrudge him it? He wouldn't have made it, as Louis Hacker points out, without tremendous ingenuity, a supreme knack for management, and a monomaniacal devotion to thrift. A colleague said, "Carnegie never wanted to know the profits. He always wanted to know the cost." The dedication of a patriotic book he wrote in 1886 read:

TO THE
BELOVED REPUBLIC
UNDER WHOSE EQUAL LAWS I AM
MADE THE PEER OF ANY MAN, ALTHOUGH DENIED
POLITICAL EQUALITY BY MY NATIVE LAND,
I DEDICATE THIS BOOK WITH AN INTENSITY OF GRATITUDE
AND ADMIRATION WHICH THE NATIVE-BORN CITIZEN
CAN NEITHER FEEL NOR UNDERSTAND.

The South stood outside the mainstream of an American economy shifting into a higher gear. Even without the war, it wouldn't have had in place the necessary architecture— including the transportation network and banking system—to keep up with the North. But the ruination of the war was like a pre-atomic-age Nagasaki. The South's share of the nation's wealth collapsed, from 30 percent before the war to 12 percent in 1870. Planters no longer made up a disproportionate share of the wealthiest Americans. Federal policies—from the tariff that favored Northern manufacturers to the pensions that were available for Union veterans but not Confederate further dis-advantaged the region. The North flinched from more radical reconstruction schemes that would have involved confiscating and redistributing planter property, out of a respect for property rights and fear of unleashing a class-based politics impossible to limit to the South. On the contrary, Northern financial interests were eager for Southern cotton production to recover and con-tribute to foreign exchange. Reconstruction petered out.

In this reduced state, and eventually left to its own devices, the South clung to a retrograde labor system that looked advanced only compared to slavery. It transitioned from slavery to share-cropping, in what amounted to debt peonage. Merchants wanted sharecroppers to have to buy their goods, so prevented them from growing anything but cotton, which you can't eat. The natural tendency was for everyone in the South to default to cotton any-way, out of familiarity, even though its value was falling; in the decades after the war, its price dropped from forty-three cents a pound to five cents a pound. The cycle of debt kept black farm-ers locked down, and so did racist repression. The South swam in cheap labor that relieved it of the need to find innovative substi-tutes for brawn. "Instead of installing machinery to do the work," an operator of a lumber mill commented, "we always undertook to do it putting in another cheap negro."

The elite in the South still feared the potential dislocations that widespread industrialization promised to the region's social system, so they kept a lid on it. The region churned out less than 10 percent of the nation's industrial output—much of it relatively crude, such as lumbering—while it had 30 percent of the nation's population, according to Licht. In a famous lament, the editor of the *Atlanta Constitution* wrote of a funeral and how all the implements at it were manufactured elsewhere: "The South didn't furnish a thing on earth for that funeral but the corpse and the hole in the ground."

The postbellum epoch in America was characterized not just by the onrush of industrial and financial progress, but by chaos and conflict. It was a time of booms, busts, and panics, of labor unrest and violent crackdowns by management, of growing power for the masters of finance, of spectacular stock manipulations, of mergers creating massive corporate entities, some almost entirely dominating the field in their markets.

Amid all this turmoil, though, we had become the richest country on earth. That wealth wasn't distributed evenly—far from it. The top 1 percent in 1890 held about half the property. Still, as Walter Licht notes, real wages rose some 70 percent from the end of the Civil War to 1890. Skilled workers in America were much better off than comparable workers elsewhere. Less-skilled workers were at least a little better off. And America was highly mobile. "A number of studies," historian Charles R. Morris writes, "show quite high rates of farm laborers becoming farm owners, blue-collar workers becoming managers, and countinghouse clerks rising to very senior positions." It was a period of progress, uneven and at times unfair, but progress all the same.

It's impossible to know exactly what Abraham Lincoln, who rode the muddy roads of the circuit on a horse, would have made of the new industrial age illuminated by Thomas Edison's lightbulb and connected by Alexander Graham Bell's telephone. A common interpretation is that he would have rued the creation of a Frankenstein monster of business predation, his unwitting progeny, his vision of small-scale capitalism gone horribly awry. "He was not consciously aware of the significance of the whole economic program of industrial capitalism," intones Louis Hacker. The French author Cyrille Arnavon noted that Lincoln's war broke the slave aristocracy but also "initiated the prodigious industrial expansion of the northern states that resulted in the clearest crystallizations of the capitalist economy." According to Arnavon, "Abraham Lincoln's ambiguity rests on this historical situation." Daniel Walker Howe believes that "the triumph of the northern bourgeoisie ushered in an era very different from anything Lincoln could have expected or wanted."

But these are guesses, usually based on the presumption that Lincoln would have turned up his nose at postbellum America like all subsequent purveyors of polite opinion. Of course, we can't be certain what specific policies Lincoln would have favored in the turn-of-the-century context.

Would he have been a labor union man? Those who like to think so might point to speeches in Connecticut as a kind of encore to his smashingly successful Cooper Union address in February 1860. Stephen Douglas had criticized a strike by Massachusetts shoemakers, blaming it on tensions between the North and South. Lincoln stuck up for the strikers: "I am glad to know that there is a system of labor where the laborer can strike if he wants to!" Of course, the larger point was less about trade unionism than the desirability of free labor itself: "If you give up your convictions and call slavery in upon you instead of *white* laborers who *can* strike, you'll soon have *black* laborers who *can't* strike."

Would he have joined Teddy Roosevelt in harrying the business trusts? Roosevelt, a determined Lincoln body snatcher, certainly thought and said so. "The official leaders of the Republican party today," he thundered in 1913, after he turned his back on the party to run for president as the nominee of his own personal Progressive Party, "are the spiritual heirs of the men who warred against Lincoln." It's a neat trick to transform the friends of Northern industry and finance into descendants of the planter aristocracy that hated both.

This we do know. Lincoln defended wage labor at a time when it was becoming increasingly prevalent. (Although he did talk of wage labor, anachronistically, as something people should graduate out of.) He was desperate for industrial development. Throughout his political career he favored giving it the advantage of the protective tariff, and indeed, prior to the Civil War, factory production had steadily risen. He exulted in new technologies. He gave no pride of place to agriculture. He wanted a sophisticated national banking system. He never attacked wealth. He objected to the very notion of class conflict. He considered property in all its forms (except slavery) sacrosanct. He worked with the biggest corporate entities of his age, the railroads, when corporations had already long been the subject of attack as tools for "the rich, and never for the poor." In fact, as a politician, he pretty much never told the railroads "no."

If every jot and tittle of the new order can't, of course, be attributed to Lincoln, its fundamentals can. There's no lack of consciousness, no ambiguity about it. Postwar America constituted the rough working-out in the real world of the Lincolnian economic vision.

That doesn't mean he would have surveyed the ever-shifting, continent-wide drama in its entirety and approved of it all. It does mean that he would have eschewed prominent schools of criticism. He certainly wouldn't have sympathized with the agrarian reaction. He would have recognized in William Jennings Bryan—the scourge of "the idle holders of idle capital"—a version of the same rustic romanticism at the bottom of Jeffersonian and Jacksonian economic populism. Bryan bellowed in his classic "Cross of Gold" speech at the 1896 Democratic convention, "You come to us and tell us that the great cities are in favor of the gold standard; we reply that the great cities rest upon our broad and fertile prairies. Burn down your cities and leave our farms, and your cities will spring up again as if by magic; but destroy our farms and the grass will grow in the streets of every city in the country." For Lincoln, this would have been eloquence as emetic.

Nor is Lincoln a natural enlistee to progressivism, although all the way from TR to Barack Obama, progressives have been after him like Mormons baptizing the dead. Lincoln wouldn't have taken to progressivism's view that the Founding was an inconvenient anachronism, or to its contempt for the idea of natural law—true for all time, in all circumstances—securing individual rights. Lincoln would have recognized in the roll call of villains in Franklin Roosevelt's 1932 Commonwealth Speech the people whom he had encouraged and identified with: "a mere builder of more industrial plants, a creator of more railroad systems, and organizer of more corporations." And Roosevelt's goal of "distributing wealth and products more equitably" would have been anathema to him. Nonetheless, FDR bestowed upon Lincoln the honor of being a posthumous father of the New Deal.

By the 1930s, the American economy had undergone several more revolutions, removing it yet further from that of Lincoln's day. In World War II, its formidable industrial capacity made the difference in a global conflict the sweep and destructiveness of which would have astounded the statesmen of the nineteenth century. As in the Civil War, the United States largely manufactured its enemy into oblivion. It could do so partly because it had mustered its own strength in the Civil War era, avoiding national dismemberment and embracing economic modernity. It wouldn't have beaten the Axis on the strength of agricultural staples, a bristling sense of honor, and sheer martial pluck—in other words, the Confederate approach. American factories belched out tens of thousands of tanks and landing crafts, hundreds of thousands of airplanes, millions of guns and shells, and on and on.

What William Seward had said in the heat of the sectional conflict in the mid-1850s proved prescient: "Political ties bind the Union together—a common necessity, and not merely a common necessity, but the common interests of empire—of such empire as the world has never before seen. The control of the national power is the control of the great Western Continent; and the control of this continent is to be in a very few years the controlling influence in the world." Eighty years later it proved so.

America emerged from the inferno with an unheard-of global strength and an economy that went a long way toward achieving what had been Lincoln's ultimate end of creating the widest possible field for individual advancement. The Lincoln fundamentals can be seen in mid-twentieth-century America at a hundred years remove from his life—in a country that had the world's most powerful economy, that continued to move away from agriculture, that was highly educated, that stood for freedom and finally began to fully embrace it at home, and that rested on a foundation of cultural orderliness. America had become the greatest middle-class society the world had ever known.

In short, we achieved a prosperity consistent with America's—and Lincoln's—ideals. The question, in the spirit of Benjamin Franklin's after the Constitutional Convention, is if we can keep it.

Chapter 6

"Work, Work, Work": Recovering the Lincoln Ethic

Among democratic nations, new families are constantly springing up, others are constantly falling away, and all that remain change their condition. . . .

—Alexis de Tocqueville, *Democracy in America*, 1840

The Lincoln of our public consciousness is the nineteen-foot-tall benevolent god of the Lincoln Memorial, presiding in his Greek Doric temple among the honeyed words of the Gettysburg Address and the Second Inaugural. It is a monument to Lincoln the war leader, Lincoln the Great Emancipator, Lincoln the martyr, who as soon as he breathed his last, "belonged to the ages," in the immortal words of Secretary of War Edwin Stanton at his deathbed.

The gawky young man looking for a chance, the circuit-riding lawyer, the Senate candidate curled up on a seat on a train, trying to get some shut-eye, even the president awaiting news at the War Department telegraph office would be bemused at his secular deification.

It is altogether proper that we celebrate Lincoln the war leader and the emancipator. He transfixes us, and always will. The events stretching from Secession Winter in 1860–61 to the assassination at Ford's Theatre constitute the greatest drama in American history this side of the Revolution. But they aren't all there is to Lincoln. Long before any shots were fired, he was committed to a vision that would create the predicate for modern America.

Lincoln believed in a dynamic capitalism that dissolved old ways of life. He thought all men were created equal and deserved the opportunity to make the most of themselves. He urged them to make the effort to do so. He found in America's constitutional system and its free institutions the best possible platform for the realization of this vision. This is the Lincoln that is too often lost—and must be found—to truly understand him and, really, to understand who we are as a people.

Or at least who we *should* be as a people. In the 1850s, Lincoln bitterly regretted our national backsliding. In that excoriating letter to George Robertson in 1855, he wrote "we are not what we have been." He said that "we have grown fat," and "that the fourth of July has not quite dwindled away; it is still a great day— *for burning fire-crackers*!!!"

It is hard not to have the same autumnal feelings about the current state of the American Dream. It is flabby and declining from its former glories. This is not the work of one president, one party, or any one factor easily reversed by a magic-bullet public policy. It has been a long-running process, a concatenation of economic and social trends augmented by government failures and inefficiencies. We are on the path to a class society inimical to our ideals and our history. *We are not what we have been.*

The temptation is to cushion our fall in a cosseting social

democracy. This has been our drift, and lately our lurch. But social democracy is where the vitality of great nations goes to die. It is something that nations settle into rather than embrace in a rising spirit. It tends to suppress growth and take the edge off individual initiative, never mind the question of whether it is fiscally sustainable. All around the Western world, the welfare state is in crisis and our aging population means we face the same grim math. The social democratic model promises gentle decline—at best.

If this is not going to be our future, the challenge facing us is quite basic: How do we revitalize the wellsprings of America as a Lincolnian republic? How do we preserve those qualities that have made our country an unsurpassed vehicle for the pursuit of happiness?

That pursuit revolves around making the most of our capabilities in Lincoln's "race of life." There are few better benchmarks for our success as a society than whether we are creating the greatest possible opportunity for the maximum number of people, as free and independent actors, treated with inherent dignity and worth, to succeed. If we are, we are well and truly American. If we aren't, we are merely another country, an extensive and powerful one to be sure, one where we light firecrackers on the Fourth of July, but not one animated by the restless quest for self-improvement that has been our hallmark.

Foreign visitors in the nineteenth century remarked on what the American journalist Hezekiah Niles called "the *almost universal ambition to get forward*." The English writer Frances Trollope—mother of the novelist Anthony—wrote that in Cincinnati, "I neither saw a beggar, nor a man of sufficient fortune to permit his ceasing his effort to increase it." Harriet Martineau, another English writer, observed, "When a few other neighbours besides frogs, gather round a settler, some one opens a grocery store." Alexis de Tocqueville wrote, "An American taken at random will be ardent in his desires, enterprising, adventurous, and above all an innovator."

The visitors didn't always approve of the relentless and unembarrassed quest of Americans for what Trollope described as "that honey of Hybla, vulgarly called money." She thought "neither art, science, learning nor pleasure can seduce them from its pursuit." But the words of these writers convey a big, bustling, unstoppable country of striving—materialistic, yes, but also open, frank, democratic, and at the end of the day, very, very successful.

Striving is desirable in and of itself, regardless of the effect it has on the country's growth. It is *good* for us, and it is written into the country's DNA. Charles Murray writes in his classic book, *In Pursuit*, "What allows man to fulfill his own nature in the Founders' vision is the process of individual response to challenge, risk, and reward." They were right. Ideally, Arthur Brooks points out in his book-length study of happiness, work brings a sense of productivity, control, and success—all key ingredients of happiness. "By all the evidence that science has been able to muster," Murray writes, "people *need* to be self-determining, accountable, and absorbed in stretching their capacities, just as they need food and shelter."

As Lincoln put it to that aspiring lawyer so long ago, "Work, work, work, is the main thing." We need to ensure that government and society create the most favorable environment to reward work and support aspiration, and that more people don't fall by the wayside of the bustling highway of American life. For our purposes here, there are a few key questions: Where were we in the immediate aftermath of industrial America's triumph in World War II, and why? Where are we now? What might Lincoln do about it? Which party is best positioned to give concrete expression to a truly Lincolnian agenda?

We emerged from World War II into the sunny uplands of a social and economic golden age that boosted millions into the middle class. A few years after the return to peace, we churned out half of the world's manufacturing output, and produced almost 60 percent of its steel and 80 percent of its cars. We underwent a revolution in educational achievement, thanks in part to the G.I. Bill. By 1950, more than twice as many people were earning college degrees as in 1940. In 1950, almost 90 percent of white Americans had nonfarm jobs, more than a third of which were white-collar. With the civil rights revolution, which finally fully extended to blacks the promise of the Declaration, the South fully joined the American mainstream. After a long detour, it was in a position to take the maximum possible advantage of its low costs for labor and land.

On top of this, the bourgeois virtues remained solidly intact. Divorce rates that had crept up since 1900 began to fall a couple of years after World War II. The marriage rate hit a high in 1946. And these couples had children at an astonishing rate; in 1964, about 40 percent of the population had been born since 1946.

It is hard not to see this era, for the most part, in a gauzy glow. But the economic dispensation of the post–World War II world couldn't and didn't last. For one thing, the advantage we had over the rest of the world in manufacturing couldn't be sustained, since a swath of the developed world had been flattened by the war. Japan and Germany would inevitably recover. Communist regimes cut off a substantial proportion of the world from the market, a condition that would come to a blessed end with the fall of the Berlin Wall. The United States owned an enormous advantage in education, as economist Luigi Zingales notes—44 percent of the world was illiterate, but only 2.2 percent of Americans were; 8.2 percent of the world had high-school degrees, but 37 percent of Americans did. This education gap, too, would end.

Putting it slightly differently in his book *The Great Stagnation*, the George Mason economist Tyler Cowen says we picked all "the low-hanging fruit" in prior centuries. We had free and fertile land widely available for anyone with the pluck to take advantage of it. We had spectacular technological breakthroughs from roughly 1880 to 1940 that transformed economic life in a way that, even with the computer revolution, hasn't been replicated since. We were pulling kids into higher education who just needed the chance, as opposed to the marginal new students of today, who are often woefully unprepared. We did the easy stuff, and what's left now is harder.

The starting point for our current economic discontents is that growth, overall, slowed in recent decades. This slowdown—which holds true for basically all advanced economies since the early 1970s—comes in the context of growing inequality. The widely cited research of economists Thomas Piketty and Emmanuel Saez shows that the percentage of income held by the infamous top 1 percent rose above 20 percent before the Great Depression. It dropped precipitously after the Depression and World War II, hovering around 8 percent in the 1960s and 1970s, before beginning to rise again, to 18 percent in 2008.

Even if growth has slowed overall and even if inequality has grown, all has not been wrack and ruin for the American middle class. As Scott Winship of the Brookings Institution points out, calculating income trends over time is hideously complicated, since so many variables—changing family size, the value of health-care benefits, the entry of so many low-skilled immigrants—complicate the picture. According to Winship, if you make all the necessary adjustments, the median American family is twice as rich today as it was in 1960, although much of that gain occurred before 1979.

Nonetheless, trends in the middle and the bottom of the income distribution are dismaying. By the crudest measures, the income of the lowest fifth has been essentially flat since 1973 and the same is true of median male wages. Adjusting for various factors makes the picture look a little better, but there's no question male high-school graduates without a college degree have been hit hard. In the decades prior to the mid-1970s, high-school graduates had been catching up a little to college graduates in earnings. Since then, the earnings differential has been sliding the other way. The gap in median income between a man with a bachelor's degree and with a high-school degree doubled since 1979, from roughly $12,000 in 1979 to about $25,000.

What is going on? The simplest and most tendentious explanation—the American government has been seized by the rich, who have distorted it to increase their share of the economy at the expense of everyone else—is false. Median-income growth has been roughly the same in Canada, France, Germany, and Sweden over the last 30 years. And European countries have seen growing inequality, as well. The top 1 percent accounts for a greater portion of federal income taxes today (about 40 percent) than it did in the 1970s (less than 20 percent), under a tax system that is more progressive than that of any other advanced nation.

Much of the run-up in pay at the top can be attributed to globalization. There is more of a premium on excellence, because the rewards for succeeding in a global market are so much greater. Meanwhile, technology is eliminating lower-skill jobs, and the global labor market puts downward pressure on wages and moves some jobs offshore. We can make more with fewer hands. Manufacturing employment has been declining, even as manufacturing output as a percentage of GDP has held steady. With an education system universally considered inadequate, economic change has been outrunning our capacity to provide the human material suitable for it, with lamentable consequences.

Inequality in itself isn't a problem, so long as everyone has a good chance of moving up. We like to pride ourselves on our economic mobility. Few things are as all-American as the up-from-the-bootstraps success story. But we aren't quite as fluid as we think. We are less mobile than many Western European countries and than other major English-speaking countries. Our income distribution is "sticky" at the bottom, meaning that people starting out at the bottom are more likely to stay there than would be suggested by random chance. And sticky at the top.

The lack of mobility at the bottom is a function of the economic struggles of lower-skilled men, but also of culture. The rise of illegitimacy, the decline of work, and the erosion of an ethic of delayed gratification all undergird stagnation at the bottom and augment the advantages of those at the top who largely avoid these cultural pitfalls. A gross and steadily increasing inequality in cultural capital is more telling and significant than any economic statistics.

Out-of-wedlock childbearing, especially, undermines economic aspiration. Today the illegitimacy rate is 73 percent among blacks, 53 percent among Latinos, and 29 percent among whites. For the first time, more than half of births to mothers under the age of thirty are out of wedlock. This is quite simply a social catastrophe. Illegitimacy is a generator—and perpetuator—of poverty, while growing up in a two-parent family brings enormous social advantages. Children in intact families perform better in school, and are less prone to behavioral problems of all kinds.

Marriage and child-rearing bear so directly on the status of the American Dream because commitment to the old norms is being redistributed upward. Brad Wilcox of the University of Virginia has carefully demonstrated how the highly educated (with a college diploma or higher) are less likely to divorce, less likely to have children out of wedlock, and less likely to commit adultery than the moderately educated (high-school degree or some college) and the least educated (no high-school diploma). From 1982 until today, the percentage of nonmarital births among the moderately educated exploded from 13 percent to 44 percent. The figure for the highly educated is only 6 percent.

The advantages of the highly educated are self-reinforcing because they marry one another at a greater rate than they did before—itself a driver of inequality. These highly educated parents pass along their attitudes, habits, and knowledge to their children. One sociologist calls the parenting style of the upper middle class "concerted cultivation." It is focused unceasingly on every aspect of preparing their children to make their way in a high-achieving world. Well-educated parents spend much more time than they used to caring for their children, and parents in nuclear families spend more time—increasingly more—than single parents. The gap in educational achievement between kids of high- and low-income families has been growing.

While highly educated people enjoy a virtuous circle—marrying one another, and transferring their advantages to their children—high-school-educated men suffer a vicious one. The economic pressure on these men makes it harder for them to marry; the lack of marriage, in turn, denies them the social stability that creates the so-called marriage premium of higher earnings.

Lower-skilled males have been dropping out of the labor force for the last three decades. In other words, they weren't available for a job even if one was open. Many of them worked fewer hours than they had before, and they were more likely to be unemployed. These trends held even when the economy was booming. So what are the men doing? Men without a high-school degree have been spending more time on leisure, while college graduates have been spending less. Among lower-skilled men without a job, the extra time went to sleeping and watching television.

The starkest indicator of the travails of the working class is the collapse of life expectancy among its less educated members. According to a study published in the journal *Health Affairs*, adults without a high-school degree have life expectancies that have reverted almost all the way back to the level for all adults in the 1950s and 1960s. Among whites, the gap between college-educated women and women without a high-school degree is ten years, and between men with those levels of educational attainment, thirteen years. It's almost as if they don't live in the same country.

In a lecture about Lincoln, historian Jean Baker notes the contrast between a photograph of Lincoln in 1846 after his election to Congress and one of Dennis and John Hanks, who lived in the old Lincoln household back in Indiana. Lincoln is posing in a studio in a frock coat and satin vest. The two Hanks stand outside a log cabin in Conestoga boots and shabby clothes. Lincoln looks like a lawyer; they look like hillbillies. You might not believe that they knew one another, let alone that they had once lived under the same roof.

It is stark visual demonstration of the gap between their two worlds, a gap that Lincoln wanted to close by extending the reach of bourgeois America. The same gap, in a different form, increasingly yawns between today's upper middle class and above and the people they have left behind in down-at-the-heels communities in Middle America, in the inner city, anywhere, really, where education and self-discipline are lacking.

So, what would Lincoln do today? His essential formula wouldn't have to change much: Economic growth. Policies to enhance the market and ensure that it is as fluid and flexible as possible. Education. An ethic of self-reliance, free of control by or dependence on others. And a commitment to order and self-regulating conduct. We should be a strenuous society that demands individual exertion and rewards it, and that is open to all, without favor or prejudice. We should be a country where you can make your way and you *have to* make your way.

Of course, the world has vastly changed a century and a half later. We are about as far in time from Lincoln in his political prime as he was from the America of the early 1700s, when all of 275,000 Anglos lived here and the colonies were still legislating against Catholic priests. Today no one wears stovepipe hats. Lawyers don't ride horses to work. We have gone from an industrial to a postindustrial economy, and computing is the steam power of our change.

We can't say with certitude how Lincoln would react if he were dropped into our America. I don't want to be guilty of Cuomo-style ideological body snatching. But if we take Lincoln as we find him in the nineteenth century and assume no major changes in worldview, we can tease out the broad contours of, or at least certain hypotheses about, an updated Lincoln platform. In what follows, I describe the major items with a broad brush and a focus on the economy and individual advancement. I fill in some of the details with my own policy preferences, without presuming that Lincoln would have necessarily endorsed any of them.*

EMBRACE WHAT IS NEW. Lincoln the modernizer wouldn't have any patience for an economics born of nostalgia or of distrust of the workings of the market. That was the province of his ideological opponents, a George Fitzhugh scorning free competition for elevating the ethic of "every man for himself," a John C. Calhoun fretting that "modern society seems to me to be rushing toward some new and untried condition." Lincoln would have been delighted by the rise of Silicon Valley and entranced by the iPhone, fascinated by robotics and thrilled by the astonishing advances in biotech. If the latest agricultural implement captivated him, the world of high-tech would have been a delightful dream. What is the Internet but the greatest means ever devised by man to conquer time and space, the same end that Lincoln sought through the new technologies of his day?

We have seemingly magical devices at our fingertips, yet our growth has been halting. Reviving it will require an era of economic reform of the sort we have undergone before, and not too long ago. Beginning in the late 1970s, the United States reacted

---

* I want to be clear: I don't necessarily agree with everything I believe Lincoln would think about our current predicament, and I'm sure he wouldn't agree with everything that I do.

to a crisis of slow growth with a renovation of its private sector and reaped an economic boom.

It dumped what historian Walter Russell Mead disparagingly calls "the blue model." The American business landscape in the mid-twentieth century was controlled by a few big firms, free of foreign and often domestic competition, comfortable in the swaddling of extensive government regulation. This environment afforded ample room for far-reaching and costly unionization. As foreign competitors rose up, and as consumers demanded more choice and the regulations favoring big business were rolled back, the private sector became more nimble and less bureaucratic. As Mead notes, it ended lifetime employment, paid productive workers more, moved away from defined-benefit pensions, automated jobs, and ran free of the old constraints of unionization.

These changes had painful social costs, but so did the transition from an agricultural to an industrial economy and so did the transition from slavery to free labor in the South (to say the least). On the foundation of this reform of the private sector, the United States managed to maintain its 21 percent stake of a much more competitive global economy, at the same time its output per person outstripped that of Japan and many European countries. The challenge during the current period of disappointing growth—extending across the Bush and Obama years and reaching a nadir with the bursting of the housing bubble—is to wrench the entire economy onto as efficient a footing as possible and to clear away hindrances to economic change.

The public sector exists in a mid-twentieth-century time warp. It is heavily unionized, incredibly generous with benefits for its employees, and bureaucratic in its practices and unresponsive to customers. It should be modernized, a process that it resists through sheer political clout. Both the education and health-care sectors—growing rapidly, dominated by government, and squeezing the middle class with ever-escalating costs—should be brought into the twenty-first century and subjected to the tempering fire of competition. The tax system should be reformed to cut rates and limit loopholes and deductions toward the goal of reducing disincentives to save, invest, and work. The transformation of the insurance and finance sectors into quasi-public utilities through regulation should be resisted and reversed. So long as these large swaths of American economic life are unreformed, we will underperform.

We can't know what particular domestic economic agenda Lincoln would have signed up for. We can know he would have favored whatever market-oriented economic change he thought best suited to the development of human capacity and the increase of national wealth. Stagnation was anathema to him, and with technology driving an ongoing revolution in communications and drawing together commercial markets as never before, today he presumably would have had less patience for it than ever. Lincoln's famous admonition in an 1862 message to Congress, "as our case is new, so we must think anew, and act anew," applies with especial force to a twenty-first-century country saddled with so many residual twentieth-century practices and structures.

EMPHASIZE EDUCATION. Lincoln talked of the importance of education from the first, although not with much specificity. He lived out his own commitment to it in his early years, with all his reading and self-directed study. His son Robert, on the other hand, didn't have to rely on his own personalized schooling.

When President Lincoln pushed back against Massachusetts Republicans who wanted too many appointments as he was forming his government in 1861, he mollified them with some flattery. He attested "that he considered Massachusetts the banner State of the Union, and admired its institutions and people so much that he had sent his 'Bob' . . . to Harvard for an education." From illiteracy to Harvard in two generations isn't so bad.

The Lincoln family experience constituted an exaggerated version of the norm for something like 100 years. From roughly the late nineteenth century to the 1970s, Americans stood on a rapid up escalator of educational attainment, with children getting much more schooling than their parents. Now research shows that a driver of inequality is the fact that educational progress has failed to keep pace with technological advance. Several decades ago, we had the best-educated young people of any country in the world. Lately, we have been falling back in terms of educational attainment compared to other countries in the Organisation for Economic Co-operation and Development (a club of more than thirty advanced democracies).

The answer can't simply be more spending. We spend more per pupil than most countries around the world, substantially exceeding the OECD average. While we have more than doubled per-pupil spending the past four decades, results have largely stayed flat. The high-school graduation rate is lower than it was in the late 1960s, and reading and math scores on the National Assessment of Educational Progress haven't changed for seventeen-year-olds since the early 1970s. We could double spending all over again, and so long as we were pouring the money into the same system, we would get the same dismal result.

The education status quo, conceived in the industrial era and set in amber there, should be dynamited. It is particularly atrocious in urban areas. Parents should be empowered with a system of choice and provided with the information to pick the best schools. Funding should follow the child, with leaders of schools given freedom from union contracts and entangling regulations so they can work to create the best possible environments conducive to learning and to attracting students.

Higher education, too, desperately needs reform. It is too expensive and too often fails to deliver value. The cost of attending college has roughly tripled since 1980. It is too inefficient at graduating students. Four-year institutions graduate less than 40 percent of their students in four years, and less than 60 percent in six. It is too irrelevant to the job market. Many college graduates end up in jobs that don't require a degree, including about half who majored in the humanities. It is too lax. Richard Arum and Josipa Roksa, in their book *Academically Adrift*, found that "American higher education is characterized by limited or no learning for a large proportion of students."

We should rethink the current architecture of financial aid, which helps drive up costs in a never-ending cycle, and find other ways to credential young people besides a BA, with an accent on practical, job-focused training. The signer of the law that gave us land-grant colleges devoted to the workmanlike subjects of "agriculture and the Mechanic Arts" would understand the imperative to make postsecondary education as economically useful as possible.

The magnitude of the overall challenge in education is such that our default should be to think big, and think radical. We either improve our schooling, or eventually settle into a permanently stratified society.

RESIST DEPENDENCY. Lincoln resented his father for making him labor and keeping the proceeds for himself. He preached a gospel of work, and wanted as many people as possible participating in the commercial economy. He made the basic principle of working for your living—not taking from others, or living off others—a foundation of his antislavery advocacy. Allen Guelzo goes so far as to write that Lincoln defined slavery "as any relationship which forestalled social dynamism and economic mobility."

Lincoln might find it strange that the American government, which he envisioned as a support for economic advance and an instrument of freedom, would create a system largely about people living, in whole or part, on others. The central business of American government is not building things or "investing." It is not fostering opportunity, or even defending the country. It is taking money from some people and giving it to others. It transfers resources from the young to the old, and from the rich to the poor, in the vast shuffle of wealth that is the modern welfare state.

Some of this is utterly unobjectionable. The fight over whether we would have a safety net for the disabled, the indigent, and the elderly was settled long ago. But the welfare state has expanded inexorably to climb up the income scale and to widen its reach. Nicholas Eberstadt of the American Enterprise Institute points out that adjusting for inflation and population growth, entitlement payments of all kinds have grown on average at 4 percent a year for five decades and now constitute two-thirds of federal spending. About half of Americans live in households receiving government benefits, up from roughly 38 percent in 1998.

Consider the rise of food stamps. Beneficiaries increased from about 17 million people in 2000, to some 30 million in 2008, to roughly 47 million in 2012. From 1 in 50 Americans on food stamps at the program's national inception in the 1970s, 1 in 7 Americans are on them now. Even though unemployment was low from 2001 and 2006, spending on food stamps doubled in those years. Loosened eligibility requirements, and promotion of usage by all levels of government, drive an increase regardless of economic conditions.

Or the course of Social Security Disability Insurance. From 1960 to 2011, the number of adults receiving benefits under the program grew from fewer than 500,000 to more than 8 million. This runaway growth makes no sense given amazing advances in health and medical care, and how much less hazardous most work has become. Eligibility standards have been relaxed and there has been an influx of younger workers under the vaguer, more subjective categories of disability involving mental health and musculoskeletal disorders.

As the welfare state grows, it must necessarily reduce the stigma that once attached to receiving "relief." It can't help but to chip away at individual initiative and work effort, both because it pays people for not working and takes away their benefits when they earn more. It depends on a present-oriented framework instead of a future-oriented one, since it funds current consumption at the price of increased fiscal burdens on subsequent generations.

The advent of the welfare state is one of the signal political innovations of the modern age. We can't know how Lincoln would have regarded it in all its permutations. It's hard to see him, though, considering the routine acceptance of able-bodied adults (who aren't war widows or orphans) living off the labor of others as anything other than shocking—offensive to common sense and harmful to the recipient. He might detect in it a whiff of the moral stink of the plantation, in its insulting assumption that people who are otherwise healthy and in possession of their senses can't take responsibility for themselves. He was tough enough on his relatives who merely had to ask for loans because they weren't sufficiently enterprising. Imagine what he would have said had they been on the dole.

BUILD INFRASTRUCTURE. Unstintingly, from the beginning of his career to the end, Lincoln favored funding better transportation infrastructure, whether it was improving the pathetic little Sangamon River or building a grand railroad project spanning the continent. It was all toward the end of reducing transit costs, and easing travel and commercial transactions. In aggregate, this project was a runaway success. It transformed American life. In its specific expressions, the Lincoln program was a mixed bag. At one point it brought Illinois to its fiscal knees. It funded pork. It aided and abetted the corrupt builders of the transcontinental railroad. It nonetheless did more good than harm, and Lincoln would surely be interested in developing a comparable program.

If he were back in Congress, he might be found on the House transportation committee. He would have a great interest in ports and bridges, highways and airports. Needless to say, if we should be doing more to maintain and build our infrastructure, we should do it intelligently. Lincoln would surely be astounded by all that the contemporary government does to put roadblocks in the way of even its own projects. A welter of environmental regulations makes it impossible to build anything of consequence without extravagant bureaucratic review and lawsuits. He would be intrigued by innovations like congestion pricing, and mindful of how new technologies are enabling telecommuting and other ways around having to get in a vehicle and drive somewhere.

Whatever the means, Lincoln's end would be the same as ever—to create efficiencies and reduce costs in traveling and shipping. In the nineteenth century, he wanted to unlock the country's potential. For him, there would be more potential yet to unlock.

FUND OTHER BASIC SUPPORTS FOR GROWTH. Lincoln lent aid to transportation improvements on the theory that they were transformative and couldn't necessarily get the capital on their own otherwise. A direct analogue today is basic science and research. It can pay massive dividends but on a time frame that is too long for any one company to fund the work. So much federal spending is erroneously touted as "investment." In this case, it actually is.

The act creating the Department of Agriculture signed by Lincoln in 1862 was intended in this vein (long before the department became a conduit for food stamps and farm subsidies). The department was "to acquire and to diffuse among the people of the United States useful information on subjects connected with agriculture in the most general and comprehensive sense of that word, and to procure, propagate, and distribute among the people new and valuable seeds and plants." Think DARPA—the famously innovative Defense Department research agency—but for farmers.

Lincoln the tinkerer, patent holder, and informal adviser to the War Department on weapons technologies would no doubt be an unrestrained enthusiast for government doing its small part to expand the horizons of our understanding and capabilities.

REJECT CLASS POLITICS. The entire thrust of Lincoln's economics was growing the pie for everyone and resisting zero-sum arguments positing an inherent conflict between classes. "By increasing total wealth," Daniel Walker Howe writes, "the Whigs hoped to avoid having to equalize its distribution." It's not as though Lincoln was unfamiliar with inequality or arguments about its supposed blight on the republic. Some estimates have the top 10 percent increasing its share of the nation's wealth from roughly 50 percent to more than 70 percent between the late eighteenth century and 1860. Representatives of the labor movement lamented that "the profits of . . . improvements in the arts, instead, as would seem just, of *tending to benefit and relieve the whole of its members in the burdens of their toil*, go only to the enrichment of *a few*, and depression of a great majority."

Lincoln rejected this kind of politics then, and he would do so now. Nothing in Lincoln's record suggests that he ever would deliver anything like President Obama's 2011 Osawatomie, Kansas, speech arguing that the rich are a clear and present threat to the middle class and to our democracy. In a reply to a workingmen's association in New York in 1864, Lincoln struck his characteristic tone: "Property is the fruit of labor—property is desirable—is a positive good in the world. That some should be rich, shows that others may become rich, and hence is just encouragement to industry and enterprize."

WELCOME IMMIGRANTS. Lincoln wasn't beyond the occasional Irish joke. The compilation of his humor, *Abe Lincoln Laughing*, has about a dozen jokes or stories involving Irishmen. He told one in his temperance lecture. Illustrating the foolishness of long-way-off promises of good or threats of evil, he recounted someone catching an Irishman in an act of theft and admonishing him, "Better lay down that spade you're stealing, Paddy—if you don't you'll pay for it at the day of judgment." The Irishman replies, "By the powers, if ye'll credit me so long, I'll take another jist."

But Lincoln was broadly pro-immigration, even if he played the politics delicately. Incredible ferment on the issue rocked the 1850s. After a massive wave of immigration, 20 percent of the population was foreign-born by 1860. In reaction, the Know-Nothing party wanted a twenty-one-year waiting period before immigrants could be naturalized, among other restrictions on their political participation, and opposed public support for Catholic schools. Although Lincoln recoiled from the Know-Nothing agenda, he didn't want to offend the party's adherents, either. Republicans hoped to absorb them into their coalition.

At an 1855 meeting of antislavery forces in Decatur, Illinois, he participated in the drafting of a platform that was anti-nativist, but diplomatically so. The platform stated that "we shall maintain the Naturalization laws as they are, believing as we do, that we should welcome the exiles and emigrants from the Old World, to homes of enterprise and of freedom in the New." At the same time, it made a bow to the anti-Catholic fears of the Know-Nothings by opposing "all attacks upon our Common School System, or upon any of our Institutions of an educational character, or our civil polity by the adherents of any religious body whatsoever."

Lincoln and his fellow Republicans had a keen eye on the German-American vote, which was especially important in the Midwest. The national Republican platform in 1860 contained two so-called Dutch planks, one of which opposed "any change in our naturalization laws, or any state legislation by which the rights of citizens hitherto accorded to immigrants from foreign lands shall be abridged or impaired." In the presidential election, Lincoln won enough backers of the Know-Nothing candidate in 1856, the former president Millard Fillmore, to prevail in the key states of Pennsylvania, Illinois, and Indiana, while picking up some immigrant voters at the same time.

Lincoln vented his true feelings in a letter to his friend Joshua Speed in 1855. "I am not a Know-Nothing," he wrote. "How could I be? How can any one who abhors the oppression of negroes, be in favor or degrading classes of white people?" In an 1859 letter to the German-American editor Theodore Canisius, he struck a similar theme: "Understanding the spirit of our institutions to aim at the *elevation* of men, I am opposed to whatever tends to *degrade* them."

With another Irish joke, Lincoln made the point that the immigrant couldn't help his status. He said that in a conversation with an Irishman tending his garden, he explained what the Know-Nothings were trying to do and asked him why he had not been born in America. "Faith," the Irishman replied, "I wanted to, but me mother wouldn't let me."

Clearly, Lincoln's default position today would be generosity toward immigrants. The effectively permanent status as second-class citizens of millions of illegal immigrants would be anathema to him. I think the way to square a Lincolnian liberality with the national interest would be to secure the border and workplace so as to check any new flow, then grant amnesty to illegal immigrants too embedded in their communities to leave the country. As for legal immigration, our policy should be reoriented around skilled workers. In a twenty-first-century economy, it's no longer a matter of welcoming Lincoln's characteristic immigrant trio—

Hans and Baptiste and Patrick—and giving them a plot of land. Without the requisite skills, immigrants often end up a net fiscal drag on government and compete with the most vulnerable, low-skilled workers. With those skills, though, they can enliven Lincoln's vision of immigrants and their new country in a mutually beneficial and elevating embrace.

EXPLOIT OUR RESOURCES. Lincoln would probably favor drilling, mining, and fracking to the utmost. If the discovery of gold in California was in his mind a testament to Yankee ingenuity to be celebrated, the advent of horizontal drilling and hydraulic fracking to tap untold new sources of oil and natural gas would have been a miracle for the ages. This is the kind of thing for which Lincoln, literally, thanked God. His 1863 Thanksgiving address said, "Needful diversions of wealth and of strength from the fields of peaceful industry to the national defence, have not arrested the plough, the shuttle or the ship; the axe has enlarged the borders of our settlements, and the mines, as well of iron and coal as of the precious metals, have yielded even more abundantly than heretofore."

No one talked about climate change in the 1860s, so it's possible he would have a change of heart. He might support subsidies to green energy, since they are justified in the same terms as the subsidies he favored in his day—as needful support for a cutting-edge industry. (It is worth noting that green energy will be a minuscule contributor to our energy consumption for a long time; the Energy Department estimates it will only go from about 9 percent of our energy consumption today to about 11 percent in 2035.) But he would surely recognize in the budding oil-and-gas revival the same sort of potential for reducing costs, albeit on a smaller scale, of the transportation revolution of his time. With the United States projected to become the world's largest oil producer by 2020, Lincoln would be tempted to begin drafting a proclamation of thanksgiving forthwith.

PAY ATTENTION TO THE INTERESTS OF THE COMMON WORKER. "Whatever is calculated to advance the condition of the honest, struggling laboring man," Lincoln said in 1861 on his way to Washington, "so far as my judgment will enable me to judge of a correct thing. I am for that thing." It is a rule, no doubt, that he would hew to still.

How to uphold it involves an enormous economic debate. A devoted tariff man, Lincoln might seek retaliation against China's predatory trade practices today, even if the global position of the United States has been utterly transformed since the mid-nineteenth century. The left focuses on renewed unionization, but unions have proved adept at disadvantaging the private industries where they are most concentrated. There are obviously no simple answers, but there are a number of things that we can do to advance "the condition of the honest, laboring man" that are consistent with broader economic efficiency and growth.

We should focus on market-oriented changes to make health insurance more affordable, since its ever-escalating cost is a millstone on ordinary workers and a contributor to inequality. No unnecessary regulatory barriers should be put in front of good, roughneck jobs, especially in the energy sector. The welfare state's reliance on the regressive payroll tax—to maintain the fiction that Social Security and Medicare merely pay back what people put in—should be rethought.

We should stanch the flow of poorly educated immigrants, who compete for jobs with and suppress the wages of low-skilled workers (these were the effects of the wave of immigration in the 1840s and 1850s, and one of the reasons it stoked such a strong political reaction). And, to counteract the way the age-old entitlements disproportionately burden families with children (their children will be the workers who pay for entitlements for everyone else), the tax code should have an even more generous child tax credit. It will benefit all families, but especially those struggling most with costs.

Regardless, the Lincoln standard is the right one, consistent, as he said in that same 1861 talk, with achieving "the greatest good to the greatest number."

SUPPORT CAUSES OF SOCIAL RENEWAL. Lincoln's Whigs self-consciously sought a higher civilization. The crusading of a Michelle Obama or Michael Bloomberg on obesity is in the same key as Whig social movements, and has the same odor of elitism. Emerson lampooned the Whigs in the same terms as the critics go after the First Lady and the New York City mayor—as "nannies." He wrote that their "social frame is a hospital" where they dress everyone in "slippers & flannels, with bib & pap spoon" and administer "pills & herb tea," among other Whig remedies.

It's not hard seeing Lincoln the temperance advocate finding the nudging and nagging from on high about weight and diet congenial (although he didn't care what he himself ate). But he surely would have found it odd that almost all the moralizing tendencies of society are now directed toward health, and very few toward the habits that directly affect the ability of people to get ahead.

It is well established that adherence to rudimentary cultural norms is the most effective of all antipoverty programs. If the head of a family graduates from high-school, works full-time, and waits until age twenty-one and marries before having children, it almost guarantees his family will avoid poverty. According to Ron Haskins and Isabel Sawhill, only 2 percent of the families who adhered to all three of these norms were poor in 2007 (a year of low unemployment, it must be stipulated). Of the families who adhered to one or two, 26.9 percent were poor. Of the families who adhered to none, 76 percent were poor.

In her book *What Money Can't Buy*, University of Chicago poverty expert Susan Mayer found that once basic needs are met in poor households, it is the values of parents, rather than additional income, that are most important to the prospects of children. Even if their families are poor, children whose parents are honest, diligent, and reliable—among other things—tend to do well. Basically, they benefit from middle-class values before they are middle class.

It seems certain that Lincoln would be alarmed by the unraveling of middle-class morality in contemporary America, and loathe to accept its inevitability. Mores can change. It happened with temperance. Historian Charles Sellers notes the astonishing amount of alcohol imbibed annually by Americans over the age of fourteen in 1830—9.5 gallons of hard liquor and 30.3 gallons of hard cider and other drinks, for 7.1 gallons of absolute alcohol all told. By 1845, the amount of absolute alcohol had fallen to 1.8 gallons, diminished by a mass temperance movement that spread the word about the social and personal costs of alcoholism. The *Temperance Recorder* warned, "The enterprise of this country is so great, and competition so eager in every branch of business . . . that profit can only result from . . . *temperance.*"

Our own social renewal has to come first from civil society.

A cultural revival must rely on cultural institutions. Yet they have been mostly missing from the field. As Yuval Levin writes, "American social conservatism has almost entirely lost interest in the cause of order—in standing up for clean living, for self-discipline and restraint, for resisting temptation and meeting basic responsibilities. The institutions of American Christianity—some of which would actually stand a chance of being taken seriously by the emerging lower class—are falling down on the job, as their attention is directed to more exciting causes, in no small part because the welfare state has overtaken some of their key social functions."

Government should pitch in at the margins, with what might be called a bourgeois paternalism. It should be confident in promoting the qualities necessary to success in a free society. It's not as though government doesn't already align itself with certain values, and advance them through suasion and law. It has launched effective crusades against drunk driving, domestic violence, and smoking and on behalf of recycling. Yet government is neutral or implicitly hostile toward the twin bedrocks of American aspiration: work and family.

If you are an able-bodied person of working age who is interacting with the government—either as a ward of the state or a subject of the criminal justice system—you should get a good dose of the basic values that might keep you from indigence or lawlessness in the first place. Every means-tested welfare program, not just Temporary Assistance for Needy Families (successor to the old Aid to Families with Dependent Children welfare program) but food stamps and others, should have a work requirement (for either actual work or a closely supervised job search). Parole and probation should be much more restrictive. Mark Kleiman of the

University of California, Los Angeles suggests an ankle bracelet to monitor compliance with conditions, with swift and certain punishment for breaking them. And so on.

Government should tell people that marriage is important, as poverty expert Robert Rector of the Heritage Foundation argues. National leaders should speak about it, something that Bill Clinton did quite courageously in the 1990s. We should tell kids in high-school of the disastrous consequences for their lives of having children out of wedlock. We should include similarly frank information at every government-funded family planning clinic. We should run public-ad campaigns touting marriage as an indispensable tool for fighting poverty. We should reduce the rewards of single parenthood in the welfare system.

The first step is to frankly acknowledge the cultural contribution to our lack of mobility. For Lincoln, our social breakdown would represent America going back to seed. In the rustic world he left, Jean Baker writes, illegitimacy was more common than in the middle-class world he joined. It was back in that world that his relatives "idled away time." For Lincoln, our social ills would be reason to redouble his commitment to improvement—since we have so much to improve.

ELEVATE THE CULTURE. A vast apparatus of cultural uplift undergirded mid-nineteenth-century America, grinding away to improve minds and inculcate good habits. Whatever else they taught, the readers that Lincoln absorbed as a boy provided a basic moral education. *Lessons in Elocution* contained "Selected Sentences" such as: "there is nothing truly valuable which can be purchased without pains and labor" (*Tattler*). "You must love learning, if you would possess it" (Knox). "Good manners are, to particular societies, what morals are to society in general—their cement and their security" (Chesterfield).

Murray's *English Reader*, which Lincoln thought so highly of, stipulated in its preface: "That this collection may also serve the purpose of promoting piety and virtue, the compiler has introduced many extracts which place religion in the most amiable light and which recommend a great variety of moral duties. . . . The compiler has been careful to avoid every expression and sentiment, that might gratify a corrupt mind, or, in the least degree, offend the eye of innocence. This he conceives to be peculiarly incumbent on every person who writes for the benefit of youth." Another collection, *The Kentucky Preceptor*, forewarned readers: "Tales of love, or romantic fiction, or anything which might tend to instil false notions into the minds of the children have not gained admission."

These were books put in the hands of children. Charles Sellers writes (not favorably) of the more general spread of "potent agencies of middle-class acculturation": "Wherever Yankees migrated they outstripped natives in wealth and culture while pressing their example through multiplying churches, colleges, schools, libraries, voluntary associations, and a new perceptual realm of mass literacy and cheap print. Voluntary associations spread rapidly across the North to promote missions and Sunday schools, enforce morality and temperance, aid and uplift the poor, and maintain libraries and lyceum lecture series for cultural self-improvement."

What do we have that is remotely comparable to such middle-class cultural evangelism? The ethic of the schools, from kindergarten through college, is a watery stew of environmentalism and multiculturalism. Who, to put it in Sellers's words, is enforcing morality or uplifting the poor? Who even thinks in such terms? Rather than joining the voluntary associations that once made America so distinctive, we are increasingly bowling alone, in the evocative phrase of political scientist Robert Putnam. American males, especially in the working class, are becoming ever more cut off from any institutions whatsoever. Once an instrument for the spread of information and instruction in the most literate country in the world, print is giving way to all things audiovisual, and its associated schlock. The overwhelmingly influential popular culture is a sewer and is proud of it.

It's not clear what can be done about any of this. The popular culture in particular won't change until such time as the country's cultural elite has a crisis of conscience, assuming, that is, it has a conscience.

Suffice it to say, Lincoln would be confounded that so much of our common life is meant to degrade rather than elevate.

LOOK TO THE FOUNDERS. Lincoln's attitude to the Founders, as discussed earlier, bordered on the worshipful. He spoke of George Washington in his Lyceum address in 1838, and ended with the high-flown hope "[tha]t during his long sleep, we permitted no hostile foot to pass over or desecrate [his] resting place" and "we revered his names to the last." His temperance address a few years later soared even higher. Noting that it was Washington's birthday, he wound up with an extravagant encomium: "Washington is the mightiest name of earth—*long since* mightiest in the cause of civil liberty; *still* mightiest in moral reformation. On that name, a eulogy is expected. It cannot be. To add brightness to the sun, or glory to the name of Washington, is alike impossible. Let none attempt it. In solemn awe pronounce the name, and in its naked deathless splendor, leave it shining on."

Although these youthful sentiments were highly rhetorical, they weren't *entirely* rhetorical. The Founding became even more important to Lincoln's political advocacy as he matured. If Churchill mobilized the English language and sent it into battle, Lincoln did the same with the Founders. His truest blows against his opponents in the 1850s and 1860s were those he struck while wielding the Declaration of Independence. The purposes he identified in the Founders and their handiwork are continually relevant.

He believed that they drew us back to the deepest principles of our republic in the Declaration. And they gave us, of course, our foundational law in the Constitution. At any time and place in American history, there are those who find the Constitution an unacceptable encumbrance to their designs. In Lincoln's day, it was the abolitionists and the secessionists, both coming at the same controversy from opposite directions. For the abolitionists, the Constitution did too much to protect slavery; for the secessionists not enough. The abolitionists condemned the Constitution and sought extraconstitutional action to smite slavery. William Garrison burned the Constitution in 1854, and deemed it an "infamous bargain." The secessionists, on the other hand, left the Union to write their own.

Lincoln had no use for the impatience with the constraints of constitutional government of either of the two opposed forces. During the war, he called the radicals in his own party "the unhandiest devils in the world to deal with," even if "their faces are set Zionwards." Unlike his more heedless friends, he would honor the Constitution even when it obstructed his most cherished ends. In his final speech of the 1858 Senate campaign, he said, accurately enough, "I have neither assailed, nor wrestled with any part of the constitution. The legal right of the Southern people to reclaim their fugitives I have constantly admitted. The legal right of Congress to interfere with the institution in the states, I have constantly denied." When Lincoln issued the Emancipation Proclamation, he did it as an inherently limited war measure. Allen Guelzo notes how he never lost sight of its prospective legal vulnerability once the war ended. He finally looked to the Thirteenth Amendment—an inarguably constitutional measure—as a "King's cure for all the evils."

Lincoln believed in the perpetual vitality of the Founders. They are never dusty, old, or out-of-date. Lincoln embraced change, but always around the central axis established by them. We must constantly rededicate ourselves to their essential principles, to free institutions and to the equality of all men, and if we do, those principles will ensure the vibrancy and justice of our society. "We understood that by what they then did," Lincoln said in Chicago in 1858, "it has followed that the degree of prosperity that we now enjoy has come to us."

Lincoln thought the American system depended ultimately on public opinion. He talked of how if the arguments of Douglas were accepted, it would "tend to rub out the sentiment of liberty in the country." If we ever lose Lincoln's reverence for the Founders, it will tend to do the same, to our detriment and shame.

Lincoln himself is so revered that nearly everyone wants to make a claim on him. And his tradition is capacious enough that nearly everyone can. Democrats make theirs largely on the basis of their positive view of government.

President Obama says that Lincoln understood that government can aid private economic growth and opportunity rather than impede it. About this, he is undeniably correct. On the other hand, it is not true that everything government does aids growth. The liberal fallacy is to believe Lincoln would have favored almost every iteration of government and expansion of it, just as they do. Old-age entitlements funded by young workers that are clearly unsustainable? He'd fight to perpetually expand them. Massive peacetime deficits? All in favor. Government-dominated health care? Why not? Steeply progressive taxes on the rich, justified as a matter of basic justice? Sign him up. Subsidies for farmers? Yes! Perpetually expanding welfare? Absolutely. Costly regulations? Certainly. Red tape obstructing development? But of course.

Lincoln favored an active government, not a blunderbuss government. The debate over the role of government in Lincoln's time was, in large part, over how pro-business it would be. And much of the action was at the state level. It is a grievous mistake to extrapolate from his position in that debate and portray him as an inchoate Great Society liberal, favoring every new federal program and every new business-impeding regulation.

The default of the Democrats is to government action rather than individual initiative, turning Lincoln on his head. Self-reliance is typically translated, in their argot, into the swear phrase of the "you're on your own" society. They style themselves pragmatic problem solvers, yet whatever the problem, the solution is always more government. They in effect want to replicate the ill-fated fiscal experience of Illinois in the 1830s on a much grander scale, with the federal government running trillion-dollar annual deficits and locked into entitlements that promise worse yet to come.

What Lincoln might hate most about our government, the transfers to individuals, including able-bodied, non-elderly adults who should be in the workforce, has been the project of liberal Democrats. They have been on the side of the cultural change that has dethroned the two-parent family, and their allies in the media and the culture scream bloody murder whenever someone suggests the importance of recovering lost mores. They style themselves the party of civil rights, but the concrete expression of this cause is a collection of race-conscious policies. They are champions of a "living Constitution" unmoored from any serious commitment to the document. They believe in a zero-sum economics and, for all their future-oriented rhetoric, protect the structure of government programs as they were handed down to us in the 1930s or 1960s. For Democrats, any line back to Lincoln is interrupted by the rise of progressivism. It is in progressivism, and its default to rule by experts, that modern Democrats have their roots.

Their case for an essential identification with Lincoln comes down, in a nutshell, to the belief that Lincoln would have favored funding high-speed rail. And maybe he would have—if he had precisely the same romance for trains that he had 150 years ago when they were the hot new thing. (There's nothing to be said for the economic merits of high-speed rail.) Regardless, this is a remarkably impoverished understanding of Lincoln. Lots of people have favored subsidies for public works throughout our history. That doesn't make all of them, or really *any* of them, Lincolnian in their understanding of America, or in their deepest purposes.

The immediate objection to any Republican claim on Lincoln, in turn, is the party's record on civil rights. Its presidential standard-bearer in 1964, Barry Goldwater, opposed the 1964 Civil Rights Act (although a greater proportion of Republicans than Democrats voted for it in the House and the Senate). Goldwater had a good civil rights record as a businessman and local politician back in Phoenix. He opposed the federal legislation as a senator out of genuine constitutional concerns. But he and other conservatives opposed to the act on the same grounds missed the most important point. Southern states were in blatant violation of both the Fourteenth and Fifteenth Amendments guaranteeing equal protection under the laws and the right to vote, and Congress had the explicit constitutional power to act.

In the historical context, the Civil Rights Act and its companion, the 1965 Voting Rights Act were the last spasm of the Civil War. The South had frustrated the imposition of black civil rights during Reconstruction in a low-grade insurgency that successfully rumbled on into the 1960s. Black civil rights weren't going to be vindicated anytime soon, absent the application of federal power again. Yes, there was already a people's movement that was having some success against segregation, but without the Civil Rights Act, it probably would have been decades more of repression in the South, and blacks—rightly—weren't willing to wait, nor was the rest of the country willing to make them.

The hostile interpretation of the party's trajectory ever since is that Republicans have held the South based on their implicit racism, that they are the de facto heirs of the segregationist George Wallace. Political scientist Gerard Alexander has written persuasively in opposition to this charge. The Republicans made their first breakthrough in the South at the presidential level not in 1964, but in 1952. That's when Dwight Eisenhower took states on the periphery of the South (Virginia, Florida, Tennessee, and Texas) and Republicans began to make inroads among middle- and upper-income voters associated with the "New South." In 1964, Goldwater prevailed only in the states of the more racially polarized Deep South (and his native Arizona), but this was an exception that didn't represent the pattern of the Republican growth in the South. Over the years, the party tended to over-perform among transplants to the South and younger voters, both groups presumably with more progressive racial views.

"In sum," Alexander writes, "the GOP's Southern electorate was not rural, nativist, less educated, afraid of change, or con-centrated in the most stagnant parts of the Deep South. It was disproportionately suburban, middle-class, educated, younger, non-native-Southern, and concentrated in the growth-points that were, so to speak, the least 'Southern' parts of the South. This is a very strange way to reincarnate George Wallace's movement."

Republicans steadily gained strength in the South in the 1980s and 1990s at the same time that the region shed its racism, and in fact the party didn't win more than half of congressional seats in the South until 1994. The broad trend was that as the region became more prosperous and open, more populated and economically diverse, and less agricultural and bigoted—in short, as it evolved in a direction Lincoln would have wanted long before—it became more Republican.

The other objection to a Republican claim on Lincoln is the contemporary party's libertarian bent, exemplified by its patron saint, Ronald Reagan. His view of government accorded much more with that of Jefferson or Jackson than of Lincoln. Yet, a profoundly humane man and natural storyteller with deep-felt ideas that he communicated with common sense and eloquence, Reagan succeeded brilliantly in Lincolnian terms. He restored the commercial vitality of the country after the stagnation of the 1970s. He was a paladin of individual economic achievement and a friend of the middle class who never scored political points off the rich. He urged staying true to the country's founding documents and grounded his deep-felt patriotism in them. He waged a war for freedom, on a global scale. Reagan left the world freer and the country wealthier and more dynamic in a triumph of statesmanship with deep Lincolnian resonances.

Widening the ambit of opportunity was his goal, just as it was Lincoln's, although the means changed. For Reagan, the task wasn't to leverage government support for the modernizing edge of the American economy but to reform and pare back government so it was no longer blunting that edge. At a time of underdevelopment, Lincoln sought to remove the physical impediments to joining together the national economy; at a time of onerous government, Reagan sought to remove obstacles created by burdensome policies and rank economic mismanagement—on inflation, taxes, and regulation.

Reagan is the default model of contemporary Republicans. He is the Second Founder of the party, and understandably so. But it behooves the party to forge a connection to its original founding figure that has more to it than mere ancestry and annual Lincoln Day dinners.

Today's Republicans will never have Lincoln's positive attitude toward government, nor should they, given that we have a much different *kind* of government today than in the mid-nineteenth century. It is vastly more extensive. It is more exacting and obstructive. It is redistributive. The Republicans are the ones keeping alive a Jacksonian reflex toward negative government, hostility to debt, and hatred for special government favors for the well connected. That is all to the good, and necessary. On the other hand, there are few Republicans today outside of Ron Paul who, in their implicit acceptance of the welfare state, don't support a much greater level of government than Lincoln could have imagined.

Developing a Lincoln-inflected agenda within its limited-government framework is absolutely essential for the party. It has no future unless it is a party of aspiration. It needs Lincoln's emphasis on uplift, delivered in his populist voice. It needs an economic agenda that is broader and deeper than tax cuts. It needs to engage with the struggles of the working class and do it more seriously than in ritualistic denunciations of "elites." It needs to understand that a dynamic capitalist society depends on character, and on character-shaping institutions. Preserving such a society is not merely a matter of limiting government and its dampening effect on enterprise, but of fostering individuals who are disciplined, ambitious, and skilled enough to rise within it. It needs a policy toward the big banks that finds a balance between necessary financial risk-taking and government-backed recklessness, and that communicates that Republicans aren't the tools of Wall Street. It needs to be the party of "the sober, industrious, thriving people."

In short, it needs to become the Party of Lincoln in a sense more meaningful than a long-standing nickname.

The current predicament of the party bears some relation to that of the Whigs, who had to scrape for their presidential victories and faced an adversary, in Andrew Jackson, who had seized on powerful democratic symbols and had a technical advantage in the business of vote-getting. Republicans have won a majority of the popular vote in only one of the last six elections. Demographically, they are swimming upstream, and in important respects they feel stuck in a bygone era—the 1980s—when in fact the world has turned many times since then. Their ability—and sometimes even their desire—to make themselves appealing seems to wane as the task of doing so becomes more urgent in an increasingly treacherous political landscape.

Given its occasional attraction for off-putting rhetoric and suicidal tactical extravagance, the party would be well served to heed the lessons of Lincoln's tone and of his statesmanship. Lincoln was a champion of a kind of nonjudgmental morality. In his temperance address, he extolled the virtues of drunks and defended the point of view of liquor merchants. For all his condemnations of the slave system of the South, he always said that Southerners were just as the rest of us would be in their circumstances. He maintained an unbending moral standard without ever descending into moralism. This is a tricky balance.

Lincoln maintained it partly out of a belief that it was the only way to convince anyone of anything. He said in the temperance address, "When the conduct of men is designed to be influenced, *persuasion*, kind, unassuming persuasion, should ever be adopted. It is an old and a true maxim, that a 'drop of honey catches more flies than a gallon of gall.'" Once he grew out of his "skinnings" that made people cry and his anonymous newspaper articles that brought on duels, he wasn't needlessly inflammatory. He could still be tough and even excoriating, but always to make a point, never simply to wound.

This approach was buttressed by his Madisonian realism about human nature—rarely surprised by human foibles, Lincoln wasn't inclined to be denunciatory about them. A Wisconsin journalist named J. S. Bliss remembered a little incident after Lincoln's election in 1860 but before he had left for Washington that demonstrated the keen insight of a man fully attuned to the ways of the world.

Bliss was with Lincoln in his office at the Capitol in Springfield when Lincoln's son Willie came running in and demanded twenty-five cents to buy candy. The president-elect said he could give him five cents only, which he took out of his vest pocket and put on his desk. Willie stormed off, turning his back forever on the thoroughly unacceptable and insulting five cents. Lincoln predicted his boy would be back. Bliss wondered why. "Because," Lincoln explained, "as soon as he finds I will give him no more he will come and get it." After the matter had been forgotten and as they were conversing, Bliss recounts, "*Willie* came cautiously behind my chair and that of his father—picked up the *Specie*, and went away without saying a word."

On much weightier matters, his judgment was almost as unfailing. Contemporary Republicans—especially the right of the party—can forget that they need prudence along with their principle. Lincoln never did. The genius of his political leadership was how uncompromising he was in his ultimate goal and how compromising he was in the course of getting there. He combined strategic fixity with tactical flexibility (and exactly the same can be said of Ronald Reagan).

He outraged abolitionists and radicals throughout the war by moving against slavery only very cautiously, countermanding orders by commanders on the ground for local emancipations when he thought they would outrage border-state sentiment and jeopardize the larger war effort. Yet his wasn't the prudence of a mushy middle. He was adamant about maintaining the antislavery integrity of the Republicans when Stephen Douglas seemed alluring to party leaders in the East. During the secession winter of 1860–61, when the air in Washington was thick with proposals for compromise, he refused to give away the principle of nonextension of slavery (when push came to shove, he wasn't at bottom a compromiser like Henry Clay). And the war had to be won, despite the terrible human cost, despite the political pressure for a settlement. "I expect to maintain this contest until successful, or till I die, or am conquered, or my term expires, or Congress or the country forsakes me" is not the voice of split-the-difference moderation.

When a political leader has the right touch to know when to push and when to relent, when his ability is joined to a larger purpose, and when that purpose is just and true, well, then, that constitutes statesmanship of the highest order.

Most important for Republicans now is to commit themselves to that larger purpose, a society of equality of opportunity where all can rise. Limiting government, although as important as ever in an era of spiraling debt, can't just be an end in itself. It must be joined to a larger vision of a dynamic, fluid society. The party shouldn't only be the party of low taxes, but of affordable health care and education. It should identify with the economic interests of the middle class more than of its richest donors and make it clear that it doesn't believe that everyone is an entrepreneur or budding entrepreneur, that it knows most people are ordinary wage and salary earners and they, too, have a place in the party's imagination. It should speak to the poor, not because it will ever win many of their votes, but so there's no mistake that it wants them up and out of poverty and in the American mainstream.

An agenda of uplift is in the party's direct electoral interest. If it can forge a more pocketbook- and aspiration-oriented economics, it will have a better chance of appealing to Latino voters. As a general matter, the better off people are, the more likely they are to vote Republican. If they are married, they are more likely to vote Republican. The party benefits if it can help create and sustain as many middle-class families as possible.

I believe that the Republican Party of today would, still and all, be the best vehicle for Abraham Lincoln. I'm not disinterested, though. I confess to a love for Lincoln. I can sense the rigor of thought of my late, great boss William F. Buckley Jr.—not to mention the wit and the taste for rhetorical combat—in his slashing polemics. Any writer or editor should relish that the first step Lincoln took to improve himself was to pick up a book, and that he counted the printing press as one of the world's greatest inventions. No matter how often I delve into it, I don't tire of the story of his rise. It is so American it should be draped in red, white, and blue bunting. In its essence, it is about the achievement of human potential, and all the more inspiring because it enabled him, in time, to devote himself to making it possible for others, too, to reach for their potential.

I look to Lincoln and think, "I want my party—his party—to be like *that*," to identify with workers and families, to propose a compelling agenda to advance their interests, to sell it with a winsome populist touch, to be pure in principle but wise as serpents in execution, to make the bedrock of it all the Declaration and the Founding and the truth of the equality of all men. This is asking a lot and perhaps it's more something to be "constantly labored for" than ever achieved. But it will never happen if Republicans don't value Lincoln and understand him as they should.

Whatever either or both parties do now, we shouldn't mistake the scale of our task. It is no longer the mid-twentieth century, and there is no way to magically transplant ourselves back to it. We have to manage in a much less forgiving environment, where we aren't the last economy standing after a global cataclysm and where, even in the best case, some people are going to have a much harder time than they would have had fifty years ago. What

we need, in a nutshell, is more rigor. We need it both from institutions and from individuals, and despite the formidable obstacles:
Reforming the economy and government will mean overcoming
the powerful pull of inertia; improving education will require
besting entrenched interests deeply vested in the status quo; and
restoring the national character will test the regenerative capacity
of American culture.

In the spirit of Lincoln, our project should be equal parts
modernization (opening the vistas of the economic future) and
recovery (of the American character and of bourgeois virtues).
After all this time, Lincoln's intellectual and moral case for the inherent worth of individual initiative, and for our free institutions
and free economy as the foundations for it, is as important as ever.
Lincoln's enduring relevance is in his embodiment, expression,
and realization of the American Dream. Nearly two centuries
ago, a boy picked up an axe and imagined something better. Fired
by ambition for himself and eventually for others, he made his
way in the world, and then changed it. He saved the republic and
did all he could to make it a bustling empire of commerce, the
hotbed of millions of dreams, schemes, and aspirations.

Across all the decades and despite all the momentous changes,
we still live in that republic. In 1861, Lincoln told Congress, "The
struggle of today is not altogether for today—it is for a vast future
also." That future was our windfall. We diminish and squander
it at the risk of losing what it means to be American, and losing
touch with the wellsprings of human accomplishment. It is up
to us. In how we react to the new challenges to the American
Dream, we shall nobly save, or meanly lose, what Lincoln and
generations of patriots bequeathed to us.

Notes

A note on the notes: These endnotes are not exhaustive. This is not an academic book. But I wanted to be sure to give readers enough information so they know where to go to find out more, and also to be sure to fully acknowledge my debt to all those professional historians on whose work I depended.

INTRODUCTION

3   "the hardest set of men he ever saw": Benjamin P. Thomas, *Lincoln's New Salem* (Carbondale, IL: Southern Illinois University Press, 1988), 79.

3   "Go to the devil, sir!": Michael Burlingame, *Abraham Lincoln: A Life* (Baltimore: The Johns Hopkins University Press, 2008), 67.

6   a trend that holds across the Western world: Peter Wehner and Robert P. Beschel Jr., "How to Think about Inequality," *National Affairs* 11 (Spring 2012), 94–114.

6   Men with only a high-school diploma: Scott Winship, "Nobel Laureate Joseph Stiglitz is All Sorts of Wrong on Inequality," *The Empiricist Strikes Back*, April 9, 2011, http://www.scottwinship.com/1/post/2011/4/nobel-laureate-joseph-stiglitz-is-all-sorts-of-wrong-on-inequality.html.

6   not quite the highly mobile society: Scott Winship, "Mobility Impaired," *National Review*, November 14, 2011, 30–33.

7   Social capital: W. Bradford Wilcox and Elizabeth Marquardt, eds., "When Marriage Disappears: The New Middle America," *The State*

of Our Unions: 2010 (Charlottesville, VA: National Marriage Project and Institute for American Values, 2010).

8   "Well, Governor": Merrill D. Peterson, *Lincoln in American Memory* (New York: Oxford University Press, 1994), 10.

9   One of the more egregious examples: Mario Cuomo, *Why Lincoln Matters: Today More Than Ever* (Orlando: Harcourt, 2004).

10   "Lincoln's legitimate offspring": Willmoore Kendall, "Source of American Caesarism," *National Review*, November 7, 1959, 461-62.

10   Lincoln inflicted: Frank S. Meyer, "Lincoln without Rhetoric," *National Review*, August 24, 1965, 725-27.

10   why Lincoln didn't forestall: John Hawkins, "An Interview with Ron Paul," *Right Wing News*, March 31, 2010, http://www.right-wingnews.com/interviews/an-interview-with-ron-paul/.

11   to protect human bondage: Thomas L. Krannawitter, *Vindicating Lincoln: Defending the Politics of Our Greatest President* (Lanham, MD: Rowman & Littlefield, 2008), 292, 230-31. He has a good discussion of all the issues, and pushes back against the conservative critics in his chapters "Was the Civil War Caused by Slavery or Economics?" and "Was Lincoln the Father of Big Government?"

12   gigantic privatization: I draw on the arguments Guelzo makes in an informative Heritage Foundation paper called "Abraham Lincoln or the Progressives: Who was the *real* father of big government?" *The Heritage Foundation*, February 10, 2012, http://www.heritage.org/research/reports/2012/02/abraham-lincoln-was-not-the-father-of-big-government.

15   unstoppable dynamo of economic development: Kevin Phillips in *The Cousins' Wars: Religion, Politics, Civil Warfare, and the Triumph of Anglo-America* (New York: Basic Books, 1999), 470, and Paul Kennedy in *The Rise and Fall of the Great Powers* (New York: Random House, 1987), 200-01, 423, both have useful discussions of the growth of post-Civil War America.

CHAPTER I

Notes

18   "more hopeful and confident": F.B. Carpenter, *Six Months at the White House with Abraham Lincoln* (New York: Hurd and Houghton, 1866), 97–98.

20   "My how he could chop": Louis A. Warren, *Lincoln's Youth: Indiana Years, Seven to Twenty-One, 1816-1830* (Indianapolis: Indiana Historical Society, 1959), 142–43. Facts drawn from this book are sprinkled throughout the chapter.

20   "back side of this world": Burlingame, *A Life*, 17.

21   "from the days of the Phoenicians": George Rogers Taylor, *The Transportation Revolution, 1815-1860* (White Plains, NY: M.E. Sharpe, Inc., 1951), 5. The beginning of Taylor, 3-6, has a rundown of conditions in the early 19th century. So does Bruce Levine, *Half Slave and Half Free: The Roots of Civil War* (New York: Hill and Wang, 2005), 51–56.

23   "a marvel of learning": Warren, *Youth*, 25.

24   "when a mere child": Burlingame, *A Life*, 37.

25   a restless and seeking mind: Burlingame, *A Life*, 45, and Daniel Walker Howe, *Making the American Self: Jonathan Edwards to Abraham Lincoln* (New York: Oxford University Press, 2009), 138. They both recount memories of Lincoln's early ambition.

25   "Honest Thomas": David Herbert Donald, *Lincoln* (New York: Touchstone, 1996), 21-26, 33, and William Lee Miller, *Lincoln's Virtues: An Ethical Biography* (New York: Knopf, 2002), 68-71. They both have details about Thomas. So do Warren's *Youth*, 10-19, 193, and Burlingame's *A Life*, 2-26.

28   Lincoln's great-grandfather: Facts about Lincoln's ancestors are drawn from Mark E. Neely Jr.'s *The Last Best Hope of Earth: Abraham Lincoln and The Promise of America* (Cambridge, MA: Harvard University Press, 1993), 2-3, and Donald's *Lincoln,* 21.

28   Despite much adversity: Donald's *Lincoln*, 22, and Warren's *Youth*, 86, 115, 121.

29   rural isolation: Warren's *Youth*, 23, 41, and Burlingame's *A Life*, 23, describe just how isolated.

30   "no market for nothing": Michael Burlingame, *The Inner World of Abraham Lincoln* (Chicago: University of Illinois Press, 1994), 41.

Notes

30   The "rusticity": Jean H. Baker, *" 'Not Much of Me' ": Abraham Lincoln as a Typical American* (Fort Wayne, IN: Louis A. Warren Lincoln Library and Museum, 1988), 7.

30   "The son's ambitions juxtaposed": Howe, *Making*, 138–39.

31   a tiny schoolhouse: Burlingame's *A Life*, 18–19, 30–34, has a detailed description of the schools and Lincoln's early diligence. So does Warren, *Youth*, 83.

34   He read the Bible: Warren's *Youth*, 21–31, 76–80, 105, 212, provides an exhaustive account of his reading. Burlingame's *A Life*, 36–45, does as well. Douglas L. Wilson, *Honor's Voice: The Transformation of Abraham Lincoln* (New York: Vintage Books, 1998), 57, and Donald's *Lincoln*, 33, describe opposition to Lincoln's reading from those around him.

36   hire Lincoln out: Donald's *Lincoln*, 32, 43, and Burlingame's *A Life*, 42–44, recount his youthful working life.

37   "we were all slaves": Burlingame, *Inner*, 36.

37   maximum height for a stump: Taylor's *Transportation*, 15, 56–64, 143, 158, authoritatively describes the changes wrought by the coming of the steamboat.

38   the riverine commercial current: Warren's *Youth*, 144–49, is especially good on Lincoln and the rivers. He tells the story of Lincoln's flatboat trip with Gentry, 182–86.

39   Two yoke of oxen: Ibid, 207.

40   "He never once": Burlingame, *A Life*, 10.

40   the merchant Denton Offutt: Ibid, 52–57. I draw on Burlingame's account of Lincoln and Offutt.

41   People moved into Illinois: Thomas, *New Salem*, 12–41. His book on Lincoln's new home is a little gem.

42   running strongman contest on the frontier: Wilson's *Voice*, 142–43, 67, describes his physicality and his humor. Burlingame's *A Life*, 78, has the story about Johnson Elmore. Thomas's *New Salem*, 67, has the story of Babb McNabb's rooster.

43   *"only plenty of friends"*: Donald, *Lincoln*, 42.

43   "how rapidly his life opens": Miller, *Virtues*, 24.

Notes

43   convinced him to run: Donald, *Lincoln*, 41. Burlingame's *A Life*, 71, has the uncouth quote.

43   become a viable throughway: Allen C. Guelzo, *Abraham Lincoln: Redeemer President* (Grand Rapids, MI: Eerdmans, 1999), 43–48. Donald's *Lincoln*, 41–42, Burlingame's *A Life*, 66, Thomas's *New Salem*, 72–76, and Wilson's *Voice*, 87–88, also take up the saga of the Sangamon.

45   revolutionary economic potential: Levine's *Half*, 54, explains why.

46   eighth out of thirteen: Donald's *Lincoln*, 42–46, and Neely, *Best Hope*, 8, describe his first campaign.

46   the local postmaster: Thomas's *New Salem*, 94–112, has many of the charming details in this passage about Lincoln's early employment.

47   ran again for the legislature: Donald's *Lincoln*, 52–55, and Wilson's *Voice*, 151–71, report many of the facts and incidents in this passage.

49   "Grammar is divided into four parts": Wilson's *Voice*, 63–67, is good on Lincoln's study of grammar.

50   "all the teaching of grammar": Thomas, *New Salem*, 69–70.

50   "bustle, business, energy": Brian R. Dirck, *Lincoln the Lawyer* (Champaign: University of Illinois Press, 2008), 15–17. He explains well the culture of the law at this time and what drew Lincoln to the profession. Wilson's *Voice*, 101, and Burlingame's *A Life* tell the story of Bowling Green. Donald's *Lincoln*, 45–54, describes how Lincoln began to take up the study of the law.

52   for hewing timbers: Burlingame, *A Life*, 6.

52   "He used to be a slave": Burlingame, *Inner*, 36.

Chapter 2

54   never elected a governor or senator: Eric Foner's *The Fiery Trial: Abraham Lincoln and American Slavery* (New York: W. W. Norton, 2010), 33–34, describes the Whig struggles in Illinois.

55   lampooned another party-switcher: Burlingame, *A Life*, 157–58.

56   Whig during the entire existence of the party: Miller, *Virtues*, 106.

57   gentleman farmer from Kentucky: Daniel Walker Howe, *The Po-*

litical Culture of the American Whigs (Chicago: University of Chicago Press, 1984), 2-18, 123-37, Gabor S. Boritt's *Lincoln and the Economics of the American Dream* (Memphis, Tenn: Memphis State University Press, 1978), 99, and Guelzo's *Redeemer*, 53-57, discuss Clay and the broader Whig attitude.

57   "self-made man": "Mr. Clay's Speech," *Niles' Weekly Register*, vol. XLII (March 3, 1832), 11.

59   within the dominant Jeffersonian Republicans: Michael F. Holt, *The Rise and Fall of the American Whig Party: Jacksonian Politics and the Onset of the Civil War* (New York: Oxford University Press, 1999), 2-3. His book is encyclopedic. I rely on its opening sections for the story of the emergence of the Whigs, as well as Daniel Walker Howe's *What God Hath Wrought: The Transformation of America, 1815-1848* (New York: Oxford University Press, 2007).

64   "refusals, rejections, and disengagements": Miller, *Virtues*, 26.

65   couldn't work for days: Burlingame, *A Life*, 36.

65   "Throughout the nation": Holt, *American Whig*, 83.

66   "the vast majority of wealthy businessmen": Ibid.

66   the slave owner and gambler: For the contrasting depictions of Jackson and Clay, I draw on Howe's *Hath Wrought*, 248-49, 329-30, and Howe's *Political Culture*, 125-27.

67   "more civilized way of life": Howe, *Political Culture*, 266.

68   an aid to labor: Thomas, *New Salem*, 48-49.

68   "Those who have no vices": Burlingame, *A Life*, 301.

69   "By jings": Burlingame, *A Life*, 5.

69   a matter of honor: Wilson, *Voice*, 295. He is particularly instructive on the culture of fighting.

73   it is a *temperate* temperance address: Harry V. Jaffa, *Crisis of the House Divided: An Interpretation of the Issues in the Lincoln-Douglas Debates* (Chicago: The University of Chicago Press, 1959), 247-48.

74   "self-control, order, rationality": Howe, *Political Culture*, 269.

78   "old" when he was still: Burlingame, *A Life*, 249.

78   At his law office: Donald, *Lincoln*, 101.

78   "Women are the only things": Burlingame, *A Life*, 97.

Notes

79 who had learned French: Burlingame, *A Life*, 176.

80 impressive catalogue: Miller, *Virtues*, 95.

81 "then commenced the drinking": Thomas Ford, *A History of Illinois: From Its Commencement as a State in 1814 to 1847* (Carlisle, MA: Applewood Books, 1854), 104–05.

81 hoopla and revelry: On the hoopla and revelry of the Harrison campaign: Holt, *American Whig*, 106–07, and Wilson's *Voice*, 212–13. On the petty violence of politics: Burlingame, *A Life*, 95, 139–42. On Lincoln's "skinnings": Wilson's *Voice*, 206–09, and Burlingame, *A Life*, 156. On the near–duel with Shields: Wilson's *Voice*, 265–81 and Burlingame's *A Life*, 191–94.

81 "such a jollification": Thomas D. Logan, "Lincoln, the Early Temperance Reformer," *The Standard* newspaper, February 6, 1909.

85 hired French chefs: Holt's *American Whig*, 107, and Howe's *Hath Wrought*, 575, and Burlingame's *A Life*, 149–55, detail the assault on Van Buren.

CHAPTER 3

87 fought desperately: Burlingame's *A Life*, 138, 162, has the background to this episode. The Democratic newspaper's ridicule of Lincoln is in Boritt's *American Dream*, 55.

90 "the optimism of Western Civilization": Boritt, *American Dream*, 71.

90 "to use it as he will": For the economic thought of Carey and Wayland, I rely on Heather Cox Richardson's *The Greatest Nation of the Earth: Republican Economic Policies During the Civil War* (Cambridge, MA: Harvard University Press, 1997), 19–23, Guelzo's *Redeemer*, 107–08, Boritt's *American Dream*, 123–24, and Eric Foner's *Free Soil, Free Labor, Free Men: The Ideology of Republican Party before the Civil War* (New York: Oxford University Press, 1970), 36–39.

91 "The importance of property": Boritt, *American Dream*, 124.

92 "The next Sunday morning": Olivier Fraysse, trans. Sylvia Neely, *Lincoln, Land, and Labor, 1809-60* (Champaign, IL: University of Illinois Press, 1994), 8.

92   a frustrated engineer: Burlingame, *A Life, Vol. 2*, 292–93.

94   "grand moral struggle": Howe, *Political Culture*, 69.

94   wholly inappropriate in the frontier context: On Thomas Lincoln's trouble with land titles, there are details in Thomas Crump's *Abraham Lincoln's World: How Riverboats, Railroads, and Republicans Transformed America* (New York: Continuum, 2009), 13. Also, in Guelzo's *Redeemer*, 29, Fraysse's *Land, and Labor*, 10–19, and Burlingame's *A Life*, 20.

96   new links of transportation: The national debate over infrastructure in this period is catalogued in Adam J. White's "Infrastructure and American History," *The New Atlantis* 35 (Spring 2012), 3–31. It is also discussed in Charles Sellers's *The Market Revolution: Jacksonian America, 1815-1846* (New York: Oxford University Press, 1994), 77, and Howe's *Hath Wrought*, 357–60.

97   loomed large in his early life: On Lincoln's early difficulties with transportation, I rely on Foner's *Fiery*, 36, Neely's *Best Hope*, Fraysse's *Land, and Labor*, and Burlingame's *A Life*, 128 and 325–27.

97   chartering private transportation companies: John H. Krenkel, *Illinois Internal Improvements: 1818-1848* (Cedar Rapids, IA: The Torch Press, 1958), 61. This book provided helpful background on the Illinois infrastructure debate.

98   "the great depot and warehouse": I draw on Sellers's *Market Revolution*, 42–43, and Taylor's *Transportation*, 32–49, for facts and figures about the Erie Canal. Boritt's *American Dream*, 7, recounts the impact on Illinois.

99   Passed in early 1837: For the course of the System, I draw on Krenkel's *Illinois Internal Improvements*, 75, 146–55, 200–16, Boritt's *American Dream*, 8, 26–31, Burlingame's *A Life*, 92–146, and Donald's *Lincoln*, 61–62.

103 the legislature created a state: George William Dowrie, *The Development of Banking in Illinois, 1817-1863* (Urbana, IL: University of Illinois, 1913). This book is an exhaustive account of banking in Illinois in this period. I also rely on Boritt's *American Dream*, 15–21, 60. Louis M. Hacker, *The Triumph of American Capitalism* (New York: Simon and Schuster, 1940), 334, discusses the state of currency in the

country overall. So do John Steele Gordon's *Empire of Wealth: The Epic History of American Economic Power* (New York: HarperCollins, 2004), 184, and Richardson's *Greatest,* 67. Howe's *Hath Wrought,* 394, 506-07, describes Jackson and Van Buren policies. Burlingame's *A Life* has the story of the sale of the horse.

106   disregarding the interests of people: Howe's *Hath Wrought,* 274, 395, 408, has the larger political context of the tariff debate.

108   His work as a lawyer: Dirck's *Lawyer,* 37-49, Donald's *Lincoln,* 70, 145-47, Guelzo's *Redeemer,* 147-48, and Burlingame's *A Life,* 332-33, all have colorful details on Lincoln as a lawyer. Henry Clay Whitney, *Life on the Circuit with Lincoln,* (Boston: Estes and Lauriat, 1892), 178, had the ripped pants story. I drew on the searchable database of Lincoln's legal work, http://www.lawpracticeofabrahamlincoln.org, for the early, inconsequential cases and also for the section on the railroad cases that follows.

110   a key advocate for the railroads: For Lincoln and the railroads: Guelzo's *Redeemer,* 167-72, Burlingame's *A Life,* 336-37, Donald's *Lincoln,* 155-57, and Crump's *World,* 34, 81. Charles Leroy Brown's "Abraham Lincoln and the Illinois Central Railroad, 1857-1860," *Journal of the Illinois State Historical Society* 36:2 (June 1943), 121-63, tells the tale of the rise of the Illinois Central.

113   "with stock-jobbers": Neely, *Last Best Hope,* 10.

113   "lawyers and bankers": Guelzo's "Abraham Lincoln or the Progressives."

114   his *Junius Tracts*: Calvin Colton, *The Junius Tracts* (New York: Greeley & McElrath, 1844), 104-05, 111.

116   "within the reach": Louis Hartz, "Government-Business Relations," *Economic Change in the Civil War Era,* eds. David T. Gilchrist & David Lewis (Greenville, DE: Eleutherian Mills-Hagley Foundation, 1965), 84.

116   steadily vindicated in Illinois: I rely largely on Taylor's highly informative *Transportation Revolution* in this passage, 48-55, 74-75, 84-85, 102-03, and 158-64.

118   the Northern "enemy": Boritt, *American Dream,* 167.

119   They reliably fed factories: The data about the larger economic effects

of the railroads is derived from Alfred D. Chandler Jr., "The Organization of Manufacturing and Transportation," *Economic Change in the Civil War Era*, 137-51.

119 "there is more poetry": Gordon, *Empire*, 218.

119 "counter to the pre-existing order of things": Richard White, *Railroaded: The Transcontinentals and the Making of Modern America* (New York: W. W. Norton, 2011), xxii.

119 farmers needed cash: Levine, *Half*, 55. Levine has a very good rundown of these trends in his chapter "Each Person Works for Himself."

120 Chicago exploded: On these epic changes: Crump's *World*, 74, Guelzo's *Redeemer*, 168, Chandler's *Economic Change in the Civil War Era*, 139, Foner's *Fiery*, 83, Taylor's *Transportation*, 9-10, and Fraysse's *Land, and Labor*, 137.

121 "The West is agricultural": Boritt, *American Dream*, 126.

121 must have had contempt: Ibid., 166.

121 "dividing line in point of time": Foner, *Fiery*, 83, and Guelzo, *Redeemer*, 47.

CHAPTER 4

127 campaign strategy memo: Don E. Fehrenbacher, *Prelude to Greatness: Lincoln in the 1850s* (Palo Alto, CA.: Stanford University Press, 1962), 73. This is a trenchant and authoritative account of this phase of Lincoln's career, and I come back to it throughout this chapter.

129 "more natural advantages": Roy Morris Jr., *The Long Pursuit: Abraham Lincoln's Thirty Year Struggle with Stephen Douglas for the Heart and Soul of America* (New York: HarperCollins, 2008), 12. This book is useful on Douglas, as is Allen C. Guelzo's *Lincoln and Douglas: The Debates that Defined America* (New York: Simon & Schuster Paperbacks, 2008), which I come back to often in this chapter. I draw on their opening sections here.

134 main chance: I benefited from Lewis E. Lerhman's cogent discussion of all this in his valuable *Lincoln at Peoria: The Turning Point* (Mechan-

icsburg, PA: Stackpole Books, 2008), 73-77. Also, I draw on David M. Potter's *The Impending Crisis: 1848-1861* (New York: Harper and Row, 1976), 165-66. It is an impressive political history of this period and I come back to it several times in this chapter.

135 would emerge ascendant: On the role of the Know-Nothings, I draw on Robert William Fogel's *Without Consent or Contract: The Rise and Fall of American Slavery* (New York: W. W. Norton, 1994), 374-78. William E. Gienapp's *The Origins of the Republican Party, 1852-1856* (New York: Oxford University Press, 1987), 360, notes how Republicans tapped into anti-aristocratic sentiment.

136 a Southern phenomenon: For the figures on slavery in America, I rely on Levine's *Half*, 20–22, and Fogel's *Without Consent*, 29–30. James M. McPherson's *Abraham Lincoln and the Second American Revolution* (New York: Oxford University Press, 1991), 17, and Foner's *Fiery*, 17, discuss the economic value of slaves. Nevins's *The Emergence of Lincoln: Prologue to Civil War, 1859–1861* (New York: Charles Scribner's Sons, 1950), 59–60, 140–42, contrasts the South's stalwart defense of slavery with slavery's retreat elsewhere in the world. John McCardell's *The Idea of a Southern Nation: Southern Nationalists and Southern Nationalism, 1830–1860* (New York: W. W. Norton, 1981), 231–36, 251–55, recounts the South's expansionist impulse.

137 to spread slavery: McCardell, *Southern Nation*, 231-36 and 251-55.

137 a somewhat attenuated one: The first chapter of Foner's *Fiery*, " 'I Am Naturally Anti-Slavery': Young Abraham Lincoln and Slavery" has an excellent summation of Lincoln's early grappling with slavery and Fraysse's *Land, and Labor*, 4-15, discusses his youth in this context.

139 Even after Kansas-Nebraska: Lehrman's *Peoria*, 111-12, discusses Lincoln's skepticism of the natural-limits argument. Fogel's *Without Consent*, 401-02, notes the political double-edge of the nonextension position.

139 became the focus of his public advocacy: Foner's *Fiery*, 64-65, notes how Lincoln's advocacy kicked into a higher gear after Kansas-Nebraska, and 97 recounts the rejection by some Southern thinkers

of the Declaration. Douglas L. Wilson's *Lincoln before Washington: New Perspectives on the Illinois Years* (Chicago: University of Illinois Press, 1998) has an instructive chapter on "Lincoln's Declaration." Merrill D. Peterson, *"This Grand Pertinacity": Abraham Lincoln and the Declaration of Independence* (Fort Wayne, IN: The Lincoln Museum, 1991) is a useful essay. Guelzo's *Redeemer*, 4, is excellent on Lincoln and Jefferson.

144   "being all the workmanship": John Locke, *Two Treatises of Government and A Letter Concerning Toleration* (Stilwell, KS, Digireads.com, 2005), 73, 80.

145   "Free labor ideology": Bradford William Short, "The Question of the Constitutional Case against Suicide: An Historiographical and Originalist Inquiry into the Degree to Which the Theory of the Inalienable Right to Life and Liberty is Enforced by the Thirteenth Amendment," *Issues in Law & Medicine*, Vol. 26, No. 2 (2010): 91-195.

145   "a dynamic, expanding capitalist society": Foner, *Free Soil*, 11.

145   the development of proslavery: McCardell's *Southern Nation*, 50-86, informs the discussion of Southern proslavery ideology in this paragraph and the ones following.

146   the rise of wage labor: Foner's *Free Soil* is the source of the material on the debate over wage labor and primarily its opening essay, "The Idea of Free Labor in Nineteenth-Century America," but also 66-67.

149   Neither was quite right: The discussion of the economics of slavery is based on Fogel's *Without Consent*, 24–28, 64–88, 91–92. Also helpful are McCardell's *Southern Nation*, 91–127, Eugene Genovese's *The Political Economy of Slavery: Studies in the Economy and Society of the Slave South* (Middletown, CT: Wesleyan University Press, 1961), 24–28, and Douglass C. North's *The Economic Growth of the United States, 1790–1860* (Englewood Cliffs, NJ: Prentice Hall, Inc., 1961), 133.

150   one-third as many public schools: North, *Economic Growth*, 133.

151   raged much more widely: Fehrenbacher's *Prelude*, 100-07, Guelzo's *Lincoln and Douglas*, 75-106, 153-54, 164, 189, 213, and Burlingame's *A Life*, 473, all have telling and vivid details about the pageantry and the circumstances surrounding the debates.

158 into the Gulf States: Foner's *Fiery*, 72, spells out the mixed record after the Founding.
159 Louisiana generously passed a law: Nevins's *Emergence*, 151-52, and Fogel's *Without Consent*, 398, describe the crackdown.
162 banned blacks: Foner's *Fiery*, 8-13, and Burlingame's *A Life*, 104, recount the anti-black laws of states where Lincoln resided.
164 More people voted: Fehrenbacher's *Prelude*, 114-15, describes the results.

CHAPTER 5

167 wrote the first draft: Burlingame, *A Life, Vol. 2*, 738.
168 the South felt squeezed: McCardell's *Southern Nation*, 23, Michael Lind's *Land of Promise: An Economic History of the United States* (New York: HarperCollins, 2012), 121–33, and Walter A. McDougall's *Throes of Democracy: The American Civil War Era, 1829–1877* (New York: HarperCollins, 2007), 340, recount the demographic shift against the South.
169 "a cordon of free States": Richard Franklin Bensel's *Yankee Leviathan: The Origins of Central State Authority in America, 1859–1877* (Cambridge, Press Syndicate of the University of Cambridge, 1990), 20–31, 65–66, and Levine's *Half*, 42–44, as well as Nevin's *Emergence*, 334, and McDougall's *Throes*, 397, spell out the South's fear, vulnerabilities, and priorities.
170 King Cotton: Charles A. and Mary R. Beard, *The Rise of American Civilization* (New York: MacMillan Company, 1927), 55-56, and Mark Thornton and Robert B. Ekelund Jr., *Tariffs, Blockades, and Inflation: The Economics of the Civil War* (Wilmington, DE: Scholarly Resources Inc., 2004), 30-31, describe the nature and extent of the cotton economy, as do Taylor's *Transportation*, 185-86, and Levine's *Half*, 21.
171 The grass didn't grow: I draw on the comparative statistics in Richard N. Current's "God and the Strongest Battalions," in *Why the North Won the Civil War*, ed. David Herbert Donald (New York: Simon & Schuster Paperbacks, 1996), 21. Also, those in Levine's *Half*, 41, 70, the Beards' *American Civilization*, 55, Crump's *World*, 127, and

Kennedy's *Rise*, 180.

172   "a free-labor empire": McDougall, *Throes*, 399-400.

172   "widen and defend": Hacker, *Triumph*, 336.

172   a transcontinental railroad: Although I draw on others, the most important source in this passage is Heather Cox Richardson's *Greatest*, chapter six, " 'It Was Statemanship to Give Treeless Prairies Value': The Transcontinental Railroad."

174   the nation's banking: Bensel in his chapter, "Gold, greenbacks, and the political economy of finance capital after the Civil War," and Richardson in her chapter, " 'A Centralization of Power Such as Hamilton Might Have Eulogised as Magificent': Monetary Legislation," are important sources for this section. I also found helpful Richard H. Timberlake, *Monetary Policy in the United States: An Intellectual and Institutional History* (Chicago: The University of Chicago Press, 1993).

175   a sweeping protective tariff: Again, Richardson is an important source in this section, this time in her chapter, " 'Directing the Legislation of the Country to the Improvement of the Country': Tariff and Tax Legislation."

176   a land-grant college bill: Richardson's chapter " 'A Large Crop is More Than a Great Victory': Agricultural Legislation" is a source of this passage, as well as Dennis W. Johnson, *The Laws That Shaped America: Fifteen Acts of Congress and Their Lasting Impact* (New York: Routledge, 2009) and his chapter, "The Promise of Land: The Homestead Act of 1862 and the Morrill Land-Grant College Act of 1862."

177   the Homestead Act: The same chapters of Richardson and Johnson apply here, too. Burlingame's *A Life*, 51, makes the point that Lincoln was never a great enthusiast for the reform. Fogel's *Without Consent*, 350-52, and Bensel's *Yankee*, 73, are good on the Southern opposition.

179   ran free of government controls: Bensel's *Yankee* makes a persuasive case, 94-98.

179   bureaucratic control and government expropriation: Bensel's *Yankee* describes this in detail in the chapter, "War Mobilization and state formation in the northern Union and the southern Confederacy." It is

Notes

also a thread in the Richard Current chapter "God and the Strongest Battalions," and Thornton and Ekelund's, *Tariffs*.

180   "One of the great ironies": Bensel, *Yankee*, 13-14.

180   as well as could be expected: McDougall's *Throes*, 445-46, describes the calamitous state of the Confederate economy. Thornton and Ekelund's *Tariffs* discusses the inflation, 59, 74-75. Phillips's *Cousins*, 477-78, and McPherson's *Second*, 38, catalogue the devastation wrought in the South by the war, as does Gordon's *Empire*, 202.

181   The North's advantages: Kennedy's *Rise*, 179-81, and McDougall's *Throes*, 455, 494, catalogue the continued growth of the North.

182   alternative future of a Slave South: Fogel's *Without Consent* has a fascinating counter-factual analysis of what Southern victory would have meant, 413-16. Phillips's *Cousins*, 462-63, and McDougall's *Throes*, 454, detail the disastrous political consequences of the war for the South.

184   began to retreat: Gordon's *Empire*, 194, 272, has many of the facts and figures about government receding after the war.

184   "the nation's credit base": Hacker, *Triumph*, 361.

184   to the head of the class: In this latter part of the chapter I draw extensively on Walter Licht, *Industrializing America: The Nineteenth Century* (Baltimore: The Johns Hopkins University Press, 1995). Licht's *Industrializing*, xiv, 102, 127, the Beards' *American Civilization, Vol. 2*, 176, 206-08, and Phillips's *Cousins*, 466-69, describe the extent of the country's post-war growth.

185   drew people to the land: Johnson's *Laws*, 94, 100-02, reports the effects of the Homestead Act and the Land-Grant College Act.

185   to conquer the continent: White's *Railroaded* is a contrarian take on the growth of the railroads but is extremely well-informed. This passage draws on material from the first 60 pages or so. The Beards' *American Civilization, Vol. 2*, 136-37, details the lavish government support, as does Hacker's *Triumph*, 371. Phillips's *Cousins*, 469, Bensel's *Yankee*, 252, 308, and Licht's *Industrializing*, 82, describe the growth of the network during the latter half of the century. White's *Railroaded*, 393, and Lind's *Promise*, 154, tell the tale of the bust later

in the century. Finally, Lind's *Promise*, 153, Licht's *Industrializing*, 82, 152, McDougall's *Throes*, 555, and Gordon's *Empire*, 235–36, report the economic benefits of the new railway network.

187   "the western front out on the Pacific": Beard, *American Civilization, Vol. 2*, 135–36.

187   A revolution swept: For many of the facts in this passage I turned to Licht's *Industrializing* chapter "The Rise of Big Business." Bensel's *Yankee*, 249–53, and Gordon's *Empire*, 232, cover the rise of American finance.

188   the new breed: Hacker's *Triumph* has a terrific treatment of Carnegie, 413–24. I also draw on Gordon's *Empire*, 249, and Lind's *Promise*, 163.

189   outside the mainstream: My main source for the discussion of the travails of the post-war South is Licht's *Industrializing*, 118–23.

191   The top 1 percent: Licht's *Industrializing* discusses income distribution, 183–85. Charles R. Morris's *The Dawn of Innovation: The First American Industrial Revolution* (New York: PublicAffairs, 2012) discusses mobility, 285.

191   "not consciously aware": Hacker, *Triumph*, 339.

192   "prodigious industrial expansion": Fraysse, *Land, and Labor*, 184.

192   "the triumph of the northern bourgeoisie": Howe, *Political Culture*, 297.

192   certainly thought and said so: David Herbert Donald, "Getting Right with Lincoln," *The Atlantic*, 1956, http://www.theatlantic.com/past/docs/issues/95nov/lincoln/lincrite.htm.

194   a natural enlistee to progressivism: Krannawitter's *Vindicating* debunks the progressive case for Lincoln, 294–304.

CHAPTER 6

199   Foreign visitors in: Morris's *Dawn* has a good rundown of these quotes, 159–72.

200   Striving is desirable: Charles Murray, *In Pursuit: Of Happiness and Good Government* (San Francisco: ICS Press, 1994), 140–243, and Arthur C. Brooks, *Gross National Happiness: Why Happiness Matters*

Notes

for America and How We·Can Get More of It (New York: Basic Books, 2008), chapter seven.

201   the sunny uplands: James T. Patterson, *Grand Expectations: The United States, 1945–1974* (New York: Oxford University Press, 1996) has much of this data, 61-77.

201   couldn't and didn't last: Luigi Zingales, *A Capitalism for the People: Recapturing the Lost Genius of American Prosperity* (New York: Basic Books, 2012), 110, makes this argument. Tyler Cowen, *The Great Stagnation: How America Ate All the Low-Hanging Fruit of Modern History, Got Sick, and Will (Eventually) Feel Better* (New York: Dutton, 2011), makes the case for the "low hanging" thesis in chapter one.

202   all advanced economies: Cowen, *Stagnation*, 64.

202   all has not been wrack and ruin: Scott Winship, "Making Sense of Inequality," *National Review,* August 13, 2012.

203   trends in the middle and the bottom: Winship parses the data for male high-school graduates, "All Sorts." Zingales's *Capitalism*, 110, and Ron Haskins and Isabel Sawhill's *Creating an Opportunity Society* (Washington D.C.: The Brookings Institution, 2009), 35, note the growing income gap between high-school and college graduates.

203   most tendentious explanation: Winship's "All Sorts" notes the income trends hold in other advanced countries. Wehner and Beschel in *National Affairs* note the same, as well as our steeply progressive tax system.

203   attributed to globalization: Zingales's *Capitalism*, 23, observes the effects of globalization. So does Haskins and Sawhill's *Creating*, 33, pointing out that male college graduation rates have been stagnating.

204   as fluid as we think: Scott Winship, "Mobility Impaired."

204   Out-of-wedlock childbearing: The *New York Times* reported on the new illegitimacy figures on February 17, 2012. The study *When Marriage Disappears* marshalls the evidence for the importance of marriage for the outcomes of children and demonstrates how old norms are increasingly the exclusive province of the college-educated. Brink Lindsey's *Human Capitalism: How Economic Growth Has Made Us Smarter—and More Unequal* (Princeton, NJ: Princeton University

Press, 2012), chapter six, and Zingales's *Capitalism*, 163, note the divergent child-rearing practices by class.

206   dropping out of the labor force: Charles Murray, *Coming Apart: The State of White America 1960–2010* (New York: Crown Forum, 2012), 170-81, and Haskins and Sawhill's *Creating*, 43, discuss the decline of work among low-skilled males.

206   The starkest indicator: "Differences in Life Expectancy Due to Race and Educational Differences Are Widening, and Many May Not Catch Up," *Health Affairs* 31:8 (August 2012), 1803-13.

206   photograph of Lincoln in 1846: Baker, "*Not Much of Me.*'"

209   "the blue model": Walter Russell Mead, "The Once and Future Liberalism," *The American Interest*, March/April 2012.

211   "the banner State of the Union": Burlingame, *A Life*, 95.

211   escalator of educational attainment: Claudia Goldin and Lawrence F. Katz, *The Race between Education and Technology* (Cambridge, MA: President and Fellows of Harvard College, 2008), document the slow-down in economic progress in their book-length study, 4-8, 324-26. Zingales's *Capitalism*, 143, and Cowen's *Stagnation*, chapter two, note the ineffectuality of the jump of education spending in recent decades. Finally, Lindsey's *Human*, chapter seven, recounts the inadequacies of the current model of college.

212   Funding should follow: Frederick M. Hess, "Does School Choice 'Work'?" *National Affairs* 5 (Fall 2010), 35–53.

213   "forestalled social dynamism": Guelzo, *Redeemer*, 9.

213   expanded inexorably: Nicholas Eberstadt, *A Nation of Takers: America's Entitlement Epidemic* (West Conshohocken, PA: Templeton Press, 2012). The information on food stamps is from one of my own columns, "The Rise of Food Stamp Nation," *National Review Online*, July 10, 2012. Murray's *Coming Apart*, 170, and Lindsey's *Human*, chapter six, discuss the rise in usage of Social Security Disability Insurance.

214   advent of the welfare state: The pensions for widows and orphans of the Civil War dead and for disabled veterans are sometimes interpreted as a precursor to the welfare state. They indeed became incredibly expansive in the decades after the war. But they applied

to a class of people who had served the country, and they faded out
with the passing of the veterans and their families.

215   makes it impossible to build: White's *New Atlantis* essay addresses this
point.

216   creating the Department of Agriculture: The language in the act
creating the department can be found at the USDA National Agricultural Library, http://www.nal.usda.gov/lincolns-agricultural-
legacy. A report by the non-profit The American Association for
the Advancement of Science notes the decline in research funding,
http://www.aaas.org/spp/rd/fy2013/hist13pGDP.pdf.

217   "By increasing total wealth": Howe, *Political Culture*, 9. Sellers's *Market Revolution* has the nineteenth century income-distribution numbers. The labor quote is from Taylor's *Transportation*, 264.

217   the occasional Irish joke: The count is from P. M. Zall, ed., *Abe
Lincoln Laughing* (Knoxville, TN: The University of Tennessee Press,
1995), index. Burlingame's *A Life*, 413, Foner's *Fiery*, 78-133, and
Foner's *Free*, 198, 257-59, are the sources of much of the information
regarding the nativist and immigrant votes.

222   same odor of elitism: Howe's *Political Culture*, 37, has the Emerson
put-down. Haskins and Sawhill's *Creating*, 71, sets out the data on
the effect of adherence to bourgeois norms. The Susan Mayer book
is *What Money Can't Buy: Family Income and Children's Life Chances*,
2-12. The alcohol numbers come from Sellers's *Market Revolution*,
259-65. The Yuval Levin quote comes from his excellent review
of Murray's *Coming Apart* in the *Weekly Standard*, March 19, 2012.
Lindsey's *Human*, chapter seven, discusses prescriptive parole, and
any number of papers by Robert Rector make the case for work
requirements across welfare programs and for a campaign of public
suasion on illegitimacy. Finally, Baker's "*'Not Much of Me'*" notes the
contrasting rustic and bourgeois cultures during Lincoln's day.

225   A vast apparatus of cultural uplift: Warren's *Youth*, 79, 106, 167,
describes Lincoln's readers and quotes from them extensively. The
dyspeptic quote is from Sellers's *Market Revolution*, 365.

227   bordered on the worshipful: I'm indebted here to the wonderful dis-

cussion of Lincoln and the Founders in Allen C. Guelzo's *Abraham Lincoln: As a Man of Ideas* (Carbondale, IL: Southern Illinois University Press, 2009), chapter six.

232   last spasm of the Civil War: I previously published this paragraph making this argument about the Civil Rights Act elsewhere. Gerard Alexander, "The Myth of the Racist Republicans," *Claremont Review of Books*, IV:2 (Spring 2004).

Index

Index

Benton, Thomas Hart, 114
Biddle, Nicholas, 62
Birch, Jonathan, 152, 153
Black Hawk War, 3, 46, 70
Blackstone, Sir William, 51, 75
Bliss, J. S., 236–37
Bloomberg, Michael, 222
Boritt, Gabor, 90, 91, 103, 121
Breckinridge, John, 170
Breese, Sidney, 110
"Broadway Pageant, A" (Whitman), 167
Brockman, John, 75
Brooks, Arthur, 200
Brownson, Orestes, 146
Bryan, William Jennings, 193–94
Buchanan, James, 178
Buckley, William F., Jr., 239
Burlingame, Michael, 19n, 40, 78
Bush, George W., 209
Bushnell, Horace, 95
Butler, William, 48, 78

Calhoun, John C., 53, 54, 140
Campbell, James, 176
Canisius, Theodore, 219
capitalism, American, 87–123; Declaration as foundation, 143; industrial capitalism, 191–92; infrastructure and, 96; labor theory of value, 90–91; Lincoln and, 103–7, 111–13, 145, 148, 168, 198; in the North, 145, 168; as opportunity, 114–16; post-bellum America and, 185–87, 191–92; railroads and, 119; South and, 146–47, 168; Wayland's ideas, 90–91; Whig party and, 90–92, 114–15
Carey, Henry Charles, 90, 91
Carnegie, Andrew, 15, 188–89
Chapman, A. H., 29, 37
Chase, Salmon P., 168, 174
Chicago, Illinois, 120, 135, 185
Churchill, Winston, 228
cities, 21, 118–19, 120, 185
Civil Rights Act, 232
Civil War: Anaconda Plan, 168; bond drives, 188; casualties, 181; Confederate Army, 181; federal

spending, 184; industrialized North triumphs over agrarian South, 168; Lincoln on purpose of, 2; Lincoln's address to 166th Ohio Regiment, 1–3; Northern prosperity and, 181–82; Southern economic-political power and, 179–81, 182; tariffs levied for, 176; tax levied for, 11–12, 176
Clay, Clement Claiborne, Jr., 177
Clay, Henry, 56–64, 80, 85, 134, 142, 154, 238; "American System" of, 58–59; Hamiltonian economics of, 59; Lincoln's eulogy, 86, 141; re-chartering Bank of the United States, 61–62; "self-made man" coined, 57
Clinton, DeWitt, 98
Cobb, Williamson R. W., 177
Collected Works of Abraham Lincoln (Basler ed.), 2n
Colton, Calvin, 114–15
Commentaries on the Laws of England (Blackstone), 51, 75
Cooke, Jay, 188
Cooper, Thomas, 95
Cowen, Tyler, 202
Crawford, Elizabeth, 25
Crawford, Josiah, 34
Cuomo, Mario, 9, 13, 207
currency, 61–62, 87, 91, 103–5; "greenbacks," 174; Legal Tender Act and, 174–75; Lincoln and national bank, 105–6

Davis, David, 32, 53, 77–78, 97, 109
Davis, Rodney O., 23n
De Bow, James, 146, 150
DeBow's Review, 118–19
Declaration of Independence, 5, 7, 16; Lincoln and, 128, 129, 140–45, 156, 164, 228; natural rights and, 143–45, 161; "self-evident lie," 140–41
Democracy in America (Tocqueville), 197
Democratic Party: banking and, 61–62, 87–88, 175; basic tenets, 230–31; "Cross of Gold" speech,

194; as Democratic Republicans, 60; government action vs. self-reliance, 230; hard-money gospel of, 105; in Illinois, 53, 101; Jacksonians in, 61, 105, 121, 146; "negative liberal state" of, 58. *See also* Jackson, Andrew

Dickey, T. Lyle, 127–28

DiLorenzo, Thomas, 10–11

Dirck, Brian, 50

Dodge, William E., 171

Donald, David Herbert, 8, 26, 78

Douglas, Stephen, 42, 82, 129–30, 132–33, 152, 192, 229; Kansas-Nebraska Act, 133–35; Lincoln debates, 57, 125–40, 151–64; as Lincoln rival, 114, 123, 126, 127, 130–33; railroads and, 128–29, 134; slavery and, 133–35, 151–64, 237; wife Adele, 152

Douglass, Frederick, 161

Duncan, Joseph, 100

Eberstadt, Nicholas, 213

economy, 194; banking-currency and, 104, 174–75; barter economy, 29, 38; cash economy, 29, 76, 103; democratic capitalism and, 5, 168; federal spending, Civil War and post-war, 184; financiers, debt financing, and Robber Barons, 187–89; free trade and, 176; global, U.S. share, 209; globalization, 203–4; government debt, 184; housing bubble, 209; industrialization and, 15–16, 21, 107, 120, 121, 149, 168, 171–72, 193; labor market, 204; Lincoln and a robust market, 14; Lincoln and industrialization, 4, 7, 15–16, 107, 120, 121, 149, 168; as Lincolnian republic and, 199–207; of Lincoln's boyhood, 20–21, 29; Lincoln's formula for today's economic ills, 207; Lincoln's modernization of, 5, 168; Lincoln's vision, 89, 107, 116–17, 129, 165, 172, 183–84, 193; post-Civil War, 185–87 191; post-World War II, 201–2;

protective tariffs and, 193; private sector and, 209–10; revolution in business, 187–89; slowing growth of, 202–3, 209; Southern cotton sales, 170–71; technology and, 202, 204, 208, 210; unemployment and, 206; U.S. vs. Western Europe, 204; World War II and, 194–95

Edison, Thomas, 191

education: American Dream and, 205–6; class divide in America and, 207; costs, 211, 212; emphasizing today, 210–12; G.I. Bill and, 201; land-grant colleges, 176–77, 185; Lincoln policies, 44, 45, 210–11; moral, 225–26; North vs. South, 150; opportunity and, 210–11; reforms proposed, 211–12; rural America, 31–32 ; socio-cultural effects, 205, 206; U.S. advantage in, 202; U.S. slippage, 211, 227

Edwards, Elizabeth (sister-in-law), 77, 79, 80

Edwards, Matilda, 130

Edwards, Ninian (brother-in-law), 80, 113–14, 130

Eisenhower, Dwight, 232

Elements of Political Economy, The (Wayland), 90

Elmore, Johnson, 42

Emerson, Ralph Waldo, 4, 8

English Grammar (Kirkham), 49

English Reader (Murray), 34, 226

Erie Canal, 98, 99

Faust, Drew Gilpin, 3

Federalist Papers, 95–96

Fehrenbacher, Don, 126, 153

Fillmore, Millard, 219

Fisk, John Moore, 53

Fitzhugh. George, 140, 146, 208

Fogel, Robert, 149

Foner, Eric, 120, 158

Ford, Thomas, 101, 106

Forquer, George, 55

Founding Fathers, 8, 16, 141, 142, 155–58; Lincoln reverence for, 227–29

Index

Index

Jaffa, Harry, 73
Jefferson, Thomas, 20, 35, 57, 96, 142, 156, 158, 168
Johnson, Andrew, 177–78
Johnson, Lyndon Baines, 11, 12
Johnston, John (stepbrother), 69, 76–77
Junius Tracts (Colton), 114–15

Kelley, Robert, 67
Kendall, Willmoore, 10
Kentucky: banning of blacks in, 162; Clay and, 57; Lincoln attends school in, 31; Lincoln family in, 19, 22, 23, 25, 26, 27, 28–29; property rights in, 94–95; as slave state, 137–38
Kentucky Preceptor, The, 226
Kerry, John, 9
Kirkham, Samuel, 49
Kleiman, Mark, 224–25
Know-Nothings, 135, 218, 219

Lamborn, Josiah, 55
law: bankruptcy law, 61; *Commentaries*, 51, 75; land law, 94–95; Lincoln circuit riding, 109–10; Lincoln letters on, 74–75; Lincoln's belief in rule of, 72–73; Lincoln's cases, 52, 108–15; Lincoln's earnings, 110, 111; Lincoln's office, 108; Lincoln's study of, 50–52; patent law, 93–94; upward mobility and, 50. *See also* property rights
Lehrman, Lewis, 140
Lessons in Elocution, 34, 225–26
Levin, Yuval, 224
Levine, Bruce, 21, 45, 120
liberalism/progressivism, 12, 58, 231; claiming Lincoln, 9, 194, 229–30
Libertarians, 10–11, 233
Licht, Walter, 187, 190, 191
Life of Washington (Weems), 165
Lincoln, Abraham, 19n, 108; ambition of, 8, 22–23, 25, 30–31, 50, 52, 55, 67, 122, 240; animals, kindness to, 70–72; appearance, 42, 43, 46, 47, 78–79, 83, 114, 152, 206–7; aspiration and, 115; character and

personality, 2, 23–24, 35, 42–43, 69, 71, 77–78, 109, 122, 131–32; courtship of Mary Owen, 79; Declaration and, 5, 7, 16, 128, 129, 140–45, 156, 164, 228; deification of, 197; enduring relevance of, 240; the Founding and, 8, 16, 141, 194, 228; "getting right with Lincoln," 8–9, 229; individualism and, 13, 14; as inventor, 93; Irish jokes, 217–18, 219; judgment of human nature, 236–37; marriage to Mary Todd, 78–79; middle-class values, 4–5, 30, 67–70, 214–15; as non-drinker, 67–68, 73–74, 81; as non-smoker, 68; "optimism of Western Civilization" and, 90; principles of, 53–54, 67–73, 115–16, 163–64; "race of life," 199; rhetorical style, wit, verbal acuity, 33, 42, 48, 55–56, 82–83, 84–85, 153, 236; strength of, 20, 38, 42, 69–70, 81; talents and intelligence, 23–25, 35, 84–85; voice, 154; work ethic, 4–5, 18, 20, 33, 74, 75, 76–77, 200, 214–15

early and pre-presidential years: background of poverty, 4, 18, 20, 32–33, 114; Black Hawk War, 3, 46, 70; brawling by, 69–70; childhood/adolescence, 20–43; as deputy county surveyor, 47, 48, 51, 53–54; earning his first dollar, 17–18; education, 31–36, 48–52, 225–26; failure of store and debt, 46, 48; family moves to Illinois, 39–40; family moves to Indiana, 23; father and, 25–30, 36–37, 40; first legal case, 52; first white shirt, 38; as "Honest Abe," 43; jobs held, 36; law studies, 48–52; as lawyer, 52, 78, 93–94, 97, 108–15, 133; leaves home, 39–40; "Lincoln the railsplitter," 18–20; New Orleans trips, 38–39, 40–41; in New Salem, 41–52; Offutt and getting a start, 40–42; popularity and friendships, 43, 47, 50–51, 53–54; as postmaster, 42, 47–48; as reader, 33–36,

Index

Emancipation Proclamation, 229; threats to personal safety, 165; U.S. becomes world's foremost military power under, 182; as war leader and Great Emancipator, 197–98 **speeches and writings**, 217; 1829 couplet, 17; 1836 reply to Forquer, 55; 1837 first published speech, 103–4; 1838 Lyceum address, 227–28; 1847 notes on natural rights, 143–44; 1848 in Congress on transportation projects, 102; 1854 antislavery speech in Peoria, 140, 141–42; 1854 statement on the object of government, 13; 1855 letter to Robertson, 127, 198; 1855 letter to Speed, 135, 219; 1856 speech in Kalamazoo, 128; 1856 speech on work for no wages, 36–37, 52; 1857 speech in Springfield, 125; 1858 House Divided speech, 126–27, 155, 157; 1858 Lecture on Discoveries and Inventions, 7, 87, 89, 94; 1858 on all men are created equal, 128; 1858 final Senate campaign speech, 229; 1858 speech on the object of government, 13; 1859 address on return to Indiana, 121–22; 1859 address to the Wisconsin State Agricultural Society, 7, 92, 148; 1860 and 1864 addresses on property and wealth, 14, 94, 217; 1860 Cooper Union address, 24, 192; 1860 New Haven speech, 115–16, 121–22; 1861 German working men in Cincinnati speech, 178; 1861 New Jersey Senate address, 165; 1863 Thanksgiving address, 220; address to 166th Ohio Regiment, 1–3, 16; on ambition, 22; autobiographical accounts, 31, 133; "blind memorandum," 1; on campaign for Harrison, 85; on Clay, 57; eulogy for Clay, 86, 141; fragment on abolition of slavery, 139, 144, 147; fragment on America's growth, 122; fragment on tariffs, 107; Gettysburg Address, 2,

7; on his frontier surroundings, 31; lampoon of party-switcher, 55–56; letters on self-improvement and hard work, 75–77; letters on the study of law, 74–75; on a National Bank, 105–6; note on Douglas, 123; "The Perpetuation of Our Political Institutions," 72; poem on the wilderness, 29; on property, 14; Second Inaugural speech, 5, 7; on Slave States, 138; speech to the Springfield Washington Temperance Society, 68, 73–74, 236; statement on the spread of liberty to all men, 15. *See also* Lincoln-Douglas Debates

Lincoln, Mary Todd, 40, 77, 78–80, 130; ambitions for Lincoln, 80; Lincoln's courtship of, 78–79; Lincoln's post-war plans, 184

Lincoln, Mordecai (uncle), 26, 28

Lincoln, Nancy Hanks (mother), 26, 27, 28, 34; death of, 27

Lincoln, Robert (son), 210–11

Lincoln, Sarah Bush Johnston (stepmother), 23, 27–28, 30, 33, 34, 68

Lincoln, Sarah (sister), 27

Lincoln, Thomas (father), 25–30; antislavery position of, 138; compared to Denton Offutt, 40; death of, 40; estrangement from son, 40; hiring his son out, 36; legal problems, 50, 52; Lincoln's view of, 26, 28, 30–31; property rights and, 94–95; son's bookishness and, 36; travel and, 37; as unlettered, 26, 30

Lincoln, Willie, 237

Lincoln and the Economics of the American Dream (Boritt), 90

Lincoln-Douglas Debates, 131, 151–64

Lincoln platform for today, 208–40, 208n; build infrastructure, 215–16; elevate the culture, 225–27; embrace what is new, 208–10; emphasize education, 210–12; exploit our resources, 220–21; fund other basic supports for growth, 216; look to the Founders, 227–29;

Index

Index

property rights, 7, 47, 90, 94, 193
Putnam, Robert, 226

railroads, 15, 21, 117, 118, 119, 121,
  128, 137, 152, 185–87, 193; high-
  speed rail, 231; in Illinois, 99, 100,
  101–2, 110, 117, 120, 134; land-
  grant railroads, 110; Lincoln and, 4,
  9, 45, 68, 86, 100, 110–13, 119, 194,
  215; manufacturing and, 21; Pacific
  Railroad Acts, 172; Southern vs.
  Northern, 150, 171, 181; subsidies,
  12, 179; transcontinental, 128, 134,
  172–73, 186, 215
Randolph, John, 67
Reagan, Ronald, 233–34, 237
Reavis, Isham, 74–75
Republican Party, 16, 59, 62, 238;
  as "Black Republicans," 161;
  conservatives criticizing Lincoln,
  10; defining principles, 90, 116;
  domestic agenda after Southern
  secession, 172–79; homestead bills
  and, 177–79; libertarian bent in,
  233; Lincoln and, 18–19, 90, 115,
  135–36; Lincoln and revitaliza-
  tion of the party today, 231–39;
  Lincoln-inflected agenda for today, 235–39; Lincoln Senate run,
  125–26; middle-class and, 4, 238;
  as National Republicans, 60, 62;
  in the North, 120–21; opposed to
  centralization, 59; origins of, 135;
  platform of 1860, 178, 218–19;
  Reagan and Lincoln, 233–34;
  record on civil rights, 231–32;
  Southern voters and, 232–33; victory in 1860, 170
Richardson, Heather Cox, 173
Robertson, George, 198
Rockefeller, John D., 188
Roksa, Josipa, 212
Roll, John, 52
Romine, John, 35
Roosevelt, Franklin D., 10, 11, 12,
  180, 194
Roosevelt, Theodore, 12, 13, 192–93,
  194

Ross, Frederick A., 147
Rutledge, Robert B., 49

Saez, Emmanuel, 202
Sangamo Journal, 44, 82, 114, 131
Sangamon River, 40–41, 43–44
Sawhill, Isabel, 223
Scott, Winfield, 80, 168
Scripps, John, 31, 133
Sellers, Charles, 223, 226–27
Seward, William, 8, 49, 182, 195
Sherman, William Tecumseh, 186
Shields, James, 83–84
Short, Bradford William, 143–45
Simmons, Pollard, 53–54
slavery: anti-abolitionism, 72–73;
  "bloody Kansas," 135; Britain
  and, 139; compensated eman-
  cipation proposed, 10, 138; as
  cornerstone of the South, 136–37,
  147–51; Declaration and, 140; in
  Delaware, 10; *Dred Scott* decision,
  160, 169; expansion of, 158–59;
  Jackson and, 60; Kansas-Nebraska
  Act, 133–35, 139, 178; liberation
  of, cost, 181; Lincoln-Douglas
  Debates and, 151–64; Lincoln letter to Robertson on, 127; Lincoln
  on natural rights vs. political-
  social rights, 162–63; Lincoln's
  antislavery stance, 3, 5, 37,
  135–36, 137–40, 151–64, 237–38;
  Lincoln's House Divided speech,
  126–27, 155, 157; Missouri Compromise, 133, 134, 160; "nonextension" position, 139; as political
  issue, 123, 151–64; population in
  South, 169; proslavery arguments,
  145–46; Thirteenth Amendment,
  229; voluntary colonization of
  blacks, 139; Wilmot Proviso,
  138–39
Slavery Justified (Fitzhugh), 146
Slavery Ordained by God (Ross), 147
Smith, Adam, 96
Smoot, Coleman, 47, 48
social capital, 7
social democracies, 198–99, 214

Index

About the Author

Rich Lowry was named editor of *National Review* in 1997. He is a syndicated columnist and a commentator for the Fox News Channel. He writes for *Politico* and *Time* magazine, and often appears on such public affairs programs as *Meet the Press* and *Face the Nation*. His previous book, *Legacy: Paying the Price for the Clinton Years*, was a *New York Times* bestseller. He lives in New York City.